GOOGLE ADS (ADWORDS) WORKBOOK:

ADVERTISING ON GOOGLE ADS, YOUTUBE, & THE DISPLAY NETWORK

2020 EDITION

BY JASON MCDONALD, PH.D.

© 2020, JM INTERNET GROUP

https://www.jm-seo.org/

Tel. 800-298-4065

"Half the money spent on advertising is wasted, but no one knows which half."

~ John Wanamaker, 1838-1922, American Merchant

CONTENTS

INTRODUCTION

Welcome to the *Google Ads Workbook 2020*! This book teaches you how to advertise on Google without losing your shirt. My name is Jason McDonald, and I am going to teach you the do's and don'ts, in's and out's, secrets, tips, and lies about how to advertise on Google and make money doing so. Google Ads, you see, can be your best friend, or your worst enemy. You can lose your shirt or make so much money you can afford custom shirts imported from Hong Kong and purchased after a Google search and ad click for "Custom shirts for ridiculously rich people who made their money via Google Ads."

I've been advertising on Google for nearly two decades, I manage tens of thousands of ad spend in any given month, and I'm Google Ads certified.

I love Google Ads! I hate Google Ads.

I am going to teach you everything that Google wants you to know and a lot of tips, tricks, secrets, do's, don'ts and insights that Google decidedly does not want you to know about the world's largest advertising system – Google Ads (formerly known as AdWords).

Let's begin at the beginning.

Why advertise on Google? First and foremost, Google is where your customers are. Need pizza? Just Google, "Pizza near me." Need a hair transplant? Just Google, "Why is my hair falling out?" Need an industrial fan? A lawyer? Car insurance? A cage for your pet iguana? Just google, google, google – Google is so important that the verb, "to google," has even made it into the Oxford English Dictionary. Not surprisingly, smart businesses *fish where the fish are*. They advertise on Google because that's where their customers are.

Secondarily, Google owns YouTube (the world's largest video site) and Gmail (the world's largest email system). So by advertising on Google's network you can reach people on YouTube and on Gmail as they watch Taylor Swift's latest video or email

Aunt Martha about their upcoming Disney Cruise. Third, Google runs the largest advertising network across independent sites (blogs, portals, media sites, etc.), allowing you to reach customers when they're on blogs, reading the newspaper, or chatting with their friends on many subsites across the Internet. It's called the *Google Display Network* or *GDN*, and it's massive. Indeed, Google even allows you to *remarket* to your customers; turning a single click on your website into a multitude of opportunities to build your brand, acquire sales leads, and sell more stuff. And Google Play is the world's biggest marketplace for app downloads.

What does Google say about its ad platform? According to the official Google Ads website (**https://ads.google.com/**), "Get in front of customers when they're searching for businesses like yours on Google Search and Maps. Only pay for results, like clicks to your website or calls to your business." Google has worked hard to make Google Ads an easy self-serve experience, and if that's not easy enough, it offers support by real human Googlers at 844-245-2553.

What's not to like?

Well, as the old adage goes, "if it sounds too good to be true, it probably is." There's *plenty* not to like in the Google Ads platform. Confusing terminology for one. A user interface that makes a Greek labyrinth, the plan of a nuclear power plant, or the American electoral system look easy to navigate for two. So many options that you often don't know when, where, or why your ads are showing, for three. And most importantly, a huge **conflict of interest** between you and Google.

Google Ads is a pay-per-click system. That means advertisers bid against each other in the Google Auction, and they pay if – and only if – there's a click from Google (YouTube, Gmail, Google Play, the GDN) to their website.

This sounds great, but there's a dark secret inherent in pay-per-click; it's *pay-per-click*, not *pay-per-sale*. And that creates a tension between you as the advertiser and Google as the advertising platform.

Let me explain.

1. Google gets paid by the **click**; that is, Google makes money when someone clicks (or calls) on a Google ad. (And, conversely, advertisers pay Google when someone clicks or calls on an ad).
2. You as the business, however, get paid by the **conversion**, that is you make money if – and only if – that click ultimately converts to a sale.

A *click* is not a *conversion*, however, yet you pay for the former and not the latter. Google gets paid whether you make a sale or not. To be cynical, Google "rigs" its platform to obfuscate this point, "obfuscate" being a fancy word to mean that Google misleads, hides, obliterates, subterfuges, and plays many linguistic tricks to encourage you to buy lots and lots of *clicks* and not realize that, ultimately, clicks don't make you money. *Conversions* do. (To be fair, Google does explain the importance of conversions though much of the Google Ads system is really designed to emphasize clicks).

We'll circle back to the contradictions and tensions between you and Google in Google Ads in the next Chapter, but for now just keep in mind that Google is a for-profit corporation, not a charity and, understandably, it rigs Google Ads to maximize clicks and thus its profits.

Zig from the Negative, Back to the Positive

One of the things you'll learn in Google Ads is that it is non-linear. You can't explain it or understand it in a straight line; rather, you have to *zig*, and *zag*, to understand its power and its complexities. Leaving aside the skepticism about Google, Google Ads, and any conflicts of interest, let's review five ways that Google Ads is a powerful advertising tool:

Google Ads can –

1. Get your company, product, or service to the **top of Google** at the precise moment, for the precise keywords that your customers are searching for, just as they're ready to buy a product or service.

2. Get your company, product, or service onto **thousands of websites and blogs** that participate in the **Google Display Network**, allowing you to reach customers as they **browse** the Web for information.
3. **Follow your customers "around the Internet"** through **remarketing**, showing them your ads on Google, YouTube, and thousands upon thousands of independent websites in the Google Display Network.
4. Get your company, product, or service onto **YouTube**, the #1 video site on the Internet, and **Gmail**, the #1 free email service.
5. Market your **App** to interested consumers through in-App advertising.

If you know what you're doing, Google Ads can be an incredibly effective tool in your advertising and marketing toolbox!

Enter the Google Ads Workbook

To succeed at Google Ads without wasting money, you need an expert guide and an expert guidebook. That's what this Workbook is. It will teach you secrets, tips, tricks, and techniques to effectively use Google Ads to market your product or service in the most efficient manner possible. We will proceed, together, "eyes wide open," understanding that Google is like a bartender or a used car salesman that has good – *no great* – products to offer us as advertisers, even if he's incentivized to oversell us just a tad.

Google Ads is powerful, and you and I are going to learn, together, how to unleash its power to help your business in an effective and cost-efficient manner.

Isn't that exciting? I think it is. I love Google Ads, and use it for myself and my clients. And I am going to teach you how to use it *safely* and *effectively*.

Who is This Workbook For?

This workbook is aimed primarily at **small business owners** and **marketing managers**. **Non-profits** will also find it useful. If you have a product or service to sell, and you realize that your customers go to Google, to websites such as blogs or news sites, to YouTube, or to Gmail, this workbook will help you understand how to use Google Ads efficiently to "get the word out."

If you are a person whose job involves **advertising**, **marketing**, and/or **branding**, this workbook is for you. (In fact, many digital ad agencies and consultants have used this Workbook to secretly hone their skills at Google Ads). If you are a small business that sees a marketing opportunity in online advertising of any type, this workbook is for you. And if your job is to market a business or organization online in today's Internet economy, this book is for you. Anyone who wants to look behind the curtain and understand the mechanics of how to use Google Ads (including the Google Display Network, remarketing, YouTube, and/or Gmail) will benefit from this book.

Anyone who sees – however dimly or skeptically – that online advertising could help their business can (and will) benefit from this workbook.

Here's our **game plan**, Chapter by Chapter:

1. **Google Ads Basics** – an overview of the basic logic and structure of Google Ads.
2. **Google Ads Gotchas** – an emergency checkup of the major gotchas in Google Ads, and how to stop them immediately.
3. **Keywords** – how to brainstorm valuable keywords and build an organized Keyword Worksheet.
4. **The Search Network** – how to use Google Ads effectively on Google.com and its so-called "Search Partners" like YouTube, Yelp, and Comcast.
5. **The Display Network** – a deep dive into Google's troublesome partner network (officially called AdSense or the Google Display Network (GDN))
6. **Google Shopping** – yes, you can advertise products on Google. This Chapter explains the basics of participating in the Google Shopping ecosystem.
7. **YouTube Advertising** – explore the power of video to market your company, product, or service on Google's YouTube service.

8. **Google Ads Metrics**. Using Google Ads and Google Analytics to measure your return on investment.

9. **Tools for Google Ads** – a cornucopia of Google Ads learning resources, tools, blogs, and other websites to help you master Google Ads and keep up-to-date on online advertising available in the companion *Marketing Almanac*.

» MEET THE AUTHOR

My name is Jason McDonald, and I have been active on the Internet since 1994 (*having invented the Internet along with Al Gore*) and taught SEO, Google Ads, and Social Media since 2009 – online, at Stanford University Continuing Studies, at both AcademyX and the Bay Area Video Coalition in San Francisco, at workshops, and in corporate trainings across these United States. I love figuring out how things work, and I love teaching others! Google Ads advertising is an endeavor that I understand, and I want to empower you to understand it as well.

I am Google Ads Certified and manage thousands of client dollars each month on Google Ads as well as on Bing's advertising platform. I also manage ads on YouTube, Facebook, and LinkedIn plus do SEO (Search Engine Optimization) and SMM (Social Media Marketing). This makes me uniquely qualified to be objective about Google Ads; Google Ads is only one of the tools in our toolkit, and we want to use it when it's the best tool (but not when another tool like SEO, Facebook, or Twitter would be a better choice).

Learn more about me at **https://www.jasonmcdonald.org/** or at my corporate website **https://www.jm-seo.org/**. Or just call 800-298-4065, say something flattering, and my secretary will put you through. (*Like I have a secretary! Just call if you have something to ask or say*). Visit the websites above to follow me on Twitter, connect with me on LinkedIn, or like me on Facebook. *Sorry, my Snapchat feed is so crazy it's for friends and family, only.*

» SPREAD THE WORD: TAKE A SURVEY & GET $5 OR A FREE BOOK!

If you like this workbook, please take a moment to take a short **survey**. The survey helps me find errors in the book, learn from student questions, and get feedback to improve future editions. Plus, by taking the survey, I'll be able to reach out to you, and we can even become friends. Or, if not friends, at least friends on the Internet or Facebook which isn't quite the same thing, but it's still pretty good!

Here's how –

1. Visit **http://jmlinks.com/survey**.
2. Take a short **survey** about the book.
3. I will rebate you $5 via Amazon gift eCard.

[handwritten: ? – maybe $500 for feedback!]

How's that for an offer you can't refuse?

This offer is limited to the first 100 participants, and only for participants who have purchased a paid copy of the book. You may be required to show proof of purchase and the birth certificate of your firstborn child, cat, or goldfish. If you don't have a child, cat, or goldfish, you may be required to prove telepathically that you bought the book.

[handwritten: lol]

» QUESTIONS AND MORE INFORMATION

I **encourage** my students to ask questions! If you have questions, submit them via **http://jmlinks.com/contact**. There are two sorts of questions: ones that I know instantly, for which I'll zip you an email answer right away, and ones I do not know instantly, in which case I will investigate, and we'll figure out the answer together.

As a teacher, I learn most from my students. So please don't be shy!

[handwritten: can ask questions – great!]

❱ COPYRIGHT AND DISCLAIMER

I knew you just couldn't wait for the legal stuff. Calm yourself down and get ready for some truly fun reading.

This is a completely **unofficial** workbook on Google Ads and Internet advertising. No one at Google, Facebook, LinkedIn, Twitter, YouTube, Instagram, Pinterest, Yelp, Instagram, Snapchat, the White House, the Russian embassy, or any other Internet company has <u>endorsed this workbook</u>, nor has anyone affiliated with any of those companies been involved in the production of this workbook.

That's a *good thing*. This workbook is **independent**. My aim is to "tell it as I see it," giving you no-nonsense information on how to succeed at Google Ads and online advertising.

In addition, please note the following:

- All trademarks are the property of their respective owners. I have no relationship with nor endorsement from the mark holders. Any use of their marks is so I can provide information to you. Don't confuse them with me, or me with them. I'm just a poor intellectual living in Oklahoma, and they are big, rich, powerful corporations with teams of money-grubbing lawyers.

- Any reference to or citation of third-party products or services whether for Facebook, LinkedIn, Twitter, Yelp, Google Ads, Google / Google+, Yahoo, Bing, Pinterest, YouTube, or other businesses, search engines, or social media platforms, should not be construed as an endorsement of those products or services tools, nor as a warranty as to their effectiveness or compliance with the terms of service with any search engine or social media platform.

The information used in this workbook was derived at the time of publication. However, Internet advertising and marketing changes rapidly, so please be aware that scenarios, facts, and conclusions are subject to change without notice.

Additional Disclaimer. Internet marketing is an art, and not a science. Any changes to your Internet marketing strategy, including SEO, Social Media Marketing, and Google Ads, is at your own risk. Neither Jason McDonald, Excerpti Communications, Inc., nor the JM Internet Group nor my Black Labrador, Buddy, assumes any responsibility for the effect of any changes you may, or may not, make to your website or Google Ads advertising based on the information in this workbook.

Additional Additional Disclaimer. Please keep your arms and legs in the vehicle at all times, be kind to one another, and signal while turning left, especially on Thursdays.

» REGISTER YOUR WORKBOOK FOR ONLINE TOOLS

This workbook is meant to leverage the power of the Internet. **Register** your copy online to get a PDF copy of this book (with clickable links to make it easy to access online resources). You'll also get free access to my *Google Ads Dashboard* and *Marketing Almanac*, which identify my absolute favorite free tools all set out for you to use in easy click-to-go format.

Here's how to **register** your copy of this workbook:

1. Go to **http://jmlinks.com/adw2020**
2. Reenter this password: **adw2020**
3. You're in. Simply click on the link for a PDF copy of the *Workbook* as well as access to the worksheets referenced herein.

Once you register, you get access to –

- **A PDF copy of this book**. Read it on your PC or tablet, and the links referenced in the book become clickable. This is a great way to extend the book into the myriad resources such as example websites or social media pages, FAQ's, support or help from the major vendors, and videos.

- **My Google Ads dashboard** – an easy-to-use, clickable list of the best tools for Google Ads by category (e.g., keywords tools, ad preview tools, etc.).
- **The *Marketing Almanac*** – a collection of up-to-date marketing tools not just for AdWords but for SEO and Social Media in detail. While the *Dashboard* identifies my favorites, the *Almanac* compiles the universe of free Google Ads tools.
- **A Free Puppy**. OK, you won't get a free puppy. But you'll get a lot of cool, free stuff. So please register your workbook.

Jump Codes

Throughout the book, I reference the website JMLINKS.com (**http://jmlinks.com/**) plus various "jump codes." If you're reading in PDF format, the links are clickable. If you're reading in hard copy or on the Kindle, I advise you to fire up your Web browser, bookmark **http://jmlinks.com/** and then enter the codes.

Here's a screenshot:

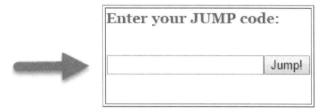

Search Engine Optimization, Social Media Marketing, and AdWords
Book Links

Welcome! My name is Jason McDonald and I provide consulting services in Internet marketing: SEO, AdWords, and Social Media Marketing.

BOOK JUMP CODES

Enter your JUMP code:

[Jump!]

If you've landed here... you must be looking for links in my books on SEO, AdWords, and/or Social Media Marketing. In each of the books, there should be numeric links that will automagically forward you to important links on the Internet.

You should know the 'secret' URL. If not, send me an email by clicking on the box to the left. Be sure to mention the class or workshop which you attended and the date.

For example, **http://jmlinks.com/16s** would mean first go to **http://jmlinks.com/** and enter "16s" in the jump code box. Your browser will then "jump" you to the referenced resource.

> **VIDEO.** Watch a video tutorial on how to use "jump" codes at **http://jmlinks.com/jump**.

❱ ACKNOWLEDGEMENTS

No man is an island. I would like to thank my beloved wife, Noelle Decambra, for allowing me to dive deeply into online marketing, and for being my personal cheerleader in the book industry. Gloria McNabb has done her usual tireless job as first assistant, including updating this edition as well the *Marketing Almanac*. My two daughters, Hannah and Ava, have inspired me to work hard on the digital world and "catch up" to a Millennial and a Generation Z. I would also like to thank my Black Labrador retriever, Buddy, for countless walks and games of fetch, during which I refined my ideas about online advertising and about life. I would also like to thank my students and clients who have given me the trust and privilege to manage their accounts in Google Ads. There is nothing quite like learning by doing, and I appreciate that opportunity.

And, again, a huge thank you to my students – online, in San Francisco, and at Stanford Continuing Studies. You challenge me, you inspire me, and you motivate me!

Let's get started!

1

GOOGLE ADS BASICS

If you were lucky enough to plan a vacation to Brazil, you'd probably buy a guidebook to the South American country such as Lonely Planet's *Lonely Planet Brazil* (**http://jmlinks.com/23f**). You might read the book on the plane ride down, and before you planned out your itinerary for what's *fun at Carnival* or a trip to *Encontro das Aguas* (where the Amazon and the Rio Negro rivers combine at **http://jmlinks.com/23w**), you'd want a general overview to the country. Your goal would be to "not get lost" in Brazil (e.g., inside the Amazon jungle), to "not get robbed," and in a positive sense, to make the most out of your investment of time and money for your Brazilian vacation. You'd marvel at the beauty, success, and intrigue of Brazil, but you'd also realize that – like all countries – Brazil has its bad neighborhoods and weird cultural quirks. *Google Ads is like Brazil*: enormous, complicated, with a scary jungle, key cities, different regions, wonderful, honest people, and scary thieves, etc. Read this Chapter on "Google Ads Basics" "as if" you were on a plane ride from your home city to the country of *GoogleAdsLandia*.

Let's get started!

TO-DO LIST:

» Search vs. Browse

» Keyword Targeting

» Bids and the Quality Score Conundrum

» Why Use Google Ads?

» Elements of Ads on Google Ads

» Google Ads Organization

» Getting Online Help with Google Ads

»Search vs. Browse

Google Ads is not one, but two, very different networks. Like the muddy *Rio Negro* in Brazil and the relatively clear *Amazon* at the *Encontro das Aguas*, it is two rivers – yes, they meet and interact, but it is two – not one – products. Google does its best to muddy the waters and confuse businesses into just throwing money at Google Ads, but your advertising dollars will be much more effective if you keep a clear head as to "which network" you are targeting, why, and at which time.

A good way to understand the two networks is to distinguish between "search" vs. "browse." We'll use as an example *Jason's Cat Emporium* of San Francisco, California, a hypothetical business that offers a) cat boarding, b) cat grooming and c) cat toys. *We don't do dogs, and we certainly don't do iguanas!* It's cats 24/7.

Turning to our target customers, we realize that there are two very different scenarios that are relevant to Google advertising.

Scenario #1 Search. The customer is pro-actively **searching** for "cat boarding." He's leaving San Francisco on a ten-week tour to Brazil, and he wants someone to take care of his prize cat, Kittles. He pro-actively searches on Google, entering in search queries such as *cat boarding San Francisco, quality cat hotels, cat sitters*, etc. This search methodology corresponds to what Google calls the "Search Network," which is Google.com plus what it calls "Search Partner" sites like Yelp.com or Comcast.net that have a strong search orientation. In some situations, YouTube search also functions in this way (e.g., "How to potty train a kitten" as a search on YouTube, for example).

Scenario #2 Browse. Here, the customer is not pro-actively searching for "cat boarding." Rather, he is reading up on blogs on cat-related issues, such as CatBehaviorAssociates.com (**http://jmlinks.com/23h**) or an article on the ChicagoTribune.com entitled, "The Last Free-ranging Cat library in Illinois" (**http://jmlinks.com/23j**). Note that he is not entering in keywords to search; rather, he is just reading blogs and newspaper sites that may, or may not, be about cats and cat care. This pattern of **browsing**, but not searching, corresponds to what Google calls the Google Display Network ("GDN" or just "Display Network" for short), which is not Google.com at all but partner sites like CatBehaviorAssociates.com and ChicagoTribune.com that agree to allow Google to place ads on their websites. (He may also be browsing YouTube videos that relate to cats). Indeed, **remarketing** (following users around the Web and showing them relevant ads) is part of this browsing process.

VIDEO. Watch an official video tutorial on the Google Search Network as well as the Google Display Network at **http://jmlinks.com/23g**. **Note**: be aware that it's overly positive and fails to explain the relevant gotchas!

Pro-actively Choose Your Network

You, as an advertiser, should be **pro-active** about which network you want to run ads on, and it really is a function of how strongly you feel people "search" for your products or services or whether you feel that they are more likely to be "browsing" for something similar to your product or service. Note that if someone is pro-actively searching for your product or service, they are much more likely to convert, as opposed to if they are just browsing blogs, websites, and YouTube and just "happen" to see an ad for your company.

VIDEO. Watch a video from Google on Campaign Types and Google Networks at **http://jmlinks.com/26d**.

As we shall see in Chapter 2 on "Gotchas," Google defaults you into *both* the Search and the Display Network, but – for most advertisers – the Display Network is much more difficult and has a *much, much, much, much, much, much, much* lower ROI (return on investment). Among the reasons (as we will explain in detail in Chapter 5 on the Google

Display Network) is that the GDN has many nefarious or I might argue, even fraudulent, websites that do nothing but generate spurious clicks. An example would be what are called "Parked Domains" such as CatCrap.com or KittyToys.com. A parked domain is essentially an "empty" website that does nothing – absolutely nothing – except serve Google ads by participating in the Google Display Network or AdSense (its official publisher counterpart at **https://www.google.com/adsense/start/**).

Although the official Google policy bans ads on Parked Domains (**http://jmlinks.com/23m**), Google seems to do little, if anything, to police this problem – perhaps because it, like the Parked Domain, makes money off of the spurious clicks! The long and short of it is that the Display Network is problematic and should generally be avoided by new advertisers.

» KEYWORD TARGETING

Keywords function very differently on the two different networks! The reason for this has to do with user behavior and what Google "knows" about the user in the different scenarios.

> **Scenario #1 Search.** The user is pro-actively searching on Google by typing in search queries. Google "knows" **user intent** (he's looking for *cat boarding*) because it "knows" the actual search term typed into Google. For this reason, keyword matching on the Search network is **tight**: you, as the advertiser, can very tightly control when your ad appears by using the attributes of quotes (""), brackets ([]), and plus signs ("+"). (*More about this in Chapter 4*).

> > **Note:** you, the advertiser, enter a "keyword trigger" such as *+cat +boarding* that Google matches to the search query entered by the searcher, *cat boarding*. Keyword matching on the Search Network is **tight**, meaning that (if you know how to correctly enter your keywords into Google Ads), you can create a very tight match between what the searcher enters and when your ad displays on Google.

Scenario #2 Browse. Here, the user may be reading the *Chicago Tribune* online, watching YouTube, or just browsing miscellaneous blogs and social media sites across the Web. He is NOT entering search terms. The most the Google knows is the content of the page he is on, but for sites like *ChicagoTribune.com, ESPN.com, USAToday.com,* etc. (all of which run Google Display Ads), Google does NOT know the user intent and is forced to compare the "page content" vs. the "keyword triggers" you as the advertiser enter into Google Ads.

> **Note:** Let's take an example like the article "10 Biggest Missteps in the Bears' Decade of Decline" (**http://jmlinks.com/23p**). Here, the question for Google is, is the relevant keyword *sports* or *Bears* or *NFL* or *football* or *Super Bowl*, etc., and is *Bears* a sports team or an animal (remember: Google is just a machine, not a person). Accordingly, keyword matching on the Display Network is **loosey-goosey**, that is, not at all tight, as Google has to "guess" at user interests, creating many nefarious possibilities that your ads will be placed on non-relevant websites. (Note: there are other forms of targeting your ads, such as *remarketing*, but for now we'll keep it simple).

> **TO-DO**. Depending on the network you are running on, you will need to understand how to control keyword match types and adjust accordingly when Google will show your ads and on what websites.

For now, just realize that keywords drive matching on Google Ads and that keyword matching is **tight** on the Search Network and **loosey-goosey** on the Display Network (*despite what Google indicates in its contradictory official documentation!*).

» BIDS AND THE QUALITY SCORE CONUNDRUM

How are ads shown on Google Ads? Generally speaking, it's a cost-per-click (CPC) system, meaning that you compete against other advertisers in an online auction to "buy" the click, and you pay, if, and only if, a user clicks on your ad. Bids function the same on both the Search and Display networks; advertisers pay per click.

Let's take a simple scenario. *Jason's Cat Emporium* is competing against other cat boarding establishments to get clients who have cats and need boarding in San Francisco as well as folks who just want cat grooming.

The Ad Auction: A Simple Model

So, imagine that Joe User goes to his computer and types into Google, *cat boarding*. At the speed of light, that query is sent to the Google algorithm in Mountain View, California, and the auctioneer (Google), says:

Incoming! I have a query, *cat boarding,* coming out of San Francisco, California. Opening bid is $1.00 for the click, do I hear $1.00?

I pipe up and say, "I'll bid $1.00 to get that click!"

The auctioneer says, "Do I hear $1.25?"

Charlie of *Charlie's Cat Boarding Inc.*, says, "Yeah! I'll bid $1.25."

The auctioneer says, "Do I hear $1.31?"

Joanie of *Joanie's Cat Boarding Inc.*, says, "Yes! I'll bid $1.31. In fact, I'll bid $2.01!"

The auctioneer says, "Do I hear $2.10?"

Silence…

The auctioneer says, "Sold! For $2.01" to Joanie's Cat Boarding.

He repeats this procedure of asking the potential advertisers for bids, having them bid against each other until he fills the top three or four slots on the Google search screen.

At the speed of light, Google then populates the Google search screen, and Joe User sees on his computer a Search Engine Results Page (or SERP), which places Joanie's ad in position #1, and positions #2, #3, and #4 on Google are populated by those who bid just a bit lower.

In reality, it's a little more complicated than this simple model because Google not only looks at advertisers' bids per click but also at their Quality Score, which is an estimation of the click-thru rate for their ad (how likely it is to get more clicks) plus factors such as ad format, and the landing page experience.

VIDEO. Watch a video tutorial on how the Google bid-per-click / pay-per-click auction works by Chief Economist Hal Varian at **http://jmlinks.com/26a**.

Here's a screenshot of the Google results page for "cat boarding San Francisco" with the ad (appearing at the top), the local snack pack (appearing in the middle), and organic (appearing at the bottom) marked. In most cases, you'll see ads at the topped marked as "Ads" and the organic or free results at the bottom. For searches with a local character you'll sometimes see the "local snack pack," and for product searches such as for "red dresses," you may see product ads on the top or far right.

Who's on Top? Ad Position

In this simple model, position #1 on Google goes to the highest bidder, position #2 to the next highest, and down to position #4. These fill the top slots. In some cases, there are additional slots at the bottom of the page, #5, #6, #7.

If or when Joe Users clicks on an ad, then that advertiser pays one penny MORE than the bid of the person just below him. So, if for example, Joanie bid $2.01 but Charlie bid just $1.10 for position #2, then Joanie would pay not $2.01 but $1.11 for that click.

That's the *simple* model. Advertisers compete against each other in the "click auction" and pay just 1¢ more than the person below them. Of course, it's more complicated than this, and Google doesn't share all the data as to what's happening behind the scenes. In fact, we are forced to trust that Google is honest and accurate with the click data, and cost per click charges; I'm not completely convinced, unfortunately, that Google is actually 100% honest on these issues, so it's best to be skeptical, measure everything, and experiment.

Here's the process from both the perspective of the searcher and of the advertiser.

1. The searcher types a **search query** into Google such as "cat boarding San Francisco."
2. Advertisers **bid** against each other to "get the click" for this search query by bidding higher to get a higher position on the page. Generally, there are three to four paid ads at the top of the page, followed by organic results (both the snack pack and organic), with a few ads at the bottom.
3. Google assembles a search engine results page (**SERP**) based on advertising (in which advertiser bid what for the click in the auction), plus organic results such as the local snack pack and regular organic results and returns this to the searcher in the blink of an eye.
4. If a user **clicks on ads**, then whichever ad they click on pays a fee to Google called the "cost per click." (*Of course, much of the time, users ignore ads and go to the organic results, which is why you must focus not only on Google Ads but on SEO!*).
5. Users land on the advertiser's website and either "bounce back" to Google, or "convert" and the process repeats.

Quality Score

Ad position and the cost-per-click auction aren't quite that simple, however, because Google calculates **Quality Score**, a mysterious part of the Google Ads algorithm. Basically, if you write a "better" ad (more tightly connected to the user search query), then Google will "reward" you with a lower CPC. So, if Joanie bids $2.01 but her ad is poorly written (not very relevant), and Charlie bids $1.10, his ad may outrank her (be in position #1, not position #2) even though he bid less. In fact, if Joanie's ad is bad, Google may refuse to show her ad entirely.

QUALITY SCORE REWARDS ADS THAT GET CLICKS

The components of Quality Score will be discussed in Chapter 4 in more detail, but for now, just be aware that a) advertisers compete against each other in the "click auction" and "pay by the click," and b) Google rewards a better quality score with a lower cost-per-click (CPC). And, as Google skeptics, just keep in mind that we want to investigate what Quality Score really means and whether it really works the way Google says it does. Don't be fooled in Google Ads by terms like "Quality Score" that sound unambiguously good for both you and for Google. "Trust but verify," as President Reagan once said about the Soviet Union.

The Quality Score Conundrum

There is, in fact, a conundrum in Quality Score which Google does not explain. Remember that Google gets paid *by the click*, while you make money *by the conversion*, which is not the same thing! So, if you write an ad that says "Cheap Cat Boarding" or even "Free Cat Boarding" or "Free Cat Boarding Plus Free Pizza for Owners" you will a) get a lot of clicks, b) improve your Quality Score, and c) pay less per click.

Google will be VERY happy!

But you will get a lot of cheap customers who are coming just because you're cheap (and you provide free pizza), that is few conversions and/or conversions from people who are not willing to pay full price for your quality cat boarding services.

The conundrum is that you are competing against advertisers who may not understand this, who follow Google's official playbook, and whose ads (*for free pizza and free cat boarding*) "crowd out" your more honest, more relevant ads.

You are forced to overbid just to stay in the game!

We'll return to this problem in Chapter 4, but for now just realize that advertisers "pay by the click" on Google and that there is a tension inherent in Quality Score between your interests (*to get the conversion*) and Google's interest (*to get the click*) plus you are often competing against a few dumb advertisers who think it's all about clicks and thereby hijack users to their pages with ads that overpromise, thus stupidly bidding up the costs for everyone else.

The system is far less perfect than Google makes it out to be.

Minimum Bids

In addition, Google has minimum bids which mean even if you are the ONLY advertiser bidding on a specific keyword phrase, you can't just bid one cent for the click. There is a non-published "minimum bid" which you must find out through trial and error. It's sort of a function of your "Quality Score," but in reality, you'll find that there is a minimum floor that you have to bid to get your ad to show on a keyword even if you are the only advertiser that wants to show up on the phrase. You can read the official Google explanation on "minimum bids" at **http://jmlinks.com/47y**, but I recommend you take it with a very big grain of salt.

Google is a monopoly and it rigs the system to maximize its revenue (not your profits), so just always be aware that you have to experiment with ad networks, ads, keywords, and bids and look at your own data. What matters is what works for you, not what the official Google propaganda says about this or that issue. Despite what Google officially says, you don't exactly pay just .01 above the person below you, and you can't just optimize for clicks to improve your so-called Quality Score!

Bear with me on this, as we'll return to bid strategy in Chapter 4. For now, just realize that generally speaking, you bid per click against other advertisers, and you pay just .01 above the advertiser below you. All of this is mediated by Quality Score, with Google rewarding advertisers that write ads that get a lot of clicks.

» Why Use Google Ads?

At this point, you may be wondering, *"Gosh, why use Google Ads at all? It sounds very complicated and seems to have quite a few 'gotchas' inserted there to take my money."*

I understand that frustration, but (*back to our analogy of a trip to Brazil*), there are many wonderful things to see, do, and take advantage of in the country of GoogleAdsLandia, if you know where to look, and know how to avoid the bad neighborhoods and cultural gotchas that can cause trouble.

> **VIDEO.** Watch a video from Google on defining your goals for advertising on Google Ads **http://jmlinks.com/26c**.

Here's a rundown of reasons why Google Ads should have a place in your online marketing strategy:

1. **Time to Market**. Google Ads can get your company, product, or service to the top of Google, quickly. You can literally set up an ad campaign in just a few hours and be up and running on Google. This allows you to react quickly to market events and get your message out and up in a much, much faster way than search engine optimization (SEO) which takes considerable time and effort.
2. **Geotargeting**. Google Ads is very effective at targeting consumers in just a specific area. You can target ONLY people in San Jose, California, for example, and you can target people in San Jose with one ad and people in Tulsa with another ad. Indeed, you can also show your ad only during certain times of the day or week through scheduling.
3. **Short Tail Queries**. You may be able to rank via SEO for a very specific search such as *quality cat boarding in the Mission District, San Francisco*, but be unable to rank for a *short tail* query such as *cat boarding*. Using Google Ads, you can strategically advertise on short tail queries that you do not rank for via SEO. Combined with geotargeting, this can be a very powerful complement to search engine optimization.

4. **Keyword Broad Match**. While SEO works well on very focused keywords, Google Ads can get your ads to show on broader, adjacent keywords. For example, you can combine a geotarget (people in San Francisco) with an "educational search term" such as "how to groom a cat" to showcase your cat grooming services. You can also get detailed reporting in Google Ads to identify relevant keyword targets for your SEO that you cannot get in any other way. When used with skill and caution, Google Ads can get your message to a broader audience than pure SEO.

5. **Keyword Research**. Google no longer provides detailed keyword data to organic or SEO users, but it does provide keyword data to Google Ads advertisers. By advertising, you can get invaluable research into the actual keywords used by users and their behavior "after the click," which you can feed back into your Google Ads and/or SEO strategy.

6. **Mobile Phone Targeting**. It's no secret that people spend more and more time on their mobile phones. The screen is very small, and Google has "crowded out" the free listings by pushing them down with ads. Using Google Ads, you can effectively advertise on mobile phones, only, again adding a powerful complement to an effective SEO strategy. You can turn "off" Google Ads on the desktop (where you rank well in the organic / SEO results), for example, and turn "on" Google Ads on the mobile phone (where you rank poorly in the organic / SEO results).

7. **Remarketing**. Using *remarketing* (explained in Chapter 5), you can "follow" your customers around the Internet as they go to sites like *YouTube, Gmail, Chicago Tribune, New York Times*, etc., showing and reshowing them relevant ads about your product or service. Remarketing is very powerful for products or services with long sales cycles like *cruises to Latin America, choosing a tax CPA*, or even *applying to law schools*.

8. **Redundancy and Branding**. Customers often buy only after seeing your brand across many experiences, so Google Ads can get your company, product, or search "into their mind" through repetition. Google Ads can work "with" your SEO efforts, "with" your social media marketing efforts and advertising, and "with" your offline, "real world" marketing efforts. Google Ads should be part of a multi-channel effort to get your brand in front of clients over and over again.

9. **Browsing / Interrupt**. While SEO works if, and only if, the person is pro-actively searching Google, Google Ads can show your ads through the Google

Display Network and YouTube to people who are NOT pro-actively looking for your product. You can "interrupt" their experience with ads on YouTube or get your ads on relevant blogs and news sites via the Google Display Network.

I hope that this nine-point list has fired up your enthusiasm for Google Ads!

SEO vs. Google Ads

Google Ads has obvious advantages, but it has one obvious *disadvantage*: it costs money to advertise. Another huge disadvantage is that people tend to ignore ads and view or click only on the organic results on Google. Many marketers conclude that Google Ads is inferior to SEO or Search Engine Optimization, the art and science of getting your product or service to the top of Google's organic results for free.

Isn't SEO better than AdWords?

Well, the answer is "it depends." I love SEO and do SEO; I've even written a book on SEO, my *SEO Fitness Workbook* (**http://jmlinks.com/seo**).

There's nothing better than getting to the top of Google for free! But SEO isn't everything, so using tactics such as geotargeting, short tail keyword matches, mobile phones or remarketing, I blend in Google Ads for a killer online marketing strategy. Ditto for other marketing efforts like social media marketing and offline advertising. Yes, you should do SEO. But you should also do AdWords, especially for **high-value keyword phrases**, mobile phone optimization, remarketing, browse, and other areas where SEO isn't the best tool for the job.

*It's not Google Ads OR SEO. It's Google Ads ** **AND** ** SEO!*

» ELEMENTS OF ADS ON GOOGLE ADS

Remember that Google Ads is two primary networks, Google Search and the Google Display Network. With that in mind, let's overview the elements to ads. What do ads look like on each network?

The Search Network

Ads on Google have the following visible components:

> **Headline 1** – 30 characters
>
> **Headline 2** – 30 characters
>
> **Headline 3** – 30 characters
>
> **Display Path** ("Display URL") – 15 characters each
>
> **Description 1** – 90 characters
>
> **Description 2** – 90 characters

Behind the scenes, there is also your final URL (the destination on your website where you want to send traffic), plus other elements such as extensions which we'll explain in a moment.

Here's a screenshot of a simple ad triggered by the search query, "motorcycle insurance:"

In addition to the standard format, there's also what's called a "Responsive Search Ad." In this format, you enter multiple headlines and descriptions and Google then mixes and matches them "on the fly" to create your ads. To learn more about responsive search ads, visit **http://jmlinks.com/52a**.

Ad Extensions

In addition to the headline, description, and path, ads on Google can also have "extensions." Among the most important are:

Sitelinks – these are blue-highlighted bits of text that can appear below an ad, and link to specific subsections of your website such as "contact us" or "cat grooming," etc.

Callouts – these are non-clickable text elements that can appear below an ad, usually meant to "call out" something special such as "Valentine's Day Specials" or "ask about our kitty services".

Structured Snippets – you select a predefined header like "Product" or "Service category" and then add callouts to specific subsections of your website.

Call extensions – these allow your phone number to appear in ads.

Lead form extension – allow persons to enter information and send messages from your ads.

Message extensions – these appear on mobile phone ads and allow customers to text message you directly from the ad.

Location – this extension type allows users to see your store's physical address.

Affiliate location – similar to the above.

Price extensions – allow users to browse products and prices in an ad, and then click directly to them on your website.

App extensions – allow you to link from your ad to your mobile app for download and installation.

Promotion Extension – use this extension like a callout extension to "shout out" a custom offer like a coupon or discount.

Google has a new type of extension called "**Automated Extensions**" which occur automatically when Google decides to feature something like a specific page on your website or a phone number. To read the official Google help file on ad extensions, visit **http://jmlinks.com/23q**. To read about the newer Automated Extensions, visit **http://jmlinks.com/39p**.

Here's a screenshot of an ad with clickable sitelink extensions:

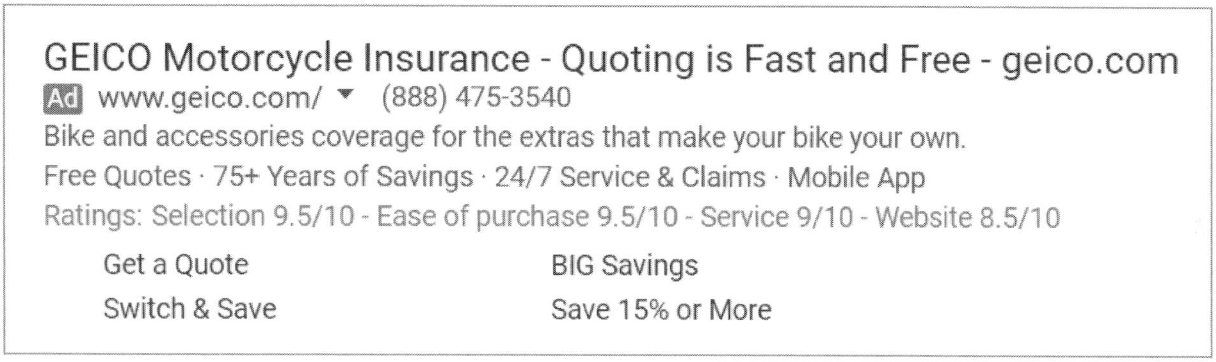

And here's a screenshot of an ad with a location extension:

Notice how DeVry has added their phone number of (866) 605-2326 as a call extension, and how the location extension shows their address in Downers Grove, IL.

And here's a screenshot with a Google shopping review extension, again getting the advertiser those nifty, eye-catching stars:

Notice how this ad has a display URL that contains a keyword (*Warehouse-Fans*), as well as call out extensions and structured snippet extensions.

The Display Network

Ads on the Display Network can be text and appear similar to the above. Or they can be graphic images, what are now called "Responsive Display Ads" (See **http://jmlinks.com/47z**). You can either upload your own or use Google's "Scan Website" tool to have it pull images from your website and create a cornucopia of possible image sizes for your ad. In addition to the text-only ads that are available on the Google Search Network, on the Google Display Network you can run the following types:

> **Responsive Display Ads** – ads that combine text, images, and URLs "on the fly" to match the many varieties of websites and ad formats across the Google Display Network.
>
> **Image Ads** – upload your own image ad creatives to the Google Display Network, and Google will strategically place your image ads across its network.
>
> **Video ads** – ads that display a video about your company, product, or service.

In addition, new ad formats are constantly popping up on the Google Network such as "App promotion ads" to promote your app on Google Shopping, shopping ads on Google shopping, dynamic search ads on Google Search Partners, and call-only ads on Google search. See **http://jmlinks.com/48a** for the Google help file on all available ad formats. But, in general, you run text-only ads on Google Search and text and image-based ads on the Google Display Network. Shopping ads are a hybrid of text and images that appear on Google.com.

To read the official Google help file on how to create "responsive display ads" for the Display Network, visit **http://jmlinks.com/23r**. Note that if you are not running on the Display Network, then you can ignore these ads format as they are not available on Google Search. Also, be aware that YouTube has specific ad requirements and formats; you can read the official Google help file on YouTube ads at **http://jmlinks.com/23s**. And to read about ad formats on Google Shopping Ads visit **http://jmlinks.com/48b**. Suffice it to say at this point that there are many more formatting options for ads on the Google Display Network, YouTube, and Google Shopping than on the Search Network.

» GOOGLE ADS ORGANIZATION

Google Ads is a hierarchy. Remember that Google is a company founded by, and run by, engineers. These are stereotypically the guys with the pocket protectors, the over-organized desks, and the Sheldon Cooper personality types that need to always "sit in their spot." (To learn more about Sheldon Cooper and ponder whether this personality type is overrepresented in the Googleplex, visit **http://jmlinks.com/23t**, but we digress).

Google Ads is a hierarchy! The more organized you are, the better you will do!

Accordingly, you will get your best performance by understanding and following Google Ads strict hierarchical rules:

> **Account**. This is the master category and contains your email login, password, and billing information. I recommend that you set up two-step verification (**http://jmlinks.com/23v**) for your Google Ads account, as thieves target Google Ads accounts because there is money to be stolen!

Campaigns. Think of a campaign as a "bucket" that holds your budget, bid strategy (but not your actual bids), network choice (Search vs. Display), geotarget, device target (mobile, desktop, tablet), and a few other odds and ends such as scheduling.

Ad Groups. Groups are the workhorses of Google Ads and should reflect your product or service categories and tightly correspond to your core keywords. Bids are also set at the group level, or at the interrelated keyword level. An example of group organization would be "cat boarding" vs. "cat grooming"; different customer needs create different search queries and should be reflected in corresponding, unique Google Ads groups

Cross-Views in Google Ads: Confusion Alert!

Google Ads is a hierarchy at a structural level. However, you can "view" across the structure in different ways. For example, you can log in to your Account, click on the "Keywords" tab and view ALL the keywords across ALL the groups of your account. However, "Keywords" live at the group level, only, so any edits that you make impact them at that level. You can also view ALL your ads at the Account level, even though both keywords and ads actually "live" at the Ad Group level.

It's confusing.

Imagine, for example, a glass building called "Account," that had two floors, called "Campaigns" and "Ad Groups." At any moment you could see "through" the building in any direction, but, for example, the "budget information" would "live" on the "Campaign floor." While you could be on the "group" floor and "see" the budget, you couldn't touch it (or edit it), without moving to the "Campaign floor."

Google Ads is like a glass building. You can "see" many things in many different ways, but you can only manage or edit them at the correct level. For example:

Budget can be edited only at the Campaign level.

Ads can be edited only at the Ad Group level.

Bids can be edited only at the Group or keyword level.

Keywords can only be edited at the Ad Group level.

Geotargeting can be edited only at the Campaign level.

and so on and so forth…

This is confusing to people as you can "view" things in Google Ads in ways that do NOT reflect the structural organization. I recommend you ask yourself "what level does this live at?" when you're having a problem editing something, and go to that level by clicking on the appropriate tab. See the official help file on best practices for account organization at **http://jmlinks.com/23u**.

> **VIDEO.** Watch an official video tutorial on best practices for Google Ads account organization at **http://jmlinks.com/48c**.

At this point, don't freak out about the organizational issues at Google Ads. Like working in a big, fancy glass building in San Francisco, over time, the organization will make sense to you and become second nature.

» GETTING ONLINE HELP WITH GOOGLE ADS

My companion *Marketing Almanac* has a cornucopia of resources on Google Ads, including tools and help documentation. That said, here are the official resources where you can "ask a question" of Google Ads.

> **Help**. Help is hidden in Google Ads under the "Question Mark Icon" in the top right of the screen. Click on it and then select "Get Help."
>
> **Live chat and Email Help**. These can be found in the "help" section as indicated above.

Phone Support. Click on the "Question Mark Icon," then, "Get Help," and you should see a phone number. In the United States, the number is 866-246-6453. Live technical support is available 9 am – 8 pm Eastern Time.

You can also access the Google Ads help files at **https://support.google.com/adwords**. You can post questions to the Google Ads Community at **https://www.en.advertisercommunity.com/**. Throughout, be aware that Google has a vested interest in your spending MORE (not less) money on Google Ads, so the technical support at all levels can be a bit salesy.

»» DELIVERABLE: GOOGLE ADS STRATEGY WORKSHEET

The **DELIVERABLE** for this chapter focuses on the Big Picture. Why are you interested in advertising on Google Ads? Which network (Search or Display) makes the most sense for your products or services?

For the **worksheet**, go to **http://jmlinks.com/adw2020**, then re-enter the password, "adw2020," to register if you have not already done so), and click on the link to the "Google Ads Strategy" worksheet.

2

GOOGLE ADS GOTCHAS

Google Ads is full of "gotchas," misleading elements in the platform that can cause you to advertise on the wrong keywords, run on websites you don't really like, pay more for clicks than necessary, and otherwise make your advertising inefficient and expensive. By their very nature, these gotchas are hidden to the average user. Note: we will circle back to the gotchas in the Chapters to come, but if you are currently advertising on Google, I strongly recommend that you either completely **stop all advertising** until you have completed this Workbook, or at least until after you have read this Chapter.

After all, the first principle of using advertising to *make* money is to NOT *waste* money on advertising!

Let's get started!

TO-DO LIST:

» Understand the Google Ads Contradiction

» Gotcha #1: Google Ads Alternatives

» Gotcha #2: Bad Keyword Match Types

» Gotcha #3: Artificial Intelligence

» Gotcha #4: The Google Display Network

» Gotcha #5: Conversions Across Devices

»» Deliverable: A Google Ads Gotcha Checkup

» Understand the Google Ads Contradiction

Google Ads is a multi-billion dollar source of revenue for Google. It's how Google makes the lion's share of its money, to the tune of 86% or more in any given year. In 2018, for example, Google generated about $33.7 billion in revenue for Q3, with about 86% coming from advertising both on Google itself and on its AdSense or Google Display Network. (See **http://jmlinks.com/39m**). Despite what people often seem to believe, Google isn't a benevolent, nonprofit charity that happily provides "objective" search results across the Internet. Yes, it's a great search engine. But Google is a **for-profit business** that makes its money by **selling ads** on top of its "organic" or "free" results.

Google, The Click, and The Conversion

Google wants to make money, and Google makes its money by selling clicks on ads. Advertisers bid against each other to "get the click," and Google does everything it can to bring more advertisers into the ad auction and push up the cost per click paid by advertisers. Google wants lots of advertisers, lots of clicks, and high prices for clicks.

At a structural level, this creates a *tension* between you (*the advertiser*) and Google (the *publisher*):

> Google is paid by the *click*; accordingly, Google wants ads that create lots of *clicks*.

> You, however, make money by the *conversion* (usually an e-Commerce sale or a sales lead via a web form on your website); you want ads that create a lot of *conversions*.

> Google wants you to spend a lot of money on Google Ads; Google wants you to *maximize your spend*.

> Google wants *high prices* for ad clicks; you want *low prices* for clicks.

You want to spend, as little as possible or as effectively as possible, to *maximize your ROAS* or *Return on Ad Spend*, that is, the profit you make from advertising efficiently.

The focus of Google is to get users to click on ads and to get advertisers to pay for those clicks. Everything else at Google is a means to this end.

GOOGLE ISN'T A SEARCH ENGINE; GOOGLE IS AN ADVERTISING ENGINE

Now, don't get me wrong. It's not that Google is totally evil and nefarious. Google is just a for-profit business, doing what for-profit businesses do, that is – maximizing profit. But, despite what mountains of Google webinars, help literature, Google Ads rep's, articles in the newspaper, and others will tell you, it's not true that Google has your best interest at heart or even the best interests of web searchers.

Your relationship to Google is a business one: it can be win/win, but it can also be win/lose.

Let's take an example. Suppose you are selling "Motorcycle Insurance" as an independent insurance rep in San Francisco, California. You want to attract customers who need to buy motorcycle insurance, and you know that many of them will turn first to Google, and type into Google search queries such as the following:

motorcycle insurance

motorcycle insurance agency

insurance agents that sell insurance for motorcycles

motorcycle insurance quote

motorcycle insurance cost

cheap motorcycle insurance

motorcycle insurance for Harleys

Etc.

You can view this cornucopia of search queries by just going to Google, entering the "seed keyword" of "motorcycle insurance" and paying attention to Google's search suggestions. More sophisticated tools such as the Google Keyword Planner (inside of *Google Ads > Tools & Settings > Keyword Planner*) or the Twinword.com keyword tool (**http://jmlinks.com/48e**), will give you the volumes and CPC's (cost-per-clicks). You'll find something like this:

Keyword	Volume	CPC
motorcycle insurance	22,200	$24.47
motorcycle insurance quote	5,400	$20.46
cheap motorcycle insurance	3,600	$17.35
best motorcycle insurance	1,900	$23.47
motorcycle insurance rates	1,000	$15.89
cheapest motorcycle insurance	1,900	$18.48

The cost per click as indicated by the tool is approximately $24.47 per click – meaning if a user clicks on your ad for "motorcycle insurance," you, as an advertiser, are going to pay Google – on average - $24.47 per click. As an advertiser, you are highly motivated that the person who "clicks" is also likely to "convert," that is, become a paying customer.

Now, looking at the data available above, you'll see that many people type into Google the phrase:

cheap motorcycle insurance

And some really cheap people type in *cheapest motorcycle insurance* - 1,900 cheapskate searchers per month according to the tool.

But it stands to reason that a person who types in *cheap motorcycle insurance* is likely to be poor, or at least value conscious, and less likely to buy and/or less likely to buy a premium policy. Looking to the future, you might want "cheap" to be a "negative keyword" (which we'll explain later), but just understand a negative keyword to be hidden instructions to Google:

If they enter the word *cheap*, then Google, please do NOT show my ad.

Similarly, Google would like you to advertise in a broad geographic area, perhaps not just the city of San Francisco, but the entire Bay Area or even all of California. That will generate the most clicks (and most revenue for Google). But, it stands to reason, that persons closest to your insurance agency may be more likely to perceive you as "local" and therefore actually buy. Google wants a wide geographic net, and you want to at least research whether a wide (or a narrow) geography will generate more conversions, at a lower cost.

Indeed, let's say that you realize that Harley-Davidson owners make the most profitable customers, and you might want to advertise only on phrases such as:

motorcycle insurance for Harleys

Harley insurance

Harley-Davidson insurance

Harley Davidson motorcycle insurance

Insurance for Harley bikes

etc.

You might decide that you want to be very narrow, in other words, targeting only people who are searching for Harley insurance, and only within a range of 10 miles from your face-to-face insurance agency. *Narrow may be better for you than the broad reach that Google tends to imply is better.*

Google Rewards Ads that Get Clicks

Similarly, if you look at an ad on Google, it has two lines of text, a URL and perhaps a few extensions such as your phone number or other text lines.

Here's a screenshot of an actual ad for "motorcycle insurance:"

GEICO Motorcycle Insurance - Get a Free Quote Online - GEICO.com
[Ad] www.geico.com/ ▼
Get a free cycle quote in 15 minutes or less! Discover how much you could save.
Insurance coverage: Auto, Motorcycle, Boat, Renters
Ratings: Selection 9.5/10 - Ease of purchase 9.5/10 - Website 9/10 - Claim handling 9/10

Get a Quote   Save 15% or More
BIG Savings   Switch & Save

Imagine that that ad said, "Cheap Motorcycle Insurance – Lowest Rates Around" or even better it said, "Free Motorcycle Insurance," or even better it said, "Free Motorcycle Insurance Plus a Free Pizza Just for Clicking," what would happen?

You would drive up the clicks (making Google more money).

You would, however, attract many "tire kicker" customers interested in only "free" or "cheap" motorcycle insurance, or worse "free pizza" thereby reducing your conversions.

Google would be happy. No, Google would be more than happy. Google would be ecstatic! Indeed, Google touts a metric called Quality Score (**http://jmlinks.com/25x**), and

Google would "reward" your ad with a high "Quality Score" because of its high click-thru rate. What could possibly be bad about a high quality score?

You, however, would not be so happy as your Google Ads advertising cost would go up (*more clicks*) and your *conversions* would go down (fewer quality people buying).

> Google wants you to advertise on lots of keywords.
>
> Google wants you to advertise on broad geographies.
>
> Google wants you to write ad copy that says "free" or "free pizza" and "free beer."

Now, to be fair, this is somewhat of an exaggeration. If you read the instructions to Google Ads, Google does point out that you should create *relevant* ads on *relevant* keywords, but they bury this tension between "clicks" and "conversions" enough that most people, even many advanced practitioners, and ad agency types, are unaware of this fundamental tension between Google and its advertisers.

Indeed, one of the more popular books on Google Ads says right on the cover, "Double your web traffic overnight," which could be completely useless when what you really want is to "Double your conversions" or "Increase the profit from your ad spend."

That doesn't sound so sexy on a book cover, however.

The Google Propaganda Machine

In our Internet-infused times, you may have noticed a steady uptick in fake facts, fake news, and information of questionable validity. This is true also with respect to Google Ads. With billions at stake, Google has a very loud propaganda machine explaining the benefits of Google Ads (to be fair, so does Facebook, Twitter, and even Snapchat about advertising on their platforms). If you call into Google Ads "tech support" or allow Google Ads to "optimize" your account, you may find a strong preference for tactics that expand your reach, increase your clicks, and grow your budget over tactics that increase the effectiveness of your ads as measured by conversions. The Google propaganda machine, unfortunately, tilts towards you spending more money to get more clicks.

There's lip service paid to the importance of relevance and conversions, but most of the emphasis at Google is to a) get you to advertise, and b) get you to expand your budget and your ad copy to encourage clicks. In fact, a cynic would say that much of the keyword, conversion, and placement data is hidden in Google Ads so that advertisers "trust" Google to be running ads in their interest as opposed to actually validating their performance with real data.

For an example, there's even a tool inside Google Ads called Bid Simulator. Go to *Campaigns > Ad Groups* and then hover your mouse over the Default Max CPC. You'll see a little box with a squiggly arrow in it. Here's a screenshot:

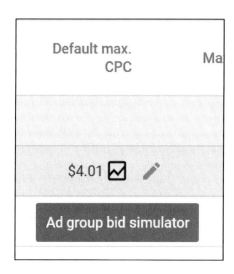

Click on the squiggly box, and Google Ads will pop up a simulation, and (*surprise, surprise, surprise* like Gomer Pyle said on the TV show), it will generally encourage you to *increase* your bid per click (often dramatically) to get just a few more clicks. You can also drill down at the keyword level and do the same process at the keyword level.

Here's a screenshot after clicking the squiggly box at the keyword level:

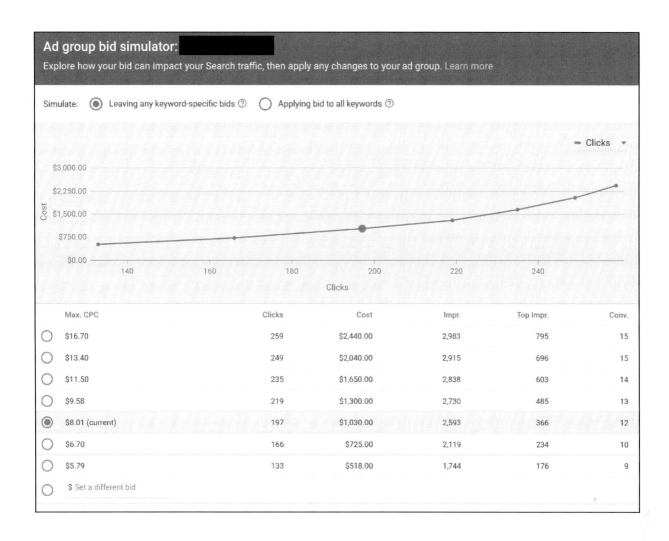

| Ad group bid simulator: ▓▓▓▓▓▓ |
| Explore how your bid can impact your Search traffic, then apply any changes to your ad group. Learn more |

Simulate: ⦿ Leaving any keyword-specific bids ⑦ ◯ Applying bid to all keywords ⑦

Max. CPC	Clicks	Cost	Impr.	Top Impr.	Conv.
◯ $16.70	259	$2,440.00	2,983	795	15
◯ $13.40	249	$2,040.00	2,915	696	15
◯ $11.50	235	$1,650.00	2,838	603	14
◯ $9.58	219	$1,300.00	2,730	485	13
⦿ $8.01 (current)	197	$1,030.00	2,593	366	12
◯ $6.70	166	$725.00	2,119	234	10
◯ $5.79	133	$518.00	1,744	176	9
◯ $ Set a different bid					

So, Google would like me to increase my bid from $8.01 to $16.70 per click, to gain three more conversions at a cost of $1410 or $470 per extra conversion. Is this good for me, or good for Google? (That depends).

You have to know what you're doing and know that Google is tilting the emphasis towards clicks to see the problem here. Indeed, most beginner advertisers don't even enable conversion tracking and may not even see that the cost per conversion is an issue.

Google tilts you to think "get more clicks," when I want you to think "get more conversions."

Even worse, in my experience, there is often not a straight-line relationship between increasing your bid per click, getting more impressions, getting more clicks, and getting more conversions. Sometimes if you bid *lower*, you actually get *more* impressions and *more* clicks, and even *more* conversions – in direct contradiction to Google's public help files!

Now, please don't think I am an extremist and think Google Ads is a scam. I'm not, and it isn't.

I wouldn't be writing a book about Google Ads if I didn't see the value in online advertising. Google Ads can be incredible! But with an eye to the tension between Google's "hunger for clicks" and your own "hunger for conversions," we can learn – together - how to maximize our Google Ads investment.

> *Just remember – always remember – that Google makes its money on clicks, and you make your money on conversions.*

With this tension in the back of our minds, let's dive into the four "Gotchas" lurking inside Google Ads.

» GOTCHA#1: GOOGLE ADS ALTERNATIVES

If you go on a Chevy lot, the car dealer will try to sell you a Chevy. He isn't likely to explain that a Toyota might be better for your needs, nor that using Uber or Lyft might be an even more effective way to secure your transportation.

Similarly, if you reach out to Google, you'll find that Google Ads is the best alternative for any Internet marketing needs. Better than –

> **SEO** or Search Engine Optimization, the art and science of getting your company to the top of Google for **free**. (See my *SEO Fitness Workbook* at **http://jmlinks.com/seo**).

Email Marketing or using email services like Constant Contact, Mail Chimp, or Aweber to build a following of interested customers.

Social Media Marketing, or using free marketing on Facebook, LinkedIn, Twitter, Snapchat and other social media networks (See my *Social Media Workbook* at **http://jmlinks.com/smm**).

Facebook Advertising. Paying to advertise on Facebook, the world's largest social media network.

YouTube Advertising. Paying to advertise on YouTube, Google's subsidiary focused on video.

Twitter Advertising. Paying to advertise on Twitter.

Review marketing. Working hard to get positive customer reviews on sites like Yelp, Google reviews, eBay, etc.

Optimizing on Amazon, eBay, or other specific websites. Some industries (e.g., books) are dominated by certain websites (e.g., Amazon), and Google advertising will do little, if anything, to influence them.

Doing Nothing at All and relying on word of mouth.

Gotcha #1 is to **"fail to consider alternatives."** Google Ads may not generate the highest ROI for your marketing investment. Generally speaking, SEO will usually far, far outperform Google Ads in terms of ROI, while other tactics like social media marketing or advertising on Facebook, Twitter, or YouTube can be cost-competitive in many instances. Indeed, word of mouth and eWom (electronic word of mouth) will nearly always outperform every other marketing vehicle. So, before you use Google Ads, or simultaneously to your use of Google Ads, be sure to maximize every other alternative that may generate a higher ROI.

Usually, a smart marketing effort will have some blood, sweat, tears, and budget in SEO, some in Google Ads, some in WOM / eWOM, some in free social media marketing efforts, and some in other advertising venues such as Facebook or LinkedIn.

Google Ads has a very loud and very powerful propaganda machine (compared, for example, with SEO or email marketing), but that loudness does not mean it generates the highest ROI for you as a small business. It just means that it has a lot of Google dollars behind it!

> **To-do.** Evaluate all your online publicity alternatives, both free and paid, and allocate your budget (both time and money) accordingly. Usually, you want a mix of more than one advertising or marketing vehicle, looking for the highest ROI across media.

» Gotcha#2: Bad Keyword Match Types

If you are advertising on Google Ads, a very common problem is Gotcha #2, "bad match types" for your keywords. We will discuss this in detail in Chapter 4 on the Google Search Network, but for now, let's discuss this basic gotcha.

We'll assume that you've done at least a little keyword research and that you understand you want to run your ads on keyword queries that are "likely" to be your customers and "likely" to be those customers near the moment of purchase.

A San Francisco insurance agent, for example, would set his geotarget to San Francisco, California, and run on keywords such as:

motorcycle insurance

insurance for Harley-Davidsons

And not

motorcycle clubs (too broad)

motorcycle (too broad!)

insurance (too broad!)

In addition, you need to understand **keyword match types** in Google Ads.

When you input keywords into Google Ads to tell Google when to run your ad, be sure to enter either a plus "+" sign, a "quote", or a bracket "[" in front of your keywords. If, for example, you want to run on the keywords "motorcycle insurance," these should be entered into Google Ads as follows:

"motorcycle insurance"

+motorcycle +insurance

[motorcycle insurance]

That is, phrase match, modified broad, or exact match. NEVER EVER enter just the words as for example:

motorcycle insurance

Despite the official Google help explanation (**http://jmlinks.com/23d**), using broad match (*just the words, without quotation marks, plus signs, or brackets*) can produce many poor matches. In this example, Google might substitute

"scooter" for "motorcycle"

so that your ad would show for

scooter insurance

which you may, or may not offer. It can be worse. For example, a keyword target entered as just *cat insurance* (no quotes, plus signs, or brackets) can end up running on search queries like *pet insurance* or even *dog insurance* generating lots of clicks but few sales or sales inquiries.

In addition, you want to pay attention to words that mean different things (e.g., "Joint repair," meaning I need a new kneecap or "joint repair" meaning I need a new CV joint for my Toyota.)

Negative Keywords

Another keyword problem is a failure to identify and input "negative keywords" that indicate people are just looking for free or cheap stuff, like the words "free" or "cheap." After all, someone looking for "free cat boarding" or "cheap cat boarding" isn't exactly the same type of customer as someone looking for "luxury cat boarding," yet if you enter into Google Ads just:

> *cat boarding*

no "+" sign, no "quote" mark and no "[]" brackets and no negative keywords like *-free, -cheap*, you are saying to the Google Ads bartender, "get me a whiskey, any old whiskey will do." Run me on

> *cat boarding*
>
> *discount cat boarding*
>
> *free cat boarding*
>
> *cheap cat boarding*

cat boarding for cat owners who don't care about their cats

etc.

Specificity, not trust, is what you need in your communications with Google Ads. So, you want to specify the correct match type and the negative keywords.

> **TO-DO** If you are currently running on broad match, I highly recommend you go through your keywords and immediately add at least plus "+" signs in front of all your keywords! If you can easily identify obvious negative keywords, add those into your Ad Groups at once.

Find Out Your Actual Keywords

To see the keywords you are actually running, click into an Ad Group (Left Column) and then click on the blue name of your Ad Group. Next, click *Search Terms*.

Here's a screenshot showing the actual search terms entered:

Search term	Match type	Added/Excluded
☐		
Search term	Match type	Added/Excluded
Total: Search terms		
☐ social media marketing books	Exact match	✓ Added
☐ best social media marketing books	Exact match (close variant)	None
☐ best books on social media marketing	Exact match	✓ Added
☐ best social media marketing books 2017	Phrase match	None

These are the *actual* terms people typed into Google, and in the column marked "clicks," you can see if they clicked (and you paid for those clicks); if you have conversions enabled, you can also see which keywords led to conversions.

- If all these terms make sense as relevant to your business, you're in OK shape.
- If, however, you see terms that are way off the mark, you have a problem caused by "Gotcha #2," *bad match types*.

Regardless, immediately tighten up your keyword matches by adding quotation marks, plus signs, and/or brackets. You can also add **negative keywords** if there are terms that clearly designate a non-customer. You want to be in control of your keywords, not Google. (More about this in Chapter 4 on the Search Network).

» GOTCHA #3: ARTIFICIAL INTELLIGENCE

Just let Google think for you. What could possibly go wrong? Google's push into Artificial Intelligence has entered Google Ads in a big way, and it's not 100% bad for advertisers. (See **http://jmlinks.com/48d**). But it's not 100% good either. It's problematic and should be used only with adult supervision.

Artificial intelligence shows up in Google in the following ways:

1. **AdWords Express**. AdWords Express is Google's "solution" for busy small business owners who are too busy to manually set up and manage Google Ads. You write your ads and it "automatically" does all the targeting and optimization for you. In general, AdWords Express produces inferior results to Google Ads, but it is less work.

2. **Keyword Suggestions**. Periodically, you'll log in to Google Ads (especially at the Overview Level) and see "recommended keywords" as Google will auto-suggest new keywords to you. 99% of the time these are junk keywords, designed to dramatically increase your ad impressions and clicks. Don't just follow the suggestions from Google blindly, but be very cautious as to its suggestions for new keywords. You can also see these directly by clicking the "Recommendations" link on the left.

3. **Smart Bidding or Automatic Bidding**. While you can set your bids per click manually, Google has options that use artificial intelligence to adjust your bids automatically. While in some cases this works well, in many others, Google overbids and artificially raises your bids without actually improving performance. To change your bidding preferences, go to *Settings > Bidding > Change Bid Strategy*. For beginners, I recommend *Manual CPC* despite what Google will tell you.

4. **Ad Suggestions**. Google will automatically create ads for you, unless you opt out. Again, because Google is motivated to "increase clicks" and you are motivated to "increase conversions," this conflict of interest can lead Google's AI to create ads that are overly enticing to users (e.g., offering "free pizza' types of inducements). To opt out of Ad Suggestions, click on Settings on the left, then Account Settings at the top, then the drop-down arrow next to "Ad Suggestions" and then "Don't automatically apply ad suggestions" and then Save.

5. **Automated Extensions**. Similar to Ad Suggestions, Google will auto-generate ad extensions which will often be oriented towards getting more clicks rather than towards more conversions. To turn these off, at the Campaign Level, click on *Ads & extensions > Automated Extensions*, then the three dots at the far right, then *Advanced options* and then *Turn off specific automated extensions*, and then enter all the various types at the prompts.

None of these Google AI innovations are inherently bad. It's just that they are experimental in nature and should only be used with "adult supervision." I personally never use AdWords Express, I always turn off the Ad Suggestions and Automated Extensions, and I am very cautious with keyword suggestions and smart bidding.

» GOTCHA#4: THE GOOGLE DISPLAY NETWORK

"Gotcha #4" is the Google Display Network or GDN. Many people do not realize that Google Ads runs on two very different networks, the *Search Network* (primarily Google but also search-driven sites like Yelp or Comcast) and the *Display Network* (a network of sites such as YouTube and Gmail but also blogs, parked domains, web portals and many nefarious sites that seem to exist primarily to steal your money).

THE DISPLAY NETWORK IS PROBLEMATIC

You can read an inaccurate and salesy pitch by Google on the Google Display Network at **http://jmlinks.com/23e**. This is akin to watching a movie trailer about Hollywood's latest horror movie or an introductory video on the latest Ford Mustang by Ford. It is NOT an independent, objective explanation of how the Google Display Network works! It is a sales piece!

The problem is that the GDN contains many badly matched and even fraudulent sites that exist solely to capture clicks and take your ad dollars. If you are not experienced, DO NOT RUN on the Google Display Network!

Default Setting: On

Unfortunately, the default setting on Google is to run on both search and display. In Google Ads' New Interface, Google has made it even harder for inexperienced advertisers to see the Google Display Network when they set up a new campaign.

When you click the blue "+" sign to set up a new campaign, then click on either "Website traffic" or "Leads," you'll see the following options:

And then you'll have to be very careful to "opt out" of the Display Network as it rears its ugly head at various points in the setup process. Here's a screenshot showing where you have to pro-actively uncheck a box to "opt out" of the Display Network:

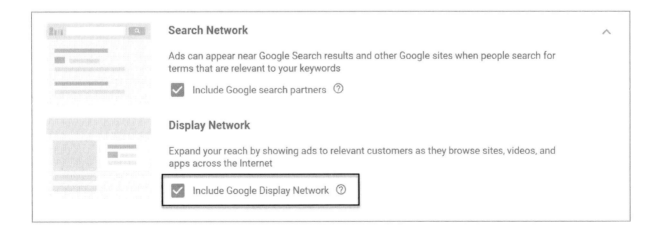

If you are running on the GDN without understanding it, you may be running on many terrible placements up to and including fraudulent sites that do nothing more than generate spurious clicks and cost you money.

To-DO. Turn off the Google Display Network and run only on the Search Network.

To disable the Google Display Network, click into a Campaign, and then click *Settings* on the left column. Next, find the *Networks* tab in the middle of the page. Click the downward chevron to expand the box, until you see:

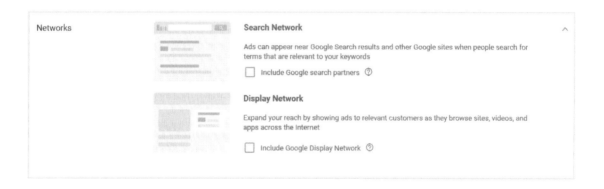

Make sure that the box under Display Network is unchecked; I also recommend you uncheck *Google Search partners* as well, though this is not as unambiguously terrible as the GDN. Google has rigged Google Ads very much to default you into the Display Network, so dig in, find your settings, and run only on the Search Network, until you pro-actively decide that the GDN has value for you.

» GOTCHA#5: CONVERSIONS ACROSS DEVICES

You may have heard that Google is now "mobile first." Google believes that because most search activity occurs on mobile devices like phones and tablets (vs. desktop computers), everyone should run full blast on mobile devices. However, the fact that a lot of *click* volume occurs on mobile phones does not mean that the best *conversion* rates occur on mobile phones. (Remember: Google gets paid off of *clicks*, and you get paid off of *conversions*). It depends on your business.

For some businesses, it is highly desirable to reach consumers on their mobile devices, getting the click from Google, and then getting a conversion on a mobile device on your website. But for many businesses, the mobile experience isn't very good, and many customers click from Google on a mobile device to your website, only to bounce and fail to convert.

Verify that Ads on Phones Actually Convert

"Gotcha #5," accordingly, occurs when you're running on phone, tablets, and desktops when you may be converting far better on only one of these platforms. In my experience, especially for complicated products like insurance, CPA service, hair transplants and the like, generally, the *desktop* conversion rate far outperforms that of the *mobile phone*. Your **TO-DO** here is to verify that your mobile conversions are as strong as your desktop conversions and turn each on or off, or adjust your bids up or down, accordingly.

The default setting is to run on –

Computers – PCs and MACS on the desktop.

Tablets with full browsers – iPad and Android tablets

Mobile devices with full browsers – mobile phones like iPhones and Android phones

You can see your impressions and clicks across devices by selecting a Campaign (or drilling down one more level into an Ad Group), and then clicking on *Devices*. You can then toggle between Campaigns and Ad Groups by clicking the blue *Level* link at the top.

You may not have conversions turned "on" yet. If not, you may show zero conversions across all device types. You can also go to Google Analytics (**https://analytics.google.com/**), then click on Segments, next turn on "Mobile Traffic" and "Tablet and Desktop Traffic." You can then compare your mobile phone traffic to your desktop traffic and look at the relative bounce rate and conversions.

Here's a screenshot, for example, that shows that cost per conversion is far worse on mobile phones and tablets vs. desktop computers:

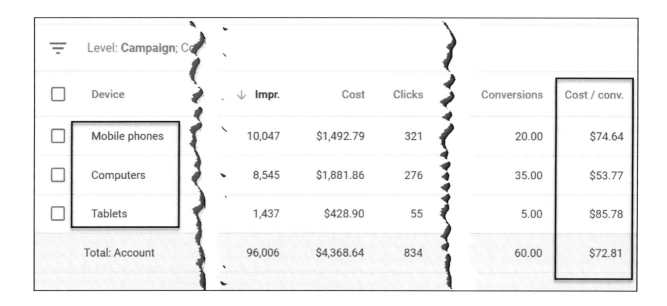

Device	Impr.	Cost	Clicks	Conversions	Cost / conv.
Mobile phones	10,047	$1,492.79	321	20.00	$74.64
Computers	8,545	$1,881.86	276	35.00	$53.77
Tablets	1,437	$428.90	55	5.00	$85.78
Total: Account	96,006	$4,368.64	834	60.00	$72.81

In this example, we'd then want to de-emphasize our ads on mobile phones and emphasize our ads on desktop computers. Despite the Google hype about mobile, we're doing better on the desktop!

A Gut Check

Note: if you don't have conversion tracking turned on, or don't understand. Don't worry. Just do a "gut check." Take out your mobile phone and browse your website. Is it likely that a customer coming FROM Google on their mobile phone and landing ON your website will convert, meaning purchase your product on an e-commerce site, or fill out a registration form on a site that wants sales leads? If so, leave your mobile turned "on" in Google Ads. If not, turn it off or at least bid it down by entering a negative percentage.

To adjust your bids on mobile, click into a Campaign (as these settings are Campaign-specific). Next, click Devices in the left column and you should see the Device targeting box appear. Having decided whether to decrease (or increase) your bids on mobile devices, select a positive or negative number in the Bid adj. (bid adjustment) column. If mobile is outperforming desktops and tablets, you can up your bid. It just depends on what's performing.

Here's a screenshot:

Do this, if, and only if, you believe (or know for a fact) that mobile traffic isn't converting for you. In some rare situations, the reverse may occur: desktop traffic does not convert, but the mobile does. In that case, then turn off or bid down the desktop by setting a bid adjustment of -100% or some lesser percentage. The point is that you need to pro-actively decide which devices to run your ads on, not let Google think for you.

»» DELIVERABLE: AN GOOGLE ADS GOTCHA CHECKUP

Now that we've come to the end of Chapter 1, it's time for your **DELIVERABLE**, a completed *Google Ads Gotcha* worksheet. This worksheet will query you as to the four "Gotchas" to make sure that you have pro-actively decided on your Google Ads strategy as opposed to being led by the nose by Google against your own best interests.

For the **worksheet**, go to **http://jmlinks.com/adw2020**, then re-enter the password, "adw2020," and click on the link to the "Google Ads Gotcha" worksheet.

This Page **Intentionally** Left Blank

(Ponder It)

3

KEYWORDS

When a user goes to the Google search engine, he or she inputs a keyword search query such as "motorcycle insurance" or "pizza near me." Because **keywords** drive Google searches, you, as an advertiser, must be very systematic in how you use keywords to trigger your ads. Choose the *wrong* keywords, and you'll waste money. Choose the *right* keywords, and you're on your way to making money. Choose the *right* keywords, block *irrelevant* queries via negative keywords and proper match types, and create *tight* Ad Groups that structurally reflect your keywords, and you'll be on your way to making a *lot* of money via Google Ads. This Chapter is a deep dive into the art and science of choosing keywords.

Let's get started!

TO-DO LIST:

» Learn Some Keyword Theory

» Brainstorm Your Keywords

» Reverse Engineer Competitors' Keywords

» Use Google Tricks to Identify Possible Keywords

» Use Third-Party Keyword Tools

» Master Google's Google Ads Keyword Planner

»» Deliverable: A Completed Keyword Brainstorm Worksheet

» Identify Your Main Keyword Structural Patterns

» Create Your Keyword Worksheet

»» Deliverable: Keyword Worksheet

Not all keywords are created equally! Let's take our hypothetical "cat grooming and cat boarding salon" here in San Francisco, "Jason's Cat Boarding Emporium, Inc." or "Jason's Cat Emporium" for short.

Cats only! No dogs allowed!

As a business, therefore, we are targeting San Francisco residents who have cats, who have money, and are interested in either our grooming services or our cat boarding services (or both). Remember that we also have an online store that sells cat toys and paraphernalia to customers across the USA.

Note: to avoid wordiness, I will use "keyword" to mean either a single word keyword such as "cats" or a multi-word phrase such as "cat boarding."

Returning to our Business Value Proposition, Jason's Cat Emporium thus has three distinct product or service offerings:

1. **Cat boarding services** – boarding cats for San Franciscans who need a place for fluffy to stay while they vacation at Cabo, or travel to New York City.
2. **Cat grooming services** – providing hair styling to cats in San Francisco so that they look their best
3. **Cat toys and paraphernalia** – an online e-Commerce offering of the very best in cat toys and products.

We suspect that our customers go to Google and type in search queries such as:

cat boarding

pet boarding

cat grooming

kitty boarding

kitty grooming

feline boarding

feline grooming

cat toys

cat collars

hypoallergenic cat litter

etc.

Now, as a potential Google Ads advertiser, we need to know a little about **keyword theory**. We want to advertise to our best customer segment (rich people who are geographically located in San Francisco who have cats that they need to be groomed and/or boarded as well cat lovers across the USA who are looking for unusual and high-quality cat toys) and avoid our worst customer segments (poor or cheap people who can't afford quality cat boarding or grooming services, or (even worse) people looking for dog grooming, dog boarding, or exotic bird services). Our high-end cat toys target folks who love their cats possibly as much, or more than, their spouses and children and for whom money is no object.

Google Ads is a Game of Words

You want to think of Google Ads as a "keyword game" played by you, Google, and your competitors to identify the most profitable keywords and eliminate money-losing keywords. It's all about focus and strategy. Take a moment to review the theoretical constructs below. These will help orient your mind to see that a "word" is not "just a word" when it comes to Google Ads.

Educational Search Query. This is a keyword query when a person is just starting out to learn something about something. Examples would be "Siamese Cats," "Where to buy a cat," or "How to Cut a Cat's Claws."

Transactional Search Query. This is a keyword query when a person isn't really in "learn mode" but rather is in "purchase" or "buy mode." (Google Ads experts often call these "buy keywords" or "late-stage keywords."). Examples would be "Cat Boarding," "Cat Boarding in San Francisco," or even "Pet Boarding." "Cat grooming" or "cat grooming service" would also be transactional keywords, albeit focused on the less valuable grooming service vs. the more profitable boarding service. Ditto for "cat collars" or "personalized cat collars."

Micro Search Query. This means a unique search query, such as "Cat Microchipping," "Luxury cat boarding," or perhaps "Iguana Boarding." "Diamond cat collar" would also fit as a micro. These queries are just a few words, but so specific as to be a very precise search term.

Short- or **Long-Tail Search Query.** This is not my favorite way to conceptualize search queries, but basically, a "short tail" is just a few words vs. a "long tail" which is more than a few words. A short tail would thus be "cat boarding," and a long tail would be "cheap cat boarding in the Castro District, San Francisco." Here's a tip: focus less on the *number of words*, and more on the *user intent*, be that educational or transactional.

Branded Search Query. Your company name, as in "Jason's Cat Emporium" or "JM Internet Group." Your **competitors' names** are also branded search terms (and can be good keywords to advertise on if you're brave).

Reputational Search Query. This is when a user is seeking to research your "reputation" and usually appends the word "review" to your company name as in "Jason's Cat Emporium Reviews."

Negative Keyword. This is a keyword that is definitely NOT your customer. For example, if someone types in "cheap cat boarding" you might consider the word "cheap" as a *negative* keyword, as it indicates the person has no money or is very budget-conscious. "Free" is a common negative keyword as it indicates a person who is not willing to pay.

Ambiguous Keyword. This is a keyword that might be your target customer but might also include some folks who are decidedly not your customer. "Pet boarding" or "Animal boarding" would be examples, as these might include both "dog people" and "cat people."

Transactions Are Where It's At

In general, as you build out your Keyword Worksheet, you're looking for **transactional keywords** that are definitely your customer vs. **educational keywords** that might indicate a person with no money or no desire to spend. Be sensitive as well to **ambiguous** keywords that could be your customers AND some non-customers and watch out for negative keywords like "cheap" or "free" that indicate poor people or people with no intention of spending money.

FOCUS ON TRANSACTIONAL KEYWORDS

Another way to think about keywords is to group them into "hot" keywords that are a) definitely your customers, and b) definitely ready to buy vs. "warm" or "cold" keywords that are a) probably not your customers, or a mix of desirable customers and non-desirable others, and/or b) persons in a frame of mind that are not quite ready to buy. Also, be on the lookout for negative keywords like "dogs," "free," or "cheap" that indicate people who are decidedly not your customers.

Volume vs. Value

Keyword **volume** has to do with how many search queries hit Google in a given time period; for example, a month. You can get this data from the *Keyword Planner* inside of Google Ads, under the *Tools* menu (marked with a Wrench icon, top right of the screen).

Value has to do with the estimated cost-per-click of the keyword. I like to think of volume and value using the analogy of "fish in a pond."

Keyword = type of fish. Is it a salmon or a tilapia? A carp or a bass? Is it *cat boarding* or *cat grooming* or *cat collars*?

Volume = number of fish in the pond. There may be 1000 tilapia in the pond, but only 100 salmon. There may be thousands of (low value) searches for *cat collars* and just a few for *luxury cat boarding San Francisco*.

Value = the price per pound in the fish market, or what people are willing to pay. Even if you know nothing about fish, the fact that organic salmon is $19.99 a pound and farmed tilapia is just $2.00 a pound is a strong clue that the former is "yummy" and the latter "not so much." The fact that the cost per click in Google Ads for *cat boarding* is more than for *cat collar* is a signal that the former has more money behind it than the latter.

You can derive this data from the *Keyword Planner* (inside Google Ads under Tools) and the Twinword.com Keyword Tool at **http://jmlinks.com/48e**. Check out the complete list of keywords tools via the dashboard at **http://jmlinks.com/dashadwords**.

VIDEO. Watch a video on how to use the Google Ads Keyword planner at **http://jmlinks.com/25a**. **Note**: be aware that must have a paid Google Ads account with some dollar spend for the tool to give detailed data! You can watch a separate video at **http://jmlinks.com/25b** that overviews alternative keyword discovery tools.

Riches are in the Niches

Generally speaking, you are looking for "high volume," "high value" keywords that are transactional. So, if you board cats, groom cats, and sell cat stuff, you are looking to advertise on *cat boarding* – YES! Definitely your customer. Plus, variations like "luxury cat boarding" or "cat boarding in San Francisco" or "Castro District cat boarding," etc.

pet boarding – Maybe! This is an ambiguous keyword (it could be dog people, after all).

cheap cat boarding – probably not, as a person who enters this into Google is indicating he has little or no money.

free cat boarding – definitely not, as a person who enters this into Google is indicating he has little or no money.

animal boarding – Maybe! This is an ambiguous keyword (it could be dog people, after all).

kitty boarding – Yes!

cat grooming – Yes!

feline boarding – Yes!

kitty grooming – Yes!

overnight cat boarding – definitely!

quality cat boarding – definitely!

dog boarding – No!

personalized cat collars – Yes!

diamond cat collars online – Yes!

personalized diamond studded cat collars money is no object – Yes, Yes!

If you were to board iguanas or exotic birds, then *iguana boarding* or *exotic bird boarding* would be excellent "riches in the niches" types of keyword queries.

❯❯ BRAINSTORM YOUR KEYWORDS

With a little keyword theory under your belt, it's time to being to brainstorm your keywords in a systematic way. Sit down in a quiet place with a good cup of coffee or tea, or if you prefer, a martini, i.e., *anything to get your ideas flowing*! Brainstorm the **keywords** that a customer might type into Google that are relevant to your company, your product, and/or your service.

Ask yourself:

> *When a potential customer sits down at Google, what words do they type in?*
>
> *Which keywords are DEFINITELY those of your customers?*
>
> *Which keywords are CLOSE to a decision to buy? Which are farther away, earlier in the sales ladder?*
>
> *Which customer segments use which keywords, and how might keywords differ among your customer segments?*
>
> *Which keywords match which product or service lines as produced by your company?*
>
> *Which keywords or helper words are definitely NOT your customers? Free or cheap, for example, are often markers of people who have little to no money, or no inclination to spend.*
>
> *Be sure to capture your synonyms – lawyer vs. attorney, boarding vs. hotel, cat vs. kitten as well as your more ambiguous umbrella terms like law firm or pet boarding.*

Conduct a Keyword Brainstorming Session

I highly recommend that you organize a formal keyword brainstorming session with your marketing team (it might be just you by yourself, or it might be your CEO, your marketing manager, and a few folks from the sales staff). Devote at least ONE HOUR to brainstorming keywords; close the door, turn off the cell phone, tell your secretary to "hold all calls" and start drinking (either coffee or martinis).

Brainstorm, brainstorm, brainstorm the keywords that customers are typing into Google. Try not to miss any possible keyword combinations!

Do this, first, individually – take out a piece of paper, and write keyword ideas down WITHOUT talking to the others in your group.

Don't be shy. Don't leave anything out. The goal is to get EVERYTHING on paper, no matter how ridiculous it might be.

Then have a group session and go over all the keywords each person has identified.

Drink some more coffee, or more martinis, and keep brainstorming – write all possible keywords on a whiteboard, a piece of paper, or a Word / Google document.

Don't censor yourself because there are no wrong answers. The goal of this exercise is to get the complete "universe" of all possible keywords that customers might type into Google.

BRAINSTORM ALL POSSIBLE TARGET KEYWORDS

For your first **TO-DO**, open up the "keyword brainstorm worksheet" in either Word or PDF, and begin to fill it out as completely as possible. For the worksheet, go to **http://jmlinks.com/adw2020**, then re-enter the password, "adw2020," and click on the link to the "keyword brainstorm worksheet."

Again, for right now, don't worry about the *organization* of your keywords. Don't police your thoughts. Write down every word that comes to mind - synonyms, competitor names, misspellings, alternative word orders. Let your mind wander. This is the keyword discovery phase, so don't exclude anything!

» REVERSE ENGINEER COMPETITORS

After you've completed this first wave of brainstorming, let's you and your group members do some searches on Google for target keywords. Take a few of the keywords you've already identified and type them into Google. As you search Google, identify your "Google competitors," that is, companies that are on page one of the Google results and therefore doing well in terms of SEO (Search Engine Optimization). Even though this Workbook focuses on Google Ads, you can use the organic results to **reverse engineer** their keywords for *SEO* and use these as possible keywords for *Google Ads*.

Here's how.

Method #1: Source Code

First, click over to their homepage or whatever page is showing up on page one of Google for a search that matters to you. Next, view the HTML source code of this page. To do this, in Firefox and Chrome, use *right click*, then **V**iew, **P**age Source. In Internet Explorer, use **V**iew, **S**ource on the file menu. Finally, find the following tags in the HTML source code:


```
<Title>
<Meta Name="Description" Content="...">
<Meta Name="Keywords" Content="...">
```


If you have trouble finding these HTML tags, use CTRL+F (on a PC vs. Command+F on a Mac) on your keyboard, and in the dialog box type *<title*, *description*, or *keywords*

For each, write down those keywords your competitor has identified that might also be applicable to you. Here's a screenshot of **http://www.globalindustrial.com/c/hvac/fans**, one of the top Google performers for the search "industrial fans" with the three critical tags circled -

(**Note**: you may not find all of these tags in competitor pages, and don't worry about what they actually do as those are questions of search engine optimization. Just use them as ways to look into the minds of competitors for keyword ideas).

Read each tag out loud to your group members. Notice how each tag in the source reveals the "thought process" behind this page, showing the "types" of fans people might search for - pedestal, wall-mounted, ceiling, etc. The goal of viewing the source of your competitors' pages is to "steal" their keyword ideas and write down any relevant keywords onto your "keyword brainstorm" document.

> **VIDEO.** Watch a quick video tutorial on how to use "view source" to reverse engineer competitors at **http://jmlinks.com/5k**.

Method #2: Ads on Google Ads

Do searches that you have already brainstormed and read the ads out loud that you see on the Google screen. Here, for example, are ads returned from the search "San Francisco Cat Boarding:"

As you read this out loud, you'll see synonyms (e.g., *cat* vs. *kitty* vs. *pet*) and helper words such as *premier, private, hotel, boarding,* and points of difference such as "large suites" or "private". Write these down on your list. For example, notice how the first ad has a headline of "Cat Hotel." Bingo! You've found a new word, *hotel* as in *cat hotel.* Be sure to click over to the companies who are advertising, and View Source looking at their TITLE, META DESCRIPTION, and KEYWORD tags.

Use Keyword Spying Tools

As you research your keywords, you can avail yourself of free / paid tools that "spy" on competitors. One of the best is SpyFu at **https://spyfu.com/,** and another is Keyword Spy at **http://www.keywordspy.com/**. Simply enter a keyword and see who's advertising, what their ads say, and some research on their keyword targets.

By entering *thepawington.com* into Keyword Spy, for example, I learn that they are advertising on:

San Francisco pet hotel

San Francisco dog hotel

Pet hotel San Francisco

Pet grooming

Cat resorts

By doing this, I get some great synonyms to "cat boarding" such as "cat hotel" or "cat resort." Who knew?

For your second **TO-DO**, open up your "keyword brainstorm worksheet," and jot down the top five competitors who appear at the top of Google for your target keywords, use the tactics above to view their source, and then write down keyword ideas taken from their TITLE, META DESCRIPTION, and META KEYWORDS tags. Be sure to input them into Keyword Spy or SpyFu as well.

Did you discover any keywords you left out in your first brainstorming session? If so, be sure to write those on your list.

» USE GOOGLE TRICKS TO IDENTIFY POSSIBLE KEYWORDS

After you have brainstormed keywords and used View Source to view the keywords of competitors, it's time to use free Google tools for keyword discovery. Here are my favorite strategies starting with Google's own free tools.

First, simply go to Google and start typing your keyword. Pay attention to the pull-down menu that automatically appears. This is called **Google Suggest** or **Autocomplete** and is based on actual user queries. It's a quick and easy way to find "helper" words for any given search phrase. You can also place a space (hit your space bar) after your target keyword and then go through the alphabet typing "a", "b", etc.

Here's a screenshot of **Google Suggest** using the key phrase "motorcycle insurance":

Hit your space key after the last letter of the last keyword (e.g., after *motorcycle insurance*) and more keyword suggestions appear. You can also type the letters of the alphabet – a, b, c, etc. and Google will give you suggestions. Here's a screenshot for the letter "b":

Second, type in one of your target keyword phrases and scroll to the bottom of the Google search page. Google will often give you **related searches** based on what people often search on after their original search. Here's a screenshot for "motorcycle insurance" -

Note the **helper words** it tells you people use to search: cheap, rates, best, "how much," comparison, cost, and average. Are these not wonderful clues as to how customers search Google? As you look at Google autocomplete and related searches, add these keywords to your master list.

Answer the Public's Keyword Tool

A third-party tool that pulls data from Google search queries is Answer the Public's Keyword Tool at **http://jmlinks.com/51e**. Ignore the creepy man, and enter a "seed" keyword such as "cat boarding." Here's a screenshot of the results page:

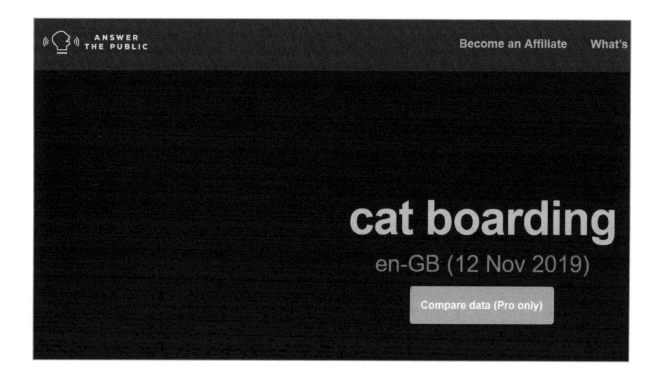

After entering your "seed" keyword, scroll down and the tool gives you the following data points:

Questions. These are questions that contain the phrase, and are generally "educational" searches such as "How much does cat boarding cost?"

Prepositions. The tool takes popular prepositions like "near" or "with" and creates phrases. Review these and look for transactional phrases such as "cat boarding near Princeton NJ."

Comparisons. This next segment takes words like "versus" or "or" and presents phrases such as "cat boarding vs. pet sitting;" review with an eye to which phrases are likely to be high value.

Alphabetical. The tool pulls every letter of the alphabet, giving you the complete universe of Google autocompletes.

Related. The tool attempts to provide related keywords such as synonyms.

You can also click on "download CSV" at the top right and download the complete dataset. The tool is a fantastic, fun, and easy way to accelerate your keyword brainstorming session. Just be on the look out for high-value keywords, as well as important synonyms such as "pet boarding" or "cat hotels" vis-à-vis your target seed keyword.

Another good tool is Keywordtool.io at **http://jmlinks.com/25z**. It basically types through the alphabet for you and gives you nifty keywords. Spend some quality time with the Google tools as well as these two suggestion tools, using your "starter" keywords and looking for synonyms and helper words. It's also a good idea to repeat this exercise on Bing as well as Amazon, as both of these search engines provide "autocomplete" suggestions. Here's a screenshot of amazon for "cat collars":

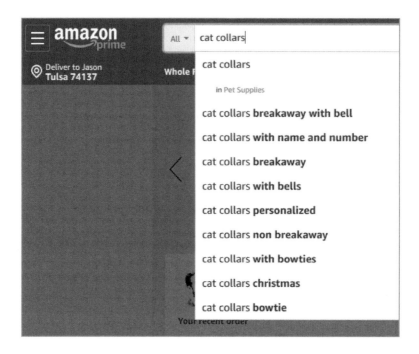

The phrase "cat collars personalized," for example, is a clue to the high-value search query for "personalized" cat paraphernalia. Thus even Amazon or Bing can give additional clues to the high value, late-stage, and/or transactional keyword phrases that should drive your Google Ads strategy.

For your third **TO-DO**, open up your "keyword brainstorm worksheet" and write down some keyword ideas garnered from these free tools. You want a messy, broad and complete list of the "universe" of possible customer keywords via your own brainstorming process, via reverse engineering your competitors, and now via Google and third-party keyword tools. The objective is to get everything down on paper.

» USE THIRD-PARTY KEYWORD TOOLS

With your rather messy list of keywords in hand, it's time to start focusing on **volume** vs. **value**. Unfortunately, the best tool (which is the *Google Ads Keyword Planner*) does not provide complete keyword data to new accounts or accounts with little spend. Here are some third-party alternatives that I recommend beginners start with.

First, I recommend that you check out the **TwinWord** keyword tool at **http://jmlinks.com/48e**. Sign up for an account, and they allow you a few free searches each day.

Type your starter keyword into the tool. Here's a screenshot for the keyword "pet boarding":

The left two columns give you "keyword ideas," such as "dog kennel" or "dog sitter." (Because we're cats-only, we can use these as ways to generate the ideas "cat kennel" or "cat sitter"). The AVG Monthly Searches gives you the volume and then the remaining columns tell you something about the competitiveness of the keyword and the relevance of that phrase to your starter keyword.

Click on "Advanced Filters" on the left and you can filter by the CPC (Cost Per Click), although unfortunately the tool does not show the CPC data directly. Click on the top right green arrow and you can save the keywords into a list, as you brainstorm your "keyword universe."

Second, check out **KWFinder** at **http://jmlinks.com/48f**. Type in a "seed keyword" such as "cat boarding" and this tool also gives you an idea column, a volume column, a CPC column, and a PPC difficult column. Here's a screenshot:

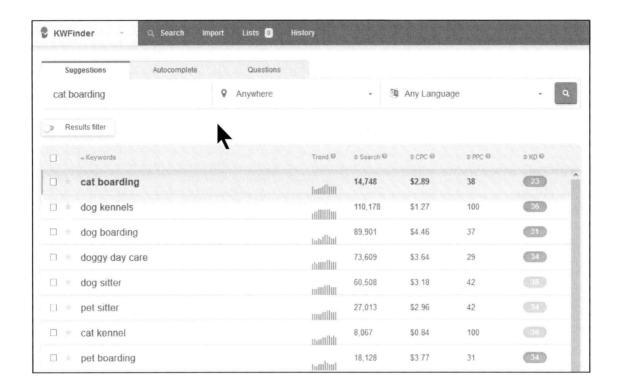

In a similar way, therefore, you can use this tool to brainstorm keyword ideas, volumes, and values (CPC amount). As you research keywords, start to pay attention to:

Keyword Groups. Begin to group your keywords around themes such as "pets" vs. "cats" or "cat sitter" vs. "cat boarding." We'll see that this idea of keyword groups (which become Google Ads groups) is a very important one.

Volumes. Which keywords have a lot of search volume, and which ones do not?

Values / CPCs. Which keywords are facing high bids as the community bids up the cost-per-click? Which ones do not?

Keyword Types. Which keywords are early-stage, educational keywords? Which ones are late-stage, transactional keywords?

Secret Fishing Holes. Be on the lookout for "secret" keyword patterns. These might be very high value and/or long-tail keywords that represent a very strong match between what customers want and what you offer. For Jason's Cat

Emporium, for example, patterns such as "luxury cat boarding" or "emergency cat boarding" might be very high value, even if they are low value, and chances are that our competitors might not have "discovered" these patterns.

Third, another good alternative to the Google Keyword Planner is the **Bing Keyword Planner.** Since Bing is a very distant #2 to Google, it "tries harder to please." Here are your steps to access the Bing tool:

1. Sign up for Bing Ads at **http://jmlinks.com/48h**. You'll need a Microsoft account, and the easiest way to do that is to sign up for a free Live email at **http://jmlinks.com/48j**.
2. The signup process is similar to Google Ads, so just follow the step by step instructions and pause any ads that it forces you to start.
3. Inside the Bing Ads interface, click on the Tools menu on the top, and then "Keyword Planner." This gets you into the interface.
4. Type in a seed keywords such as "cat boarding" where it says, "Search for new keywords."

Similar to the Google Keyword Planner, the Bing tool then gives you a column of keyword suggestions or ideas, the average monthly volume, and a suggested bid, indicating what the community is willing to pay for a click. Once you're in the interface, you can change your target keyword target by retyping a new one in the top bar and hitting "get suggestions." Here's a screenshot:

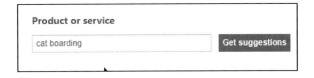

One of the best discovery features of the Bing tool is the "Ad group suggestions" feature, which groups keywords by themes. Click on the tab marketing "Ad group suggestions" to access this feature. Here's a screenshot for "cat boarding:"

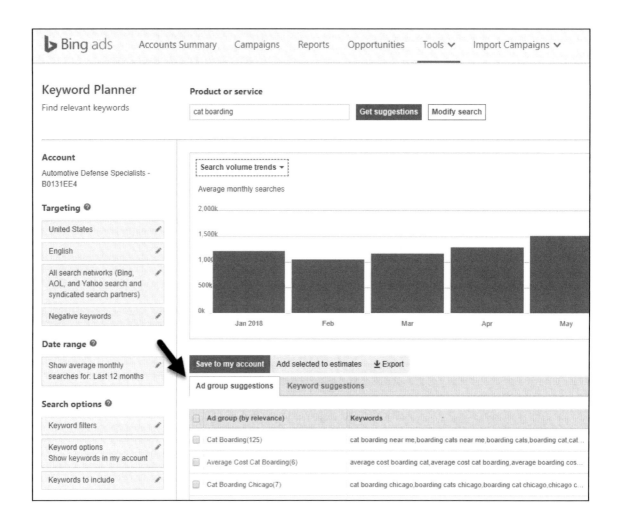

In this way, the Bing tool gives you suggestions for Ad Groups based on similar keywords such as:

Cat Boarding

Cat Sitting

Cat Kennels

Pet Boarding

Pet Sitters

etc.

It's a great way to discover synonyms such as "sitting," "kennels," or "pets" as you brainstorm your keywords.

On the left-hand column, you can adjust your geo-target, network, and keyword filters. Bing runs about 10% of Google volume, so you can generally take whatever volumes Bing is telling you and multiply by ten to get approximate Google volumes.

Paid Tools

Returning to the other tools, you can sign up for free TwinWord and/or KWFinder accounts or upgrade to a paid account for about $30/month. If you're really pressed for money, you can sign up for just a month, do your keyword research and then cancel your account. Other good paid tools are SEMRush (**https://www.semrush.com/**) and Ahrefs (**https://ahrefs.com/**) both of which offer robust keyword discovery tools. I recommend that you sign up for at least one paid third-party tool as robust keyword research is essential to success at AdWords.

» MASTER THE GOOGLE ADS KEYWORD PLANNER

Now it's time to use the most comprehensive keyword tool of them all: Google's own official **Keyword Planner.** It's free, but you'll need a Google Ads account to use it fully.

> **VIDEO.** Watch a video tutorial on how to use the Google Ads Keyword Planner at **http://jmlinks.com/17j**.

Sign up for Google Ads

To sign up for Google Ads, go to **http://ads.google.com/**. You'll need a credit card to set up an account, and the Google Ads interface will attempt to get you to start advertising right away.

Google Ads will FORCE you to set up your first campaign, with groups, ads, and keywords. Simply follow their instructions "as if" you were going to set up an ad, and immediately set your first campaign to "pause." To pause your campaign, follow the Google Ads set-up instructions to set up your account and then click on the "campaigns" tab, select the checkbox to the left of your first campaign, click "edit" in the menu, and then "pause." (You can even call Google Ads at 866-246-6453 and ask them for help on how to set up your advertising campaigns, and then *sneakily* ask them to **pause your campaigns** – just explain that you are just setting things up, right now, and you do not want to turn on any advertising at this time). The point of all this is to use a credit card to set up an active Google Ads account, and then use this account to access the Keyword Planner.

Note: do NOT ever let the "helpful" Google Ads employees "help" you set up your Google Ads Campaigns, as they will run wild and you'll overspend. We want to be much more focused and selective than the Googlers would lead us to be.

Google Goes Evil

Google now requires that you spend money to get accurate data out of the Keyword Planner. Accordingly, you may need to allocate a few hundred dollars and run some actual ads before you'll get accurate keyword information out of the tool. I know it's a bit of a pain, but once you have an operational Google Ads account, you can use the Google Ads Keyword Planner as a wonderful way to research keywords. Alternatively, you can always use the free or paid tools referenced in my Dashboard at **http://jmlinks.com/dashadwords** > Keywords.

Now, let's return to the Keyword Planner.

Access the Tool and Get Started

Inside of your Google Ads account, next, go to the "Tools" tab at the top underneath the "Wrench" icon at the top right, and scroll down to "Keyword Planner." Here's a screenshot:

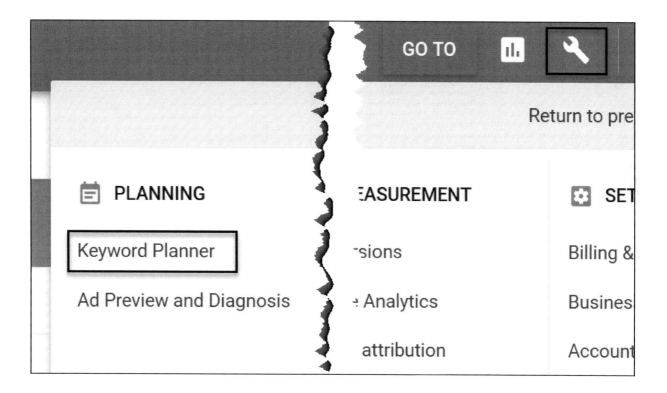

You should see two boxes, so click on the one marked "Discover new keywords." Next, enter a "seed keyword" such as "cat boarding" into the box and click the blue "Get Started" button. This gets you into the actual tool interface. At any time, you can change your "seed keyword" by clicking in the search bar and x'ing out the keyword and entering another one. Here's a screenshot:

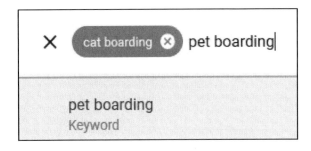

To research a keyword, click the blue "Get Results" button on the far right. It's best to research one keyword at a time. You should see a screen that look like this:

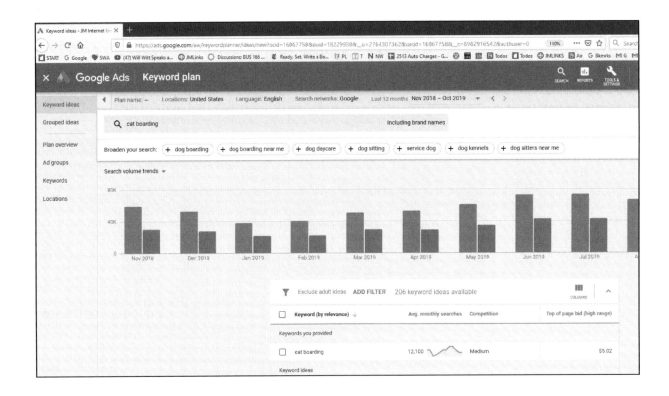

Now, let's dive into the tool's elements. Across the top, you can set your location to United States vs. Canada, UK, etc. You can also set it to a city such as New York City, but I recommend using a very big region such as a country as the tool is most useful at higher volumes. So, if you are in the United States, make sure it is set to United States. You can also set the language to English (French, German, etc.). And then you'll see

"Search networks." The default is to "Google and search partners," but you can also set this to just Google. It's fine either way.

The left column has "Grouped Ideas," "Plan overview," "Ad groups," "Keywords," and "Locations." Of these, "Grouped Ideas" is the most important. Click on that and Google will give you suggestions of interrelated ideas. This is a great way to discover synonyms, and using "cat boarding," Google gives us "grouped ideas" of:

Cat Daycare

Cat Hotels

Long Term Cat Boarding

Cat Only Boarding

Cat Resort

Looking to the future, we realize that highly focused, "niche" Ad Groups are the best way to maximize the click-thru rate and ROI of our ad spend. A focused Ad Group on "Cat Daycare," for example," might snatch those high income San Franciscans who are so neurotic about their cats that they'll pay lots of money for daytime cat care. Who knew?

Click back into Keyword Ideas on the top left, and the tool will give you four columns:

Keyword = keyword ideas similar to your "seed" keyword

Avg. Monthly Searches = estimate of how many monthly searches for this keyword against your geography

Competition = how competitive it is to advertise

Top of page bid (high range) = the bid per click necessary to get your ad to show at the top of search

If you don't see these columns, click on the "columns" icon and enable them. You're researching synonyms, high-value phrases, volumes, competition, and what you have to bid to get your ad to show. Think of Google Ads as a fishing competition. You're the fisherman or woman and you're competing against other fisherfolk to find the best fish in the easiest way at the lowest price vs. value to you. Look for "niche" keyword patterns such as "cat hotel" or "cat daycare." Click on "Download Keyword Ideas" on the top right to download your data into an Excel.

To be blunt, it's good to just click around in the interface to learn what's hidden where and to find some functions that are very useful and ignore the ones that are not. Another weird feature of the tool is that the volumes given are for "exact match" data, so if you enter "cat boarding," the volume you get at about 12,100 for the USA is applicable ONLY to searches that are exactly "cat boarding" and not inclusive of search such as "luxury cat boarding," or "cat boarding San Antonio," etc. There is, unfortunately, no option in Google to look for the "phrase volume," but third-party tools do offer this feature.

Column Data in the Keyword Planner

Now, let's dive into the results that are returned column by column. (If you don't see these columns, click on the "Columns" icon on the top right and expand to include them).

Keyword (by relevance). You should see a column on the left called "Keyword (by relevance)." This is what I call the **keyword ideas column.** Scan it and look for keyword ideas. For "cat boarding," for example," you should see not only "cat boarding" but interesting and possibly related keywords such as "dog kennels," "pet sitter," "cat kennel," and so on and so forth. Open up a Word or Google Doc and copy down those keywords that you think are highly relevant. Pay special attention to synonyms such as "pet" for "cat," or "kennel" for "boarding." **It is absolutely critical to get your synonyms!** Also pay attention to keywords like "dog," which in our case are not relevant and might become negative keywords, and others like "pet" which are ambiguous (as those could be either dogs or cats).

Discuss possible keyword ideas with your team. Also, don't be afraid to take a keyword like "pet sitter" and re-enter it in the top search bar to re-research keyword possibilities.

In this way, one "seed keyword" can beget other "seed keywords" and you can quickly use the tool to brainstorm possible keyword targets. The Keyword Planner tool is probably the best tool on the market for discovering synonyms such as "pet" vs. "dog" vs. "cat" or "kennel" vs. "boarding" vs. "hotel."

Avg. monthly searches. Google will give you the average search volumes. Remember that this is for the geographic location you set at the top (e.g., United States, Canada, or United Kingdom). Also remember that Google gives you the monthly search volume based on "exact match" and "close variants" so with "cat boarding" at 12,100 for the USA, this means around twelve thousand searches were for "cat boarding" but this wouldn't include phrases like "best cat boarding" or "cheap cat boarding." If you find a good helper phrase such as "luxury cat boarding," reenter it as a keyword to get its actual monthly search volume.

Competition. This is an attempt by Google to tell you how competitive a keyword is. The tool gives you "High," "Medium," and "Low" as metrics. Popular, high-value words like "car insurance" will get a score of "high competition," while unpopular, non-money keywords like "cat videos" will get a score of "low competition." I do not find this particularly useful, as I prefer to look at the CPC costs, so I often turn off or ignore this column.

Top of page bid (high range). This is a dollar estimate of what you need to bid (CPC) to get your ad to show at the top of the page. It's a capitalist world we live in, so Google gives you a way to see which keywords are likely to end in profitable sales and which ones are not. For "cat boarding," for example, we see a $5.02 bid for the high range. In effect, the tool gives you a way to poll your competitors who will likely bid UP transactional keyword phrases that reflect buyers who are ready to buy at high prices and bid DOWN educational or poorly formed queries that are people who either don't want to buy or who are cheap or poor. I often refer to this as the CPC bid or value column. It's very important data.

Other Stuff. You may see columns such as "Account Status," "Organic impression share," "Organic average position," and "Competition (indexed value). These are pretty useless, so I recommend you just ignore them. They are Google's poorly formed attempt to tell you whether you are ranking organically or not for these keywords.

Educational vs. Transactional Keywords

The tool can help you understand which patterns are high-value, transactional keywords and which ones are low value, educational keywords. As you research your keywords, make an educated guess and then re-enter the keyword patterns all at once across the top. For example, take "knee pain," "knee surgery," and "best knee surgeon" to compare volumes and values by entering all of them in the search bar at one time. Here's a screenshot:

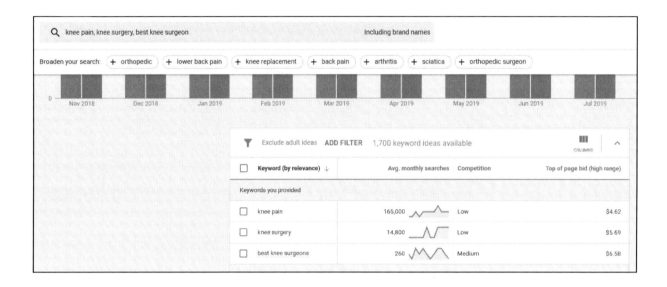

You can see that there are 165,000 searches per month for "knee pain" at a cost per click (CPC) of $4.62, vs. 14,800 for "knee surgery" at a CPC of $5.69 vs. 260 for "best knee surgeons" at $6.58. In other words, you can vividly see the trade-off between "volume" and "value." The early-stage keywords have lots of volume, but less value (lower bids per click in the AdWords auction) as they are less likely to end in a high-value transaction; the late-stage keywords have less volume but more value as someone searching for "best knee surgeons" is likely close to a transaction. Play around with your keyword patterns, as you are looking for the "sweet spot" of sufficient volume and sufficient value to justify your ad spend. Also be aware that the tool gives data only for "exact match" and is rather unreliable at low volumes. It's not particularly accurate vs. the data you'll get in your actual account once you're actually advertising, so use it as a starting point only.

Other Features

Finally, let's also look at a few other **features**. At the top middle you should see a gray "Add Filter" Click on this to view a "Filter menu." Here's a screenshot:

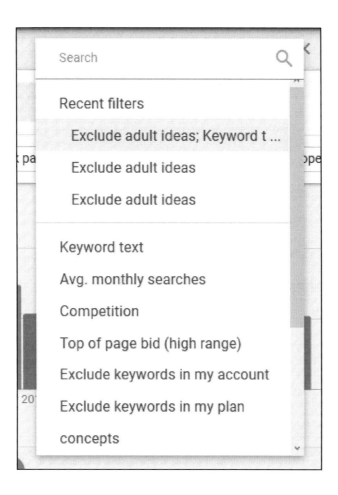

The best filters are "keyword text," which you can use to narrow down the results, and "Avg. monthly searches," which you can use to filter out low-volume search patterns. The other filters are not particularly useful.

Reverse Engineer a Website for Keywords

You can even return to the very beginning screen of the Keyword Planner by clicking on the Wrench / Tools icon > Keyword Planner, clicking into "Start with a Website," and then entering in a URL such as your home page, or a landing page, or even the URL of a competitor. This is yet another way to brainstorm keywords by "reverse engineering" a competitor.

Try it with *https://www.rover.com/cat-sitting* for example. Here's a screenshot:

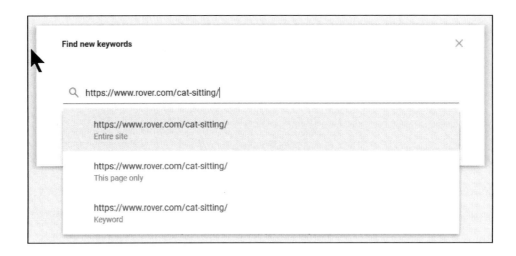

This tactic is especially good if you are a new advertiser vs. competitors who are well-established and have a very focused strategy of keywords. Try it for a competitor and see what results you get.

Building Your Keyword List

As you work on your keywords, you can click the checkbox to the left of any keyword to save a keyword into a plan or identify it as a negative keyword. You can create a new Ad Group called "Test Keywords" and put your keywords into that group, for example, However, I find this feature very cumbersome and hard to use, so I just generally copy/paste my keywords into a Google Doc or Word Doc or a spreadsheet. (You can also download keywords by clicking "Download Keyword Ideas" in blue at the top). I find that copy/paste or download into a spreadsheet works better, as I can then use my

Keyword Worksheet to organize my SEO, Google Ads, and/or Social Media keywords accordingly.

You can then click up to "Plan overview" and Google will give you some data about your keywords. I don't find this very accurate or useful but do what works for you.

What You're After

As you are using the tool to research and brainstorm your keywords, here's what you're after.

Keyword Ideas. You want to capture the "universe" of **core keywords** plus available helpers. Don't miss "attorney" for "lawyer" or "pet" for "cat," etc. Pay attention to common **helpers** like best, top-rated, or top or **negatives** like "cheap" or "free."

Keyword Volumes. Get your keyword volumes, but don't fixate on volume. Some very high-value keywords are worth advertising on or optimizing on for SEO or social media. It's not just about volume.

Keyword Values or CPCs. Use the tool to "poll the community" as to which keywords are the most valuable by seeing the bids. But realize that these are the "discovered" keywords. Be on the lookout for **undiscovered keywords** that are highly valuable such as micro or long-tail keywords that represent affluent customers ready to buy. If you repair watches for example, "watch repair" is high volume but low value, while "Rolex repair" is lower volume but much higher value. For "cat boarding," folks who search "luxury cat boarding" are clearly the folks who have money and are willing to spend it.

»» DELIVERABLE: A COMPLETED KEYWORD BRAINSTORM WORKSHEET

Now we've come to the end of this process, and you should have the first Chapter **DELIVERABLE** ready: your completed **keyword brainstorm worksheet**. For the worksheet, go to **http://jmlinks.com/adw2020**, then re-enter the password, "adw2020," and click on the link to the "Keyword Brainstorm Worksheet."

Remember the "Keyword Brainstorm" document will be messy. Its purpose is to get all relevant keywords, helper words, and keyword ideas about volume and value down on paper. In the next step, we will turn to **organizing** our keywords into a structured **keyword worksheet**. This will be our blueprint for setting up our Google Ads campaigns and groups.

» IDENTIFY YOUR MAIN KEYWORD STRUCTURAL PATTERNS

After you complete your **keyword brainstorm** worksheet, your head may be spinning (*especially if you and your team were using martinis rather than coffee as the drink of choice during the brainstorming exercise*). Now it's time to shift gears and to organize those keywords into "structural patterns" with an eye to both keyword volume and value.

Here's where we're going:

> **Brainstorm** *your keywords* **>** **organize** *them into a keyword worksheet* **>** **organize** *your Google Ads account into* **keyword-centric Ad Groups**.

Let's look at some example websites.

Most businesses have a few different product or service lines, and often a few different customer segments. Take a look at Progressive Insurance (**https://www.progressive.com/**), for example, and you'll quickly realize that they have different types of insurance offered such as auto insurance, motorcycle insurance, RV insurance, and even Segway insurance. Take a look at **https://www.progressive.com/insurance-choices/** to see the organizational structure of their website, and you'll quickly realize that the "structure" of the website reflects the "structure" of how people search for insurance. Those who are on a Harley-Davidson motorcycle are searching in one way, and those looking to insure their Segway are searching in another.

In terms of **keyword structural patterns** and **matching Ad Groups (**and website landing pages), we have:

motorcycle insurance =

> a group of keywords around *motorcycle insurance* like *cheap motorcycle insurance, motorcycle insurance quote*, etc. =
>
> an Ad Group in Google Ads =
>
> a landing page on the website.

Car insurance =

> a group of keywords around *car insurance* like *cheap car insurance, automobile insurance, car insurance quote*, etc. =
>
> an Ad Group in Google Ads =
>
> a landing page on the website.

etc.

Or, take a look at Industrial Fans Direct (**http://www.industrialfansdirect.com/**), and you'll see that they have product categories such as blowers, man coolers, ceiling, bathroom fans, etc., and that these reflect the "needs" of consumers who "search Google" using words that reflect those needs.

blowers =

> a group of keywords around *blowers* =
>
> an Ad Group in Google Ads =

a landing page on the website.

roof exhaust =

a group of keywords around *roof exhaust* =

an Ad Group in Google Ads =

landing page on the website.

etc.

With those examples in mind, it's time to look at your own keyword patterns.

Take a look at your own **keyword brainstorm document** and circle the "core keywords" that reflect your basic product or service categories. Usually, you'll see a one-to-one correspondence of a "product group" that matches a "core keyword," as you see in the examples above. And you'll also see a bunch of helper words like *cheap, best, San Francisco, quote, rate,* etc., that are often entered alongside the core keyword. People often mistakenly think that they have "hundreds" of keywords, when in fact they usually have only about five to ten **core keyword groups** or **structural patterns**, and these then form hundreds of possible keyword queries. As on *Progressive.com* and *IndustrialFans.com* as listed above, you'll see that a core keyword should become one, and only one, landing page on the website.

In terms of Google Ads, this means:

One *core keyword* will (ultimately) become one *group* in Google Ads account.

To return to Jason's Cat Emporium, we'd have:

A *cat boarding* Ad Group

A *cat grooming* Ad Group

A *cat toys* Ad Group

Looking to the future, however, if *luxury cat boarding* generates a really strong ROI, then we'd break out luxury cat boarding into its own unique Ad Group. We'd also have an Ad Group for *pet boarding*, recognizing that this is an ambiguous pattern vs. *cat boarding*. Google Ads **strongly rewards** a **tight match** between a *core keyword*, a corresponding *Ad Group*, corresponding *keyword triggers*, *corresponding ads* that contain the keyword in visible ad text, and a corresponding unique *landing page* on your website. Your keyword worksheet should group your target keywords into this structure.

In fact, Google itself strongly encourages that you organize your Ad Groups by keyword themes. Read the Google help file on Ad Group organization at **http://jmlinks.com/39n** and watch a simple but useful video on organization at **http://jmlinks.com/48g**. You'll learn the following:

A **Campaign** is where you set the network, geotarget, budget and other attributes.

An **Ad Group** is where you group together closely related keywords around a theme, and where your ads will "ultimately" live.

Each ad should also go to a **landing page** on your website that specifically relates to the keyword target. Your "cat boarding" ads, for example, should go to a page on "cat boarding," while your "cat grooming" ads should go to a landing page on "cat grooming."

We'll discuss account organization more in the next Chapter, but for now start taking your disorganized Keyword Brainstorm worksheet and organizing your keywords into thematically connected patterns that will form the basis for your Ad Groups.

Keyword Volume and Value

As for keyword *volume* and *value*, you'll then see that you take a core keyword and you can look at the volume of the entire "group" of keywords around it, as well as the value as measured in the Keyword Planner that reflects the "value" of these keywords in the sense that they are likely, or not, to end in a sale.

> **Volume** = are there a lot, or just a few, searches on Google that reflect the core keyword as a group?
>
> **Value** = if a searcher enters this search query is it of high, or low value, to your company, as measured in the likelihood that it can become a sale, and if it becomes a sale that that sale makes you a lot (or just a little) of money?

For your next **TO-DO**, download the **keyword worksheet**. For the worksheet, go to **http://jmlinks.com/adw2020**, then re-enter the password, "adw2020," and click on the link to the "keyword worksheet." Note this is a Microsoft Excel document.

> **VIDEO.** Watch a video tutorial on how to create a Keyword Worksheet at **http://jmlinks.com/17m**. Note: this video is focused on SEO, but many of the same rules apply to Google Ads.

Inside the document, list each major pattern of your keywords (which reflect a product or service grouping of your company) on a line all by itself in the first column. Return to the Keyword Planner and note both the keyword volume and keyword value (suggested bid) that correspond to each core keyword.

» CREATE YOUR KEYWORD WORKSHEET

Now it's time to fill out your keyword worksheet in more detail. In your spreadsheet, you'll be filling out columns for the following:

Core Keywords. These are the minimum words necessary to create a relevant search. If you are a watch repair shop servicing high-end watches, for example, your core keywords would be phrases such as "watch repair," "Tag Heuer Repair," "Rolex Repair," etc. This is the first column, and reflects the core, structural keyword patterns and indicates volume and value.

> **Note.** If, to your business, a phrase is important enough (e.g., *Rolex watch repair* vs. *Tag Heuer watch repair* vs. just *watch repair*), then break it out into its own core keyword group / line item on your keyword worksheet. Do this even if these words are closely related (e.g., Rolex repair vs. Hamilton repair vs. Tag Heuer repair for watches).

Helper Keywords. Common helpers are geographics like San Francisco, Berkeley, and Oakland. In the watch examples above, other helpers would be "best," "authorized," "SF" etc. that combine with the core keywords to make the actual search query (e.g., "Best watch repair SF").

Sample Search Query Phrases. Take your core keywords plus your helpers and build out some "real" search queries that potential customers might use. Group these by keyword family. For example, you'd have a keyword group called "Rolex Repair" and underneath, related keyword phrases such as "Rolex Repair SF," "Authorized Rolex Repair Downtown San Francisco," or "Best Rolex Repair Shop Bay Area," etc.

Search Volumes. Indicate the volume of searches (where available) as obtained from the Google Ads Keyword Planner.

Search Value. Indicate whether a given keyword family is of high, low, or negative value to you and your business. Does it indicate a searcher who is probably a target customer? If your answer is strongly yes, then this is a "high value" search term! Does it clearly indicate a non-customer? If so, this is a "low value" or even a "negative" search term. I often mark "hot," "warm," or "cold" next to a keyword group.

Competitors. As you do your searches, write down the URL's of competitors that you see come up in your Google searches. These will be useful as mentors that you can emulate as you build out your SEO strategy.

Negative Keywords. Are there any keywords that indicate someone is definitely not your customer? Common examples are *cheap* or *free*, as these are often indicative of people with little or no money, or little or no intention to buy something. *(These negative keywords are not so important for SEO, but for Google Ads, it is CRITICAL to identify your negative keywords.)*

Priority Order

Not all keywords are created equally. Some are **high volume** (*lots of searches*), and some are **high value** (*they are customers ready to buy something or take an important action like filling out a feedback form or calling with an inquiry*). With respect to your business, take a look at your keyword worksheet and think about which queries are a) the *most likely* to be a potential sale, b) the *most likely* to be a high-value sale, and c) the *least likely* to be ambiguous. (An ambiguous or problematic keyword is one that has several meanings, that might cross business products or services, and is, therefore, more difficult to optimize on than an unambiguous keyword. Compare *fan* for example, which could be a *hand fan*, an enthusiast for a *sports team*, or an *electrical appliance* to *blow air* with *insurance* which refers to one, and only one, type of product. *Pet boarding* or *animal boarding*, for example, are ambiguous vs. *cat boarding* or *dog boarding*, which are not)

> **VIDEO.** Watch a video tutorial on educational vs. transactional, volume vs. value keyword theory at **http://jmlinks.com/17n**.

Prioritize Your Keywords: Hot, Warm, or Cold?

Prioritize your keyword families on the spreadsheet from TOP to BOTTOM with the highest priority keywords at the top, and the lowest at the bottom.

Remember the *volume* vs. *value* trade-off. "Transactional" keywords (those close to a sale) tend to have higher *value*, but lower *volume*; "whereas educational" keywords (those early in the research process) tend to have lower *value*, but higher *volume*.

However, here's the rub: because of the see-saw between value and volume, there is no hard and fast rule as to what should be your top priority. It can't be just *volume*, and it can't just be *value*.

In fact, I recommend you use a column on the far left and call it "hot / warm / cold." Sit down with the CEO or sales staff, and play a "hot / warm / cold" game by asking IF a customer entered such-and-such into Google, would it be hot (*definitely our customer*), warm (*probably our customer*), or cold (*not our customer*)?

Prioritize the "hot" keywords at the top of the Keyword Worksheet, and the "warm" keywords towards the bottom. I often throw out the "cold" keywords entirely. This will help you see the complexity of keyword patterns as some keywords will be "easy" to see as hot / warm / cold, and others might be more challenging – perhaps they have a lot of volume, but are ambiguous, or perhaps they are high value but just so little volume, or the customers don't know to search for them.

> *The art of Google Ads is targeting the keywords most likely to generate high ROI, which is a function of BOTH volume and value as well as whether a keyword is unambiguously your customer or ambiguously your customer plus others.*

Ignore Low Volume Warnings

Another tip: the Google help files and tech support team tend to focus on keyword *volume* over *value*. You may even get warnings in Google Ads that threaten "low search volume." If a keyword patterns (such as "Rolex repair" or "luxury cat boarding") is of very high value to your company, however, I strongly recommend you build it out into a keyword-based Ad Group anyway. The algorithm and customer experience both reward very tightly organized groups, even if the volume is low. Because you pay by the click, there is no penalty for creating laser-focused Ad Groups in Google Ads! In fact, the more tightly connected the relationship among keyword target, Ad Group, Ad text, and landing page, the better you will do.

The Art of Google Ads

On the flip side, don't stress your keyword organization too much!

Your keyword worksheet is a *living* document. As you build out your Google Ads campaigns and groups and measure your rank and results, you will "tune" your advertising to work on those keywords that are high value, high volume, and you can actually out-compete the competition for. It's a process, not a static result. Online advertising, like cooking great food or preparing for a marathon, is as much *art* as *science*. Don't fall prey to **analysis paralysis**, and endlessly analyze your keywords as opposed to implementing them.

The basic concept to get is:

Keyword Group = Ad Group in Google Ads

You should identify core keywords that will be at the center of corresponding Ad Groups. For example:

Cat boarding = one Ad Group

Cat grooming = one Ad Group

Cat Toys = one Ad Group

Pet boarding = one Ad Group

»» DELIVERABLE: YOUR KEYWORD WORKSHEET

After some brainstorming, hard work, and organization, you should have your **DELIVERABLE** ready: a completed **keyword worksheet** in an Excel or Google spreadsheet. The first "dashboard" tab should be a high-level overview to relevant keywords, reflecting the structural search patterns that generate the **keyword groups**, next the keyword volumes as measured by the Google keyword tool, and finally the values measured by the Google cost-per-click data and your own judgment as to which search queries are most likely to lead to a sale or sales lead. Other tabs (which you will fill out over time) include a tab for reporting, a tab to measure your rank on Google vs. keywords, a tab for local search rank, and a tab for landing pages.

> **Note**: *I recommend one Keyword Worksheet for both your SEO project and your Google Ads project. If for now, you are only working on Google Ads, it may be more Spartan, but – long term – you want to think of both SEO and Google Ads as working together for an effective Google strategy. Ditto for Bing / Yahoo.*

In summary, the **keyword worksheet** for your company should reflect keyword *volume*, *value* (as measured by the "fit" between the keyword search and what your company has to offer), and the *structural search patterns* that reflect the "mindset" by which people search. This document will be your blueprint for building out your Ad Groups going forward.

4

SEARCH NETWORK

When people say they want to "advertise on Google," they generally mean that when a customer searches on Google for *such-and-such* product, service or company by keyword, they want their ad to appear on the Google search engine at Google.com, and nowhere else. As we've learned so far, however, Google is actually two distinct networks (*Search* and *Display*), and if you're not careful, Google can place your ads on the Display Network as well as the Search Network without your pro-active understanding. Indeed, few people realize that Google "search partners" such as Yelp, YouTube, or Xfinity are included in the "Search Network." It's confusing; perhaps by design. Who knows? Regardless, in this Chapter, we'll focus on tips, tricks, and best practices for the **Google Search Network** so as to show your ads when (*and only when*) you want them to appear on Google and its Search Partners like Yelp, YouTube, or Xfinity.

Let's get started!

TO-DO LIST:

» Review Basic Set-Up Best Practices

» Identify Transactional Keywords

» Organize Your Campaigns & Ad Groups

» Use Correct Keyword Match Types

» Write "Attract / Repel" Ad Copy

» Experiment with Responsive Search Ads

» Use Ad Extensions

» Follow CEA on Landing Pages

» Set Your Bids

» Set Logical Campaign Settings

» Choose Your Geotarget Settings Wisely

» Monitor Your Keywords, Bids, Conversions, and Performance

» Shoot Your Dogs, and Let Your Winners Run

»» Deliverable: Search Network Worksheet

» REVIEW BASIC SET-UP BEST PRACTICES

We'll assume you've set (or reset) at least one Campaign to run *exclusively* on the Search Network. Here are the steps to create a new Campaign:

1. Log in to your Google Ads account.
2. Click on *Campaigns* on the left.
3. Click the White "+" sign in the blue circle, and then "New Campaign."
4. Select "Create a campaign without a Goal's Guidance"
5. Select "Search."
6. Select "Website visits" in the checkbox.
7. On the next screen, make sure that the "Display Network" box is NOT checked (i.e., you are running ONLY on the Search Network.)
   a. You can include *Google search partners* if you like. Or if you are on a tight budget, uncheck this.
8. Follow the steps to set up an at least one Ad Group that matches one of your Core Keywords, at least one ad inside that Ad Group going to a matching landing page on your website, and keywords (as indicated below) using "+", """", or "[]" around your target keywords. (*We'll return to this, in detail, later in this Chapter*).

One annoying feature in Google Ads is the "guided set up." I recommend you fight your way through "Guided Set up" for your *Campaign > Ad Group > Ad*, and then pause this. Once you're through this, you can then use the simpler interface that lives underneath at campaign. You should see something like this:

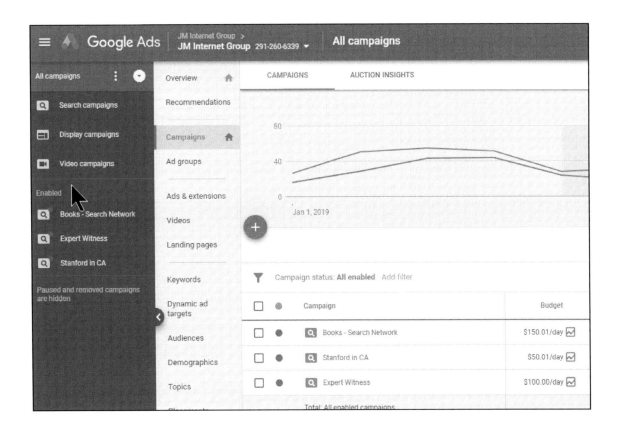

If you're resetting an existing campaign to the Search Network, click on the Campaign, and then click Settings on the left. Click into "Networks" in the middle, and make sure that Search Network is selected; uncheck the box for Google Search partners, and do NOT check the box for Display Network. At the end of this process in *Campaign > Settings > Networks* you should see this:

If you see "Display Network," your campaign is running on that network as well; reset your settings until you get "Google Search Network" and only "Google Search

Network" to show. It is a best practice to NEVER mix Search and Display targeting, despite how Google leads you in guided set up.

Google Ads is a Hierarchy

Importantly, realize that you can navigate from this basic Campaign level to various features and options. Click –

Into a **Campaign** and then **Settings** on the left to modify features such as the **Network** (Search vs. Display), **Locations** (where you want your ads to appear), **Languages** (which languages to target), **Budget** (what your daily budget limit is), **Bidding** (your bid strategy), **Start and end dates** (if you want to schedule your ads).

Into a **Campaign** and then **Devices** to manage your bid adjustments (up or down) for Computers vs. Mobile phones vs. Tablets.

Into a **Campaign** and then **Ad Groups** to create or modify Ad Groups.

Then inside of **Ad Groups** to create ads, create or manage extensions, and set keyword triggers.

As you work with Search Campaigns, always remember that Google Ads is a hierarchy. Different components "live" at different levels, beneath different "parents," and accordingly, you can manage features only at specific levels. Keywords, for example, "live" at the Ad Group level while Geotargeting "lives" at the Campaign level.

Search Partners

Search partners are sites such as Yelp.com or Xfinity.com that run Google search results. YouTube searches are now included as a search partner. These "partner sites" are considered "search" because people tend to type keywords rather than browse. For example, here's a screenshot of the "Search box" on Xfinity.com:

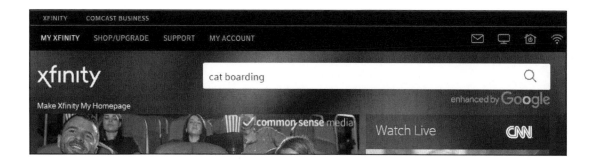

You can see "enhanced by Google" on the right. And here's the Yelp home page with Google results shown after I searched for "cat boarding" near San Francisco:

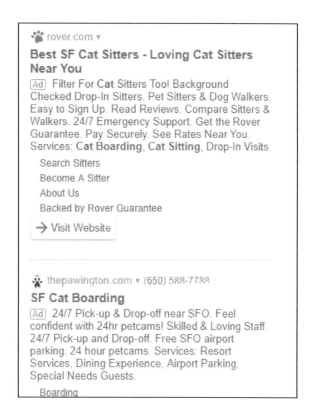

And here's a screenshot of a search for "cat boarding" on YouTube pulling ads from Google's search network function:

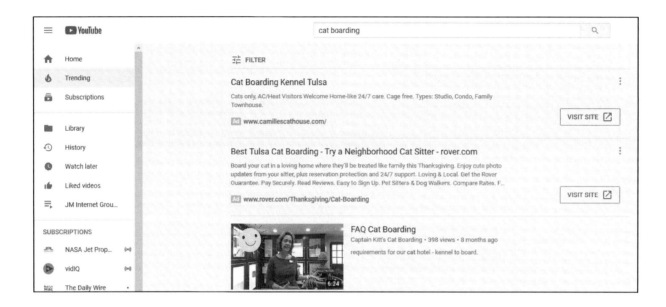

To sum up, if you select "Search Network" in your settings, your ads can appear on Google as well as Search Partner sites like Yelp, Xfinity, and YouTube.

Here's a (not-so) fun fact. *Nowhere* does Google publicly identify the companies in its Search Network. (So much for transparency, Google.) We know it's Yelp, Xfinity, and YouTube for example, but there isn't a clear list of all sites in the Search Network, nor does Google Ads identify where your ads appear if you check the box. So, if you're cynical, I'd uncheck this box to be sure your ads run only on Google.com.

As this is most conservative strategy, I usually uncheck "Search partners." Google is where the action is, and I want to run full blast on Google. If, however, you think customers will search YouTube, then I think checking Search Partners is warranted. As for Yelp, Xfinity, and partner sites, I think they're pretty lame for this function and you tend to get a lot of fraudulent bot clicks on them.

Say No to the Display Network (For Now)

If you see "Display Network" anywhere, you've done something wrong. Sometimes if you've set up a Campaign running on the "Display Network," Google Ads will not let you convert it to the "Search Network." In that case, you have to pause that Campaign and create a new one in the correct fashion. At the end of this process, you want at least one Campaign that is set to run on *only* the Search Network. In fact, you never want to "mix networks." You should have campaigns running only on the Search Network and if you decided to use the Display Network, another set of campaigns running only on the Display Network. Mixing the networks in one Campaign complicates everything, so **do not mix campaigns**.

> **VIDEO.** Watch a video from Google on the Google Search Network at **http://jmlinks.com/26d**.

» IDENTIFY TRANSACTIONAL KEYWORDS

Let's revisit your keywords and explain how to input them into your *Search Campaign > Ad Groups > Keywords*. Keywords drive search, and – therefore – *keywords* drive Google Ads on the Search Network. Here are the steps from the perspective of a customer

Customer need > search query on Google > click on ad > landing > sale / sales inquiry

Or, translated into our scenario of a San Francisco resident who needs cat boarding for Fluffy, during his vacation to Cabo San Lucas:

I need to have my cat taken care of on vacation > keyword search on Google for "cat boarding San Francisco" > see / click on ad for Jason's Cat Emporium > land on Jason's website > fill out inquiry form to check out the Emporium for my cat, Fluffy > Agree to sign up Fluffy, and the deal is done.

Using this simple process model, you can see that your steps on Google Ads begin with defining the best **keywords** to advertise on.

Step #1: Identify the search keywords that you want to advertise on.

It all starts with the keyword. The customer need "becomes" the keyword, and the keyword that the customer enters into Google needs to find a match in the keyword that you enter as a **keyword trigger** into Google Ads.

Customers enter **keywords** into Google.

Advertisers enter **keyword triggers** into Google Ads.

While Google calls both of these *keywords*, it's helpful to distinguish between the *keywords* that are entered by the searcher, and the *keyword triggers* that you, as an advertiser, enter into Google Ads. Keyword triggers as we shall see, need to be notated in Google Ads in one or more of four distinct ways:

Plus Signs (called Modified Broad Match)

+cat +boarding = telling Google to run your ad on any variations of the words *cat* and *boarding*, but no substitutions.

Quotation Marks (called Phrase Match)

"cat boarding" = any keyword query by the searcher that includes that phrase.

Brackets (called Exact Match)

[cat boarding] = the exact phrase, only, as entered into Google.

No Plus Signs No Quotes No Brackets (called Broad Match)

The "sucker choice" is to enter in the words *cat boarding* into Google Ads with no "+" sign, no "quotation," and no "[" bracket.

NEVER JUST ENTER KEYWORDS INTO GOOGLE ADS!

The reason, of course, is that if you just enter

cat boarding

Google can substitute nearly *anything* for those words, and before you know it, you're running on

dog hotels

Because to Google, the word *cat* is like the word *dog*, and the word *boarding* is like *hotel*. Entering keywords with no quotes, plus signs, or brackets is a "gotcha," so don't do it!

Core Keywords

Refer back to Chapter 3, and your Keyword Worksheet. You should have identified **core keywords** that reflect the major structural patterns of your products or services. Take a look at the Progressive.com website (**https://www.progressive.com/**), and you'll see a very structured organization of keywords in terms of landing pages on the website.

Auto / car insurance at **https://www.progressive.com/auto/**

Home insurance at **https://www.progressive.com/homeowners/**

RV insurance at **https://www.progressive.com/rv/**

Motorcycle insurance at **https://www.progressive.com/motorcycle/**

Boat insurance at **https://www.progressive.com/boat/**

etc.

In addition, as you look at their landing pages and read the text out loud, you'll notice helper keywords such as *quote, rates,* or *companies* that further make a keyword transactional. In fact, here's a screenshot of their ad running on "motorcycle insurance":

Progressive® Motorcycle | Insurance as Low as $75/year
[Ad] www.progressive.com/Motorcycle ▾
★★★★☆ Rating for progressive.com: 4.6 - 656 reviews
One Visit Could Save You Money on Motorcycle Insurance! Get A Quote. Norton Secured Site.
Golf Cart Insurance · Windshield & Glass Claims · Vehicle Insurance · Boat Insurance

And here's their ad for "boat insurance:"

You'll see that Progressive runs very specific ads for "boat insurance" that go to a very specific landing page for "boat insurance" vs. very specific ads for "motorcycle insurance" that go to a very specific landing page for "motorcycle insurance" and so on and so forth.

Check it out yourself. Do some searches relating to *car insurance, RV insurance, boat insurance*, etc., and click on the ads. Notice how many of the top advertisers send you to very defined landing pages even if they offer other products or services.

Google Ads rewards a **very organized, hierarchical structure**, as follows:

One core keyword > one specific Ad Group > one or more specific ads > one specific landing page

Identify Transactional Keywords

On your own Keyword Worksheet, you should have identified 5-10 **core keywords** plus another 10-20 helper words that ensure that your keywords are **transactional** in nature. You also want to keep an eye on keyword **volume** and **value** because, since Google Ads is expensive, you generally want to advertise only on keywords that are likely to lead to a sale. In general, (but not always), *educational* keywords should be avoided. (Or, if you decide to bid on them, place them in their own Ad Group and bid much lower per click as they have a significantly lower value.).

A San Francisco orthopedic surgeon, for example, might have core keywords such as:

Knee surgery

Knee surgeon

Hip surgery

Hip surgeon

Shoulder surgeon

Shoulder surgery

Orthopedic Surgeon

And helper words like *San Francisco, best, top, top-rated, arthroscopic, second opinion,* etc. (He will NOT advertise on "knee pain" as that "educational keyword" will have a lot of volume, generate a lot of clicks, cost him a lot of money, but end up with many bounces as these are people who are not close to the decision to engage with a knee surgeon). Also, let's say he only focuses on knees. Then he might run ads only on the "knee surgeon" pattern and avoid the more general "orthopedic surgeon" as this will pull in people looking for hip or shoulder surgeons.

In general, the tighter your focus among your keyword target, your Ad Group (and ads), and your landing page, the better you'll do on Google Ads.

Similarly, for Jason's Cat Emporium, we will identify transactional keywords such as:

cat boarding

cat hotels

long-term cat care

cat kennels

cat grooming

cat toys

And avoid educational /non-relevant keywords such as:

cat

cat vets

dog boarding

And realize that some relevant keywords are ambiguous (because they may signify other animals such as dogs):

pet boarding

animal boarding

And some helper keywords are negative (poor or cheap people):

cheap

free

To review what we learned in our Keywords Chapter, your first **TO-DO** is to build out your **keyword worksheet**, organize your keywords into core keywords, and identify transactional keywords that are also (hopefully) high volume / high value. I would also create a column and designate the core keywords as "hot" (definitely your customer), "warm" (probably your customer), "cold" (probably not your customer). It's also a good idea to notate keywords like *pet boarding* that are **problematic** because they include both your customers and non-customers. (We'll return to ambiguous keywords when we discuss writing ads in the "Attract / Repel" style).

» ORGANIZE YOUR CAMPAIGNS AND AD GROUPS

Generally speaking, **one** core keyword should be represented in **one** ad group in Google Ads. Where we're going is to see that your Keyword Worksheet will map to your Google Ads as follows:

one core keyword > one Ad Group in Google Ads

for example:

cat boarding > cat boarding group in Google Ads

pet boarding > pet boarding group in Google Ads

cat hotel > cat hotel group in Google Ads

cat kennel > cat kennel group in Google Ads

cat grooming > cat grooming group in Google Ads

DON'T LET REALITY CONFUSE YOU

While you might think that *pet boarding* includes *cat boarding* (which it does in the real world), at the "word game" level of Google Ads, you want a very tight focus between the words. Don't be lazy and clutter your Ad Groups with non-related keywords. So *pet boarding* will get its own Ad Group, *cat boarding* will get its own Ad Group, and so on and so forth.

The tighter the linkages, the better your performance will be.

Campaigns in Google Ads

But before we dive deeper into strategy and setup, let's talk for a moment about **Campaigns** in Google Ads

Conceptually, a campaign should reflect a budgetary "bucket" of how you want to spend some money in a strategic fashion. They should reflect customer segments as well. Since campaigns are where you set the *network* (Search vs. Display), plus features such as *geotargeting* and *device targeting*, you want to think strategically about your campaigns as you get started (or revise existing campaigns).

As examples:

> **Networks**. Since "search" is radically different from "browse," the MOST important campaign setting is to ONLY run a campaign on ONE network, the Search Network (not *Search Network and Display Network*) (*despite what Google tells you is the "best choice!"*).

> **Geotarget**. "Geotarget" or "location targeting" is Google Ads lingo for showing ads ONLY to people who reside in a specific area (e.g., San Francisco) and/or are searching with intent around that area (e.g., "Cat Hotels San Francisco") vs. showing your ads just to anyone, anywhere. Location targeting is set at the campaign level; accordingly, if you want to show different ads to people in different cities, then you set this at the Campaign level, and you need separate campaigns (e.g., one for San Francisco and one for Oakland).

> **Budget**. If you make a lot more money on one product (e.g., *cat boarding*) than on another (*cat grooming*), it makes sense to put them in separate campaigns as budgets can be set separately at the Campaign level.

> **Devices**. Since you can determine whether you show on mobile phones vs. desktops vs. tablets by changing these settings at the campaign level, and budgets are set at the campaign level, it makes sense to split your mobile from your

desktop campaigns if (for some reason) you want a different spend for people searching on different devices.

Ad Groups

Next, once you've set up a campaign, drill down into your **Ad Groups**. Remember:

one core keyword = one ad group in Google Ads

Also, remember that even though you can geotarget in Google Ads, city names are also often helper keywords, so you'd have *cat boarding San Francisco* in the *cat boarding* Ad Group. Finally, although structurally in Google Ads, Ad Groups "live" inside of Campaigns, Google Ads will force you to set up a group and an ad the first time when you set up a Campaign, so you often have to toggle back and forth as you set things up.

GOOGLE ADS IS A HIERARCHY

Structurally, however, Google Ads works as a **hierarchical system**:

Account (sets account information, access, controls billing, etc.)

Campaign (sets budget, geotarget, devices, etc.)

Ad Group (organized around ONE and ONLY ONE core keyword) controls ads and bids and contains the keywords.

Here's a nice graphic from Google that displays the hierarchy of Google Ads:

Account			
Unique email and password Billing information			
Campaign		Campaign	
Budget Settings		Budget Settings	
Ad Group	**Ad Group**	**Ad Group**	**Ad Group**
Ads Keywords	Ads Keywords	Ads Keywords	Ads Keywords

Source: **http://jmlinks.com/39v**.

For example, I'd have a Campaign called **Cat Emporium – Search Network** that is running on the Search Network only, geotargeting residents of San Francisco. Here's a screenshot showing the hierarchy of *Campaign > Ad Group* from inside an account:

Your Campaign are accessible off to the far left in the menu system but also appear at the top in the "breadcrumb" trail as I have indicated above. Also note how I have four ad groups, one for *cat boarding,* one for *cat hotels,* one for *cat kennels,* and one for *pet boarding* that reflect the core keywords of *cat boarding, cat hotels, cat kennels,* and *pet boarding.* I usually name my Campaigns with their network, making it easy to see what's what at a glance. By naming the Campaign *Cat Emporium – Search Network,* I can see in an instant that this is a Search Network campaign.

While you can zig and zag through Google Ads, up and down the levels, it is immensely helpful always to ask yourself "what level am I at?"

Account

    Campaign

        Ad Group

            Ads ("live" at the Ad Group level)

Keywords ("live" at the Ad Group level)

You can "view" items like keywords across levels, like looking into a glass building that has different floors, but you can only edit / change them when you are actually "at" a specific level. With respect to keywords, for example, you can "view" them across Campaigns, but you can only edit / change them at the Ad Group level. A few things, such as bids, can be set at two levels (e.g., you can change a bid at the Ad Group level or at the Keyword sublevel).

Since *cat grooming* is quite different from *cat boarding*, then I'd have a separate campaign called *Cat Grooming*, with at least one Ad Group in it, also called *Cat Grooming*. And, to advertise my cat collars, cat toys, and other cat paraphernalia via Google Shopping ads (an XML feed from my e-Commerce store), I'd also have a Campaign called *Google Shopping* with Ad Groups for the main product groupings. Since e-Commerce is nationwide and very different from the boarding and grooming functions, I'd set up a unique Campaign for that (as the geotarget would be "United States" not "San Francisco.") (See Chapter 6 on how to set up Google Shopping campaigns).

> **VIDEO.** Watch a video tutorial from Google on setting up Ad Groups at **http://jmlinks.com/26b**.

» USE CORRECT KEYWORD MATCH TYPES

Next, you need to properly understand and use Google Ads nomenclature to set your keyword targets. Google confuses this by misleading you into thinking you can just throw keywords into Google Ads willy-nilly.

Keyword Match Types

Taking our example of *cat boarding*, in your Cat Boarding Ad Group, you'd insert the keyword:

+cat +boarding

meaning, *modified broad match* in Google Ads speak.

which tells Google to run your ad if, and only if, the searcher enters BOTH the word *cat* AND the word *boarding* (as well as very close variants such as the plural *cats*, or a misspelling like *baording*). I also recommend you enter variants such as

"cat boarding"

meaning, "phrase match" in Google Ads speak

and

[cat boarding]

meaning, "exact match" in Google Ads speak

And you would **NEVER** enter just

cat boarding

as this is the **dangerous broad match** in Google Ads. If you enter just *cat boarding* (no "+" plus sign, no """" quotation marks, no "[" brackets, as Google will run away with this, and run your ads on things like *pet boarding, dog boarding, iguana boarding, dog hotels,* etc.

Here's a screenshot of keywords correctly entered into Google Ads:

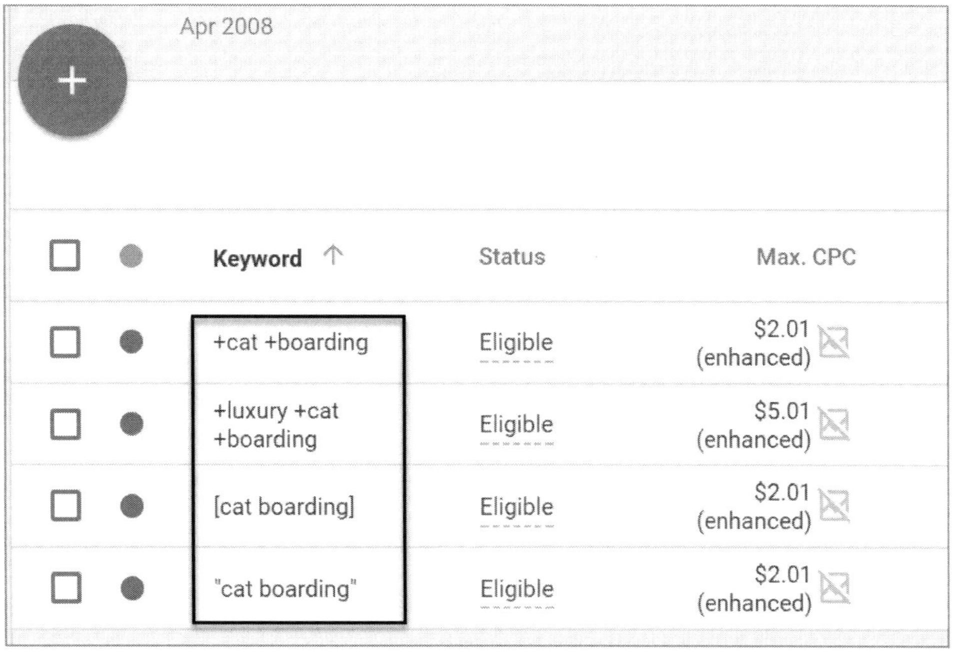

		Keyword ↑	Status	Max. CPC
☐	●	+cat +boarding	Eligible	$2.01 (enhanced)
☐	●	+luxury +cat +boarding	Eligible	$5.01 (enhanced)
☐	●	[cat boarding]	Eligible	$2.01 (enhanced)
☐	●	"cat boarding"	Eligible	$2.01 (enhanced)

Apr 2008

Enter All Three Variants

Why enter

"cat boarding"

[cat boarding]

when

+cat +boarding

is the superset of the former two keyword phrases, meaning it **includes** them by default?

Technically speaking, you do not have to enter all three variants because *+cat +boarding* captures the other two.

However, if you also enter the phrase and exact match variants, you get better reporting (you'll know exactly how many searches occur for the *exact keyword query, the phrase, and then variations of the phrase*), plus you can **set your bids differently** for these keywords. (*I've also noticed that entering all variants seems to help your performance… don't ask me why just do it*).

You can use the Google Ads Wrapper tool at **https://jmlinks.com/25c** to quickly create all variants this. Just be sure to enter your core keywords and select **ONLY** the "+Modified +Board, 'Phrase' & [Exact] Match" box. Here's a screenshot:

You can then copy / paste those into the Keywords tab / Ad Group level for the corresponding Ad Group in your Google Ads Campaign.

High-Value Keyword Phrases

Similarly, for more targeted bidding, if a phrase might have higher value to you, you can enter it as a phrase. For example:

same day cat grooming

luxury cat grooming

in-home cat grooming

The reason for this is that the addition of certain helper words indicates that the customer is more likely to be affluent, and/or willing to pay a premium.

SKAG: Single Keyword Ad Groups

Accordingly, you want the option to be able to raise your bid for these variations of your keyword. Indeed, if a phrase is really, really valuable (e.g., *same-day cat grooming*), you can even break it out into its own Ad Group for specialized management! Howie Jacobson (*Google Ads for Dummies*, 2007) likens this to a "special trailer" on a Hollywood movie set for a superstar. The industry term has become "SKAG," for "Single Keyword Ad Groups."

SKAGs are a bit of a pain to set up, but if I have a very high-value keyword phrase such as "luxury cat boarding" or "same-day cat sitting," it's probably worth it. I'd create SKAGs for:

Ad Group: Luxury Cat Boarding

Keyword patterns: +luxury +cat +boarding, "luxury cat boarding," [luxury cat boarding]

Ad copy: headline would say "Luxury Cat Boarding"

Landing Page: landing page would emphasize "luxury cat boarding"

Ad Group: Same-day Cat Boarding

Keyword patterns: +same +day +cat +boarding, "same day cat boarding," [same day cat boarding]

Ad copy: headline would say "Same Day Cat Boarding"

Landing Page: landing page would emphasize "same day cat boarding"

In this way, my very high value, very likely to convert keywords get the special treatment of SKAGs, improving my click-thru rate, quality score (thus lowering my cost per click), and conversions. SKAGS are worth it for high-value keywords! To learn more about SKAGs, visit **http://jmlinks.com/52b**.

TO-DO. Consider breaking out high-value phrases into their own keyword phrases for special bidding or reporting, or even creating a specific Ad Group for each high-value phrase.

Since SKAGs are a bit of a pain to set up, I set them up only for very high value, focused keyword patterns.

However, throughout your entire AdWords experience, Google rewards a tight focus. It's extremely important a) never to mix the Search and Display Networks, b) to have a tight relationship between a core keyword and the corresponding Ad Group, c) to write Ad Copy that regurgitates the target keyword to the user, and d) to have landing pages that also tightly reflect the search pattern. The "cat boarding" Ad Group contains ads only about "cat boarding" and has a landing page focused on "cat boarding," while the "iguana boarding" Ad Group contains ads only about "iguana boarding" and has a landing page focused on "iguana boarding" and so on and so forth. A little hard work at Ad Group organization will pay off big time in terms of cheaper cost-per-click, higher click-thru rates, and better conversions.

Google's Official Explanation

Let's return to keyword match types. Despite the official Google help explanation (**http://jmlinks.com/23d**), using broad match (just the words, without quotation marks, plus signs, or brackets) can produce many poor matches. If you just enter

cat boarding

as a keyword trigger into Google Ads (no plus sign, no quotes, no bracket), Google will substitute words: *cat* will become *pet*, *boarding* will become *vet*, and your ad will be running on *pet vets* before you know it! Google doesn't easily explain this (*for nefarious reasons?*). Who knows why, but just never ever enter "broad match" unless you are doing very aggressive keyword research, and you monitor the actual search queries very religiously.

See Actual Keyword Search Queries

Fortunately, Google does let you see the actual search queries entered by users on Google. This is a good checkup, especially if you are running on broad match (no quotes, brackets, or plus signs). Long-term, it's a best practice to check your search queries to verify that you're running on the proper keywords, and to look for new keyword ideas. (Note: you need to be running long enough for there to be data about real search queries and real clicks to your ads).

You can access the Search Query Report at either the Campaign or Ad Group level; just be aware that keywords "live" at the Ad Group level, so if you want to make changes, you'll make them in reference to an Ad Group. At either level, click on "Keywords" on the left column. This will show you the keyword triggers you have entered. Next, at the top menu, click on "Search Terms."

At this point, you can view the actual search queries entered by users, you can set a time horizon in the top right, and you can sort by Campaign, Ad Group, etc. It's best to be at the Ad Group level. If you don't see the proper columns, click on the "Columns" icon on the top middle right of the page. Here's a screenshot:

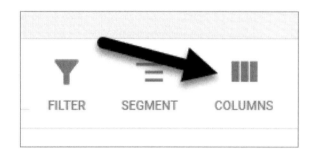

Here are the columns you want to enable:

Under "Performance:"

Impr = number of impressions the search query received, that is how many searches there were for the time horizon you select.

Clicks = number of clicks on your ad.

CTR = click-thru rate, or clicks/impressions. The higher this is, the more attractive your ad is vis-à-vis this keyword search query.

Avg CPC = the average cost per click you paid for clicks via this keyword search query.

Cost = total you spent for clicks on this search query

Under "Conversions" (if you are running conversion tracking):

Conversions = the number of people who "converted," i.e., made an e-commerce purchase, filled out a feedback form, etc.

Conv. rate = the number of conversions / the number of total ad clicks, which tells you how compelling your ad and landing page were vis-à-vis this search query.

Cost / conv. = how much you paid per conversion.

Impr. (Top) % = the percentage of total impressions for which your ad showed at the top of the page, above the organic results.

You may not see all these as options but save these columns after you set them up. I usually designate this as SIS (*Search Impression Share*) as SIS tells me how frequently my ads are running.

Now, you might not have all these metrics, so ignore any you don't have. Right now, you want to pay most attention to whether your ads are running for relevant search queries or not. Here's a screenshot for actual search queries for my ads for my Social Media Marketing Book for mid-November, 2019:

	Search term	Match type	Added/Excluded	↓ Impr.	Impr. (Top) %	Clicks	CTR	Avg. CPC	Cost
☐	marketing books	Exact match	✓ Added	618	95.31%	37	5.99%	$1.33	$49.34
☐	best marketing books	Exact match	✓ Added	588	94.22%	37	6.29%	$1.62	$59.96
☐	best books on marketing	Exact match	✓ Added	166	94.58%	15	9.04%	$2.44	$36.57
☐	best marketing books 2019	Exact match	✓ Added	164	87.80%	9	5.49%	$1.44	$12.92
☐	marketing for dummies	Exact match	✓ Added	130	90.00%	7	5.38%	$2.23	$15.58

This tells me the actual terms people entered into Google. You can see that there were 618 impressions for "marketing books," for example, that the ads ran at the top of Google 95.31% of the time, there were 37 clicks, the click-thru-rate was 5.99%, the average cost-per-click was $1.33 for a total cost for November, 2019, of $49.34. If you enable conversion-tracking, you'll also be able to see the conversion rate and cost for each query.

At this early keyword discovery and verification state, pay most attention to the keywords listed in the far-left column. Scan it for the following:

Relevant Keywords. You want to make sure that 90% of these keywords are strongly relevant and hopefully transactional to your product or service.

Negative Keywords. Be on the lookout for helpers like "cheap," "free," etc., which you can set as negative keywords because they indicate a person not likely to buy your product.

Niche Keywords. Look for really strong, focused keywords that you might want to break out into their own highly targeted Ad Group. Unusually high CTRs mean that you have a very strong keyword that might deserve being broken out into its own highly targeted SKAG (Single Keyword Ad Group).

You want to go your Search Query report for any and all *Ad Groups > Keywords > Search Terms* on an on-going basis, looking for really good, high converting keywords (which you then break out into their own special Ad Group) and really bad, low converting keywords (which you abandon or even add as negative keywords).

Stay Organized. One Keyword Group = One Ad Group

Do NOT jumble keywords into ad groups willy-nilly! For example, if you have a keyword group for *cat grooming* do NOT put keywords relating to *cat boarding* into that group. The same goes for closely related but distinct keywords:

cat kennel

cat boarding

cat hotel

In the real world, these are the SAME THING, but in Google Ads these are DIFFERENT, and each should have its own UNIQUE Ad Group. That's the best practice, but if you're pressed for time (*or just lazy*), you can put very closely related keywords into the same group. You might put all three in one Ad Group (again, *if you're lazy*), but that's not the best practice (*because you want specific ads to show for each keyword, which we'll discuss in a minute*).

> *Like a well-organized dresser, Google wants the socks in the sock drawer, the underwear in the underwear drawer, and the pajamas in the PJ drawer. Even better they want the red socks in the red socks drawer, the blue socks in the blue socks drawer, etc. Don't mix things up!*
>
> *Hey, and don't call my Mom and tell her just how disorganized my own "real world" dresser drawers are; at least my Google Ads Campaigns > Ad Groups are organized, Mom!*

Google Ads is a Word Game

Also, realize that Google Ads is a word game; do not put the keyword phrase *pet grooming* in a mangled Ad Group either. To Google Ads, "pet" is a different word than "cat," so – accordingly – it should have its own Ad Group, meaning:

cat boarding = its own Ad Group

pet boarding = its own Ad Group

animal boarding = its own Ad Group

If there is a very close synonym (such as *animal* for *pet*), it is probably OK to include both of those keyword phrases in one group. You might have:

pet / animal group = keywords that are derivations of *pet boarding* and *animal boarding*.

That said, it is **always** better to split and have highly focused Ad Groups than to combine (related) keywords into one Ad Group. I would split *pet* and *animal* into different Ad Groups.

Google Ads rewards tight, highly focused Ad Groups over unfocused keyword groups!

Also, at a conceptual level, realize that some keywords are unambiguously your customers (e.g., *cat boarding*) and others may or may not be your customers (*pet boarding*); this is a major reason NOT to mix keywords of the one into the Ad Group of the other. It's also a reason to separate them by Campaigns, so you can always bid high with a large budget on your tight Campaigns (*cat boarding* / definitely our customers) vs. bidding low with a smaller budget on your ambiguous Campaigns (*pet boarding* / maybe not our customers).

In summary, the tighter more organized the matching between the keyword group and the ad group, the better you will be in the long run.

Google Ads rewards very tight, very focused Ad Groups, organized around very tight, very focused keywords!

Branded, Reputational, and Trademarked Keywords

Branded keywords are searches that contain a brand, such as your own for example. If you're GEICO insurance, then every search that contains GEICO is a "branded" search opportunity for you. If you're ROLEX, every search that contains ROLEX is a branded search vis-à-vis your watches. And if you're Amazon or Apple, it's complicated, as some searches are truly for your brand and others are for rivers or fruits. It depends.

Searches that contain your brand plus "reviews" are what are called reputational searches as in GEICO insurance reviews. Branded and reputational keywords present unique opportunities in Google Ads. Trademark issues occur when branded terms such as the names of a company, its products, or its services, have been registered with the government for trademark protection.

At a minimum, consider **advertising on your own branded terms** such as your company name, product name, or service name. This is especially important if your competitors are advertising against your branded terms. Usually a good practice is to designate these ads as "Official Site." Here's a screenshot of the ad Progressive Insurance runs against the branded search "Progressive Insurance:"

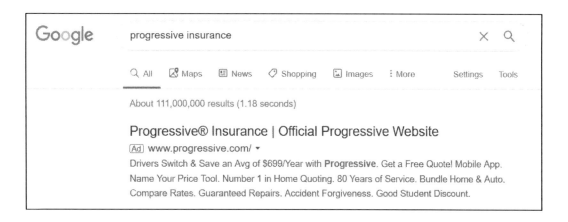

This ad presents the brand in a positive light and attempts to make sure that any person who is looking for Progressive insurance clicks into the official site, and not – God forbid – into a competitor. For this reason, I recommend you set up an Ad Group and call it "Branded Terms" and run against your own company name, phrases that include your company name, and possibly misspellings of your company name. Include product names, service names, and even the names of key employees if customers are likely to search on their names. Jeff Bezos would be an example for Amazon, for instance.

Secondarily, people who are close to a buying decision will often also search for "reviews" of your company. If you have bad reviews or a review issue, you might create an Ad Group specifically targeting reviews of your company. The keyword trigger would be your company name plus reviews, as in:

+Progressive +Reviews

"Progressive Insurance Reviews:

Now, look at the problem not from the perspective of your own company but from that of the competition. You know that people search for your competitors by name.

You know that they often search for competitor names plus the term reviews, especially when they are close to a buying decision. **Thus branded terms can be some of the most lucrative, highly transactional terms in Google ads.** You want YOUR COMPANY to be in the game, YOUR COMPANY to snag clicks that might be going to your competitors, etc.

Consider advertising on your competitor's company names, product or service names, or reputational searches such as competitor name plus review.

Be advised, however, that advertising on the branded terms of other companies is an aggressive and dangerous strategy. It is likely to piss off your competitors should they become aware of it. It is likely to create a "cease and desist letter" should they be litigious. It may even provoke a lawsuit. That said, Google says it is OK to use competitor names and competitor branded terms as keyword triggers, even for trademarked terms.

What is not OK, and illegal is to use competitor trademarked terms in your ad headline or text; ads that are intentionally confusing, ads that represent your company "as if" it were a competitor are not allowed. Indeed, if a company has registered a trademark with Google the system may pro-actively prevent you from using those terms in your ad text. It all depends. I am not a lawyer, and I am not advising that you advertise or not on competitors names, branded terms, and/or trademarks. I am merely explaining that it is commonly done in the industry, and it is often highly lucrative. Proceed at your own risk with Ad Groups and Ads that focus on competitor branded terms. Read the official Google policy on trademarks at **http://jmlinks.com/52e**, consult with your lawyer as to how aggressive you want your ads to be, and proceed accordingly.

Keyword Insertion

Google Ads has a feature called **Keyword Insertion**, formerly called *Dynamic Keyword Insertion*. In this technique, you write your ads using a snippet of code. For example, you'd write an ad headline like:

Buy {Keyword Chocolate}

and enter keyword triggers like

"Dark Chocolate Bar"

"Sugar-Free Chocolate"

"Gourmet Chocolate Truffles"

(Remember to use plus signs, quotation marks, or brackets! And note that in this methodology the capitalization does matter).

Next, if the keyword trigger / keyword query is short enough to fit into your headline, then Google Ads automatically replaces *Chocolate* with the keyword query entered by the user. If, for instance, they enter *dark chocolate bar* on Google, your ad headline would not say *Buy Chocolate* but rather *Buy Dark Chocolate Bar*

In this way, the ad appears, to the user, to be laser-focused on what he or she just entered. If you have hundreds or thousands of closely related keywords, Keyword Insertion is a time-saving option in Google Ads. (You can read the full Google help file at **http://jmlinks.com/26v**).

I would use caution when deploying Keyword Insertion, however, because, in my experience, it tends to hurt the Quality Score vs. ads that are manually written with a tight focus between the keyword trigger and the actual keyword in the ad headline / text. In addition, Keyword Insertion can allow you to be lazy and jumble up your Ad Groups to Keywords, even though a disorganized *Ad Group > Keyword* relationship will hurt your ad performance in the long run.

I'd recommend it only for large companies, with thousands of keyword patterns, and especially for very focused e-Commerce Campaigns. Google even has a feature called *Dynamic Search Ads* in which Google will automatically pull your website content or an

XML feed of your product data and write your ads on the fly. (Read about it at **http://jmlinks.com/26w**). Again, I would be very cautious about letting Google do all the hard thinking for me.

Negative Keywords

Negative keywords are "stop" words that tell Google NOT to run your ad if they are entered. *Cheap* is a common negative keyword or stop word. If you enter *cheap* as a negative word (at either the campaign or group levels), then any time someone enters *cheap*, your ad will NOT show.

> **VIDEO.** Watch a video from Google on how to use negative keywords in Google Ads at **http://jmlinks.com/26m**.

The logic is by entering *cheap* as a negative keyword (trigger), you are telling Google:

> *If they enter the word* cheap, *they are NOT my customer, they are NOT going to convert, do NOT show my ad to them, I will NOT pay for that click!*

Here's a screenshot showing where to add Negative Keywords:

SEARCH KEYWORDS	NEGATIVE KEYWORDS	SEARCH TERMS ▾
+		
☐ **Negative keyword** ↑		Added to
☐ cheap		Cat Emporium - Search Network
☐ cheap		Cat Emporium - Search Network › Cat Boarding

To add a negative keyword, just click on the blue plus sign, and type it in.

Where to Add Negative Keywords

Negative keywords can be added at two levels, so to speak:

- **Campaign Level** – if added here, then any Ad Group that "lives" in the Campaign is affected. Using our *cheap* example, then if someone entered the word *cheap* into Google as in *cheap cat boarding* or *cheap cat hotels*, then that would block the display of our ad for any of the dependent ad groups that live in the Cat Boarding San Francisco Campaign (i.e., the Ad Groups *Cat Boarding*, *Cat Hotels*, and *Cat Kennels*).
- **Ad Group Level** – if added here, then this impacts ONLY the Ad Group itself. So, if I add the negative keyword *cheap* to the Ad Group *cat boarding*, then if someone enters *cheap cat boarding*, Google will NOT run our ad, but if they enter *cheap cat hotels*, then that Ad Group is not affected, and the ad will run.

Think of negative keywords as *stop words*. If the word is entered, then Google will NOT run your ad even if other words match. Be sure on your Keyword Worksheet to identify any and all stop words that are 100% "not your customers." A detailed *negative keyword list* can save you a LOT of money in Google Ads spend! You can read the Google Ads help article on negative keywords at **http://jmlinks.com/25d**.

The Shared Library

If a keyword is always negative, across all your campaigns, I recommend drilling into the *shared library* (available by clicking first on the wrench at the top right and then clicking to "Negative Keyword Lists"). Here's a screenshot of where to find the *Shared Library > Negative keyword lists:*

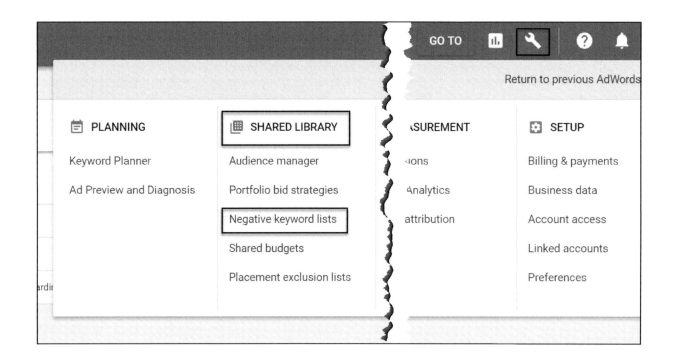

I generally create a keyword list called "Universal Negatives" which contains the negative keywords I am absolutely, positively, 100% sure that if the user enters, I do NOT want my ad to be shown. Here's a screenshot:

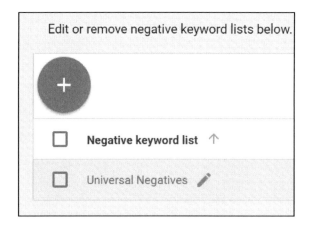

When you click in, you simply add negative keywords using the same system of

"cheap cat insurance" = phrase match

cheap cat insurance = broad match

[cheap cat insurance] = exact match

I wouldn't worry about "+" signs here. In fact, because Google's incentive is to run your ads, I generally just enter the words with no quotes, no plus signs, and no brackets. For instance, just enter:

cheap

free

In fact, Google tilts the negative keyword system to its advantage, explaining:

> Negative keywords won't match to close variants or other expansions. For example, if you exclude the negative broad match keyword flowers, ads won't be eligible to serve when a user searches red flowers, but can serve if a user searches for red flower (**http://jmlinks.com/25d**).

Thus, you need to enter plurals, singulars, and all variations of a negative keyword to stop your ads from running. After you're up and running check your "search terms," sort by impression, and scan for potential negative keywords.

Once you build out a universal negative keyword list, you want to add it to individual campaigns. To do this, here are the steps:

1. Click Campaigns on the left menu (to show all your Campaigns)
2. Select the Campaign to which you want to apply your "Universal Negatives" keyword list to.
3. Click Keywords on the left menu.

4. Click Negative Keywords on the top menu
5. Click the white plus sign in the blue circle.
6. Select "Use negative keyword list" and select your "Universal Negatives" list.
7. Click the blue SAVE on the bottom.

The easiest way to do this is to apply your "Universal Negative" list to each and every Campaign one by one. You can also select Campaigns and then apply the list to all of them at once; it isn't easy, as Google's made a convoluted mess of it in the New Interface. To learn how to do it, see the help file at **http://jmlinks.com/39s**. Once you've linked a Campaign to a negative keyword list, however, all you have to do is update the list, and it automatically updates every Campaign that is connected to it.

If, however, there are words that are negative only with respect to one Campaign or one Ad Group, then you can add them at that level by clicking on the Keywords tab at either the Campaign or Ad Group level. Here's a screenshot keywords at the Ad Group level, clearly showing how keywords can be added via a keyword list, or at the Ad Group or Campaign level:

» Write Attract / Repel Ad Copy

Now that you have your Campaigns and Ad Groups set up, plus you've added relevant keywords using plus signs, quote marks, and/or brackets as well as negative keywords at the Campaign, Ad Group, or Shared Library level, you're ready to write some ads. Ads "live" at the Ad Group level, and so by having tightly focused Ad Groups, we can now match *highly focused ads* to *highly focused Ad Groups* and *highly focused keywords* and *highly focused landing pages.*

The Purpose of an Ad

What's the purpose of an ad? If you answer, "to get clicks," well, you work for Google, or you haven't been paying attention. If you answer, "to get clicks that lead to conversions," you're on the right track, and if you answer that the purpose of an ad is to:

> **Attract** clicks from **relevant customers** that end in conversions and also **repel** clicks from **non-customers**.

You get a gold star. We want to attract our customers and repel non-customers, sometimes derisively referred to as "tire kickers" on the old car lots.

Include Keywords in Your Ad Text for Best Results

Let's investigate best practices for writing strong ad copy on Google Ads. First, remember that the Google Ads Quality Score rewards a tight match between keywords and ads, so a major first principle is to:

include your **core keyword phrase** in your ad, preferably your ad headline.

To create an ad, click into a *Campaign > Ad Groups > Ads & extensions*. Click the white plus in the blue circle. Select "Text ad," which is the easiest format and the one that gives you the most control. Here's a screenshot:

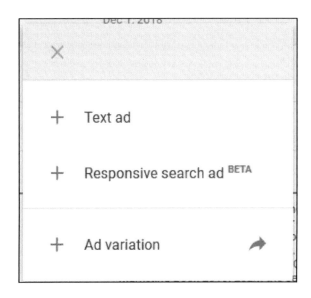

As you write the components of your ad, you want to make it clear to the searcher that you have *exactly* what they want. That means you need to do three things:

1. Include the target **keyword** in your ad, especially in at least once headline option. Google (and searchers) heavily reward ads that regurgitate the keyword.
2. Write with some **pizazz**. What's unique, exciting, and compelling about what you sell? Why should they click? Be excited, so that they are excited!
3. **Attract** your target customers and **repel** your non-customers. "We sell cat boarding but no dogs," for example.

Ads on Google Ads now include the following:

Final URL – the URL where you want to send a person after they click

Headline 1 – 30 characters

Headline 2 – 30 characters

Headline 3 – 30 characters

Display Path – the visible URL that searchers see. Note: this does NOT have to be a real URL.

Description 1 – 90 characters

Description 2 – 90 characters

Second, in addition to including your target keyword in your ad headline, you want to have some **pizzazz** in your ad copy to "get the click," plus indicate how your product or service is unique and different. For *cat boarding* in San Francisco, you might write an ad that looks like this:

Here's a screenshot of how you enter the ad into Google:

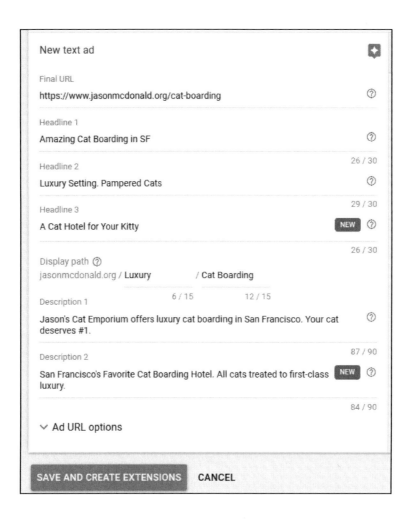

New text ad

Final URL

https://www.jasonmcdonald.org/cat-boarding   ⑦

Headline 1

Amazing Cat Boarding in SF   ⑦

                                                        26 / 30
Headline 2

Luxury Setting. Pampered Cats   ⑦

                                                        29 / 30
Headline 3

A Cat Hotel for Your Kitty   NEW   ⑦

                                                        26 / 30
Display path ⑦

jasonmcdonald.org / Luxury   / Cat Boarding

                        6 / 15   12 / 15
Description 1

Jason's Cat Emporium offers luxury cat boarding in San Francisco. Your cat   ⑦
deserves #1.

                                                        87 / 90
Description 2

San Francisco's Favorite Cat Boarding Hotel. All cats treated to first-class NEW   ⑦
luxury.

                                                        84 / 90
ᐯ Ad URL options

SAVE AND CREATE EXTENSIONS   CANCEL

And on the right, Google gives you a preview of what your ad will look like. Here's a screenshot:

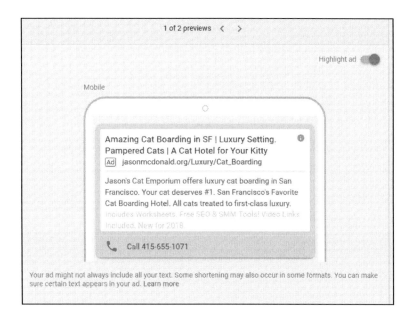

1 of 2 previews

Click the blue "Save and create extensions" to create your ad. (Ignore Google Ads if it wants you to create extensions at this point). Create at least three variations for your ads, each containing headlines with relevant keywords, some pizzazz, and a value proposition that explains why someone should click. Remember: you're trying to get relevant clicks, not a lot of clicks, so don't overpromise! "Free pizza and beer" will get lots of clicks, but is that really what you want?

The trend at Google is Artificial Intelligence (AI), so now you don't have very good control over which headlines and ad text appear, so as you write your ad headlines and text, be aware that Google will pick and choose what it thinks is the "most relevant" and may truncate some of your text.

Here's an actual ad for *Cat Boarding in San Francisco*:

The first principle is to regurgitate the keyword phrase into the ad itself, preferably the headline as this ad does. The second is to have some pizzazz as in "Skilled and loving staff" and "24-hour pet cams." Related to all this is to attract customers (preferably rich ones) with words like "Large suites" and "luxury experience" and implicitly repel certain types of undesirables (a.k.a., poor people) who can't afford a luxury experience. You can see how this Pawington ad is a true work of art: attracting the right kind of customers, repelling the others, and clearly stating its unique selling proposition.

Ah, Google Ads poetry in action.

Note as well that it's not shy. It's a bit brash, and it toots its own horn. If you don't toot your own horn, my High School English teacher once told me, no one will. Write your ad text on Google to say that you're #1, the best, on top, top-rated, luxury experience – whatever sells you as THE best match for what they are searching for (within reason).

Returning to The Pawington's ad, my main critique would be to use the Display URL to highlight cat boarding as in *pawington.com/cat-boarding/sf*. Google rewards ads that follow these principles with a better Quality Score, and the humans will more likely click on your ads if everything in them conveys that you have exactly what they're looking for; keywords and superlatives work together on this.

And, should you think I am against poor people, here's an ad for "hotels near me:"

Cheap Hotels Near Me - 60% Off Last Minute Hotels - hotwire.com
[Ad] www.hotwire.com/Hotels ▾
Travel Like A Baller, Don't Pay Like One. Never Pay Full Price On **Hotels** Again.
Chicago Hotels - from $54.00 - 3+ Star Hotels · More ▾

| Book A Hot Rate® Hotel | Try Our Hot Rate® Flights |
| Bundle Up & Save More | Car Rentals From $8.99 |

This ad is thus attracting cheap or poor people, or what my Dad would call "frugal," and repelling people who want a top of the line experience. There's no wrong or right here – you're just aiming to attract your customers and repel spurious clicks.

For your **TO-DO**, do some relevant searches for your keywords and browse the ads that pop up. Do they attract? Do they repel? Do they inspire you to click? Do they clearly convey the business value proposition? Imitation is the highest form of flattery – just remember it's not only about *getting the click*, but it's also about *not getting the (wrong) click*, too. Read them out loud to your boss, your team, your sales staff, potential customers, or if all else fails, your Mom or Dad. Which ads spur you to click? Why?

This, in combination with tight Ad Groups focused on tight keywords, is the key to success on Google Ads ad copywriting.

To repeat myself, as yes, it is that important, the best ad copy:

1. Contains the target **keyword** in it, preferably in the headline.
2. Has some **pizzazz** explaining your brand and your unique selling proposition (USP)
3. **Attracts** your target customer yet **repels** non-customers.

All within the very tight character limits of Google Ads. Good luck! (I know; It's like your worst High School English Poetry writing assignment has come true. But as you get into Google Ads, you'll start to see that good ads are like Haiku's.) In fact, PPCHero had a contest for Google Ads Haiku's, and here is the winner and a few runners-up:

New client, new goals

An empty canvas to fill

Words and ads, not paint

Click through rates are high

And conversion rates are low

Oh, CPA woes!

Fitting your message

Into just three lines. Is that

An ad or haiku?

Source: **http://jmlinks.com/39w**.

Quality Score: Don't Trust Google

Remember that Google gets paid *by the click* while you make money *by the conversion*. Google will want you to write ads that say things like *free cat boarding*, or *one night free* or something like that to encourage more clicks. In fact, if you watch Google videos or talk to Google Ads technical support, they will nearly ALWAYS tell you to write your ads in such a way as to maximize clicks.

> **VIDEO.** Watch a video from Google on how to write effective ads on Google Ads at **http://jmlinks.com/26x**.

Good advice from Google on how to write ads? Yes, definitely, with the caveat that you want to make sure you've identified *negative keywords* and thought about ways to *repel* non-customers. Don't believe everything you read or hear about ad copy, as many people think good ads get clicks when that's only half the story.

Attract & Repel: Striking a Balance

While it is true that higher click-thru rates will generate a higher Quality Score, you have to strike a balance between ads that *get a lot of clicks* and ads that *generate a lot of conversions*.

STRIKE A BALANCE BETWEEN ADS THAT GET CLICKS AND ADS THAT GET CONVERSIONS

I tend to emphasize ads that focus on conversions, and not clicks. And I tend to use very focused *Ad Groups > Ads > Keywords* as "riches are in the niches" to improve my Quality Score. That's my style. I want every ad to match the search query tightly, so I'd write individual ads for:

> *Cat boarding*
>
> *Luxury cat boarding*
>
> *Cat hotel*
>
> etc.

The tighter the match among *Keyword > Ad Copy > Landing page*, the better you will do.

You'll need to find your own style and workflow. Just be aware, however, that Google wants you to write ads that "get clicks," and I want you to write ads that "get conversions." You will be penalized a bit by Google on Quality Score by using this strategy, but it's worth it in my opinion. Remember: you want high-value conversions, not just clicks!

Quality Score

Once your Ad Groups are up and running, Google will give you some feedback on your Quality Score. Just drill into *Campaign > Ad Group > Keywords*. Next, hover your mouse over the dialogue box under Status, where is usually says *Eligible*. Here's a screenshot:

You can also enable the Quality Score column by clicking on *Columns (the three BAR icon) > Modify Columns > Attributes > Quality Score*. Here's a screenshot:

A quality score of 5 or higher is very good, and remember in some cases you may choose to accept a low-quality score for a high-value keyword for which you have written a powerful attract / repeal ad.

VIDEO. Watch an official video from Google on Quality Score in Google Ads at **http://jmlinks.com/26u**.

Note: you sometimes may get a notification that your ad is / is not running for this keyword. We will discuss this in a few moments. Also, when your Ad Groups / Keywords are new, there may not be enough data to get a Quality Score reading.

Ambiguous Yet Important Keywords

Some keywords are unambiguous, and definitely your customer, as for example, *cat boarding*. Others are ambiguous – they contain both your customers and your non-customers. An example would be *pet boarding*. Some of those folks are *cat people*, some are *dog people*, and some are *exotic bird people*, but you only want the cat people.

What do you do?

You can either choose NOT to run on *pet boarding* entirely and run only on *cat boarding*. This makes sense if you have a very tight budget, or you want to be very conservative in terms of your Google Ads strategy. (This is one of the most important reasons to have highly organized Campaigns and Ad Groups, so you can turn "on" and "off" keyword groups, leaving "on" your highest performing keywords at all times and turning "on" or "off" your lower performing keywords depending on your budget and other factors like seasonality).

But if you want to be more aggressive, you would want to run our ads on *pet boarding*, too. But we want to repel *dog people* and attract *cat people*. We can't use a negative keyword strategy as there is NOT a negative keyword; it's just *pet boarding*.

What, then, is to be done? Write attract / repel ad copy that both includes the target keyword of *pet boarding* but clearly is all about *cats*:

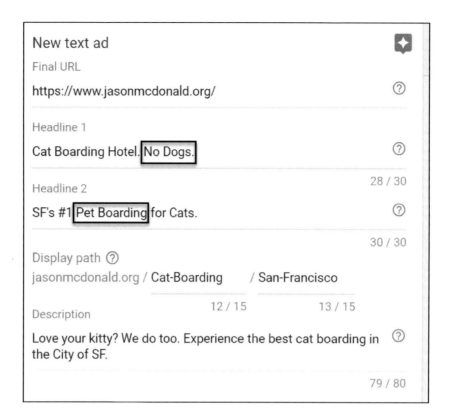

Which shows on Google as:

The idea (and hope) being that dog people will be repelled by the phrase *No Dogs*, and NOT click on the ad. Now, relative to ads that say *pet boarding* and don't use repel, or establishments that board both cats and dogs, our ad will get fewer clicks and have a lower Quality Score, compelling us to bid somewhat higher. But what's the point in getting a click from a dog person, anyway, when he'll never convert because as soon as he lands on our website, he'll learn that we do NOT board dogs?

Attract /repel, in summary, is an important strategy to writing ads, especially when you confront **ambiguous keywords** that cannot be dealt with using negative keywords. I recommend you ignore the hit to your Quality Score and pay closer to attention to whether your ads are actually running, getting clicks, and getting conversions.

» EXPERIMENT WITH RESPONSIVE SEARCH ADS

Google Ads has a new type of ads called "Responsive Search Ads," which are a hybrid between you writing your ad copy and Google doing it for you. Google has a feature called "Ad Suggestions" which is 100% AI, which I recommend you turn off. (I'll explain how in a moment). For now, let's zero in on "Responsive Search Ads."

Click into *Campaign > Ad Group > Ads & extensions*. Then click the white cross in the blue circle, and select "Responsive Search Ad." Here, rather than constructing the ad in a rigid format, you write a series of five headlines and two descriptions; Google will mix and match these to create your ads on the fly. Here's a screenshot:

Click on "Show guided steps" for a nice step-by-step guide to creating this type of ad. The main conceptual points are the same here as for regular text ads:

1. Include the target **keyword** in the headline, or in this case at least most of the headlines.
2. Write with some **pizzazz** to explain what's unique, compelling, and exciting about your product or service.
3. Attempt to **attract** your best customers yet **repel** non-customers.

Similar to text ads, you also have a final URL and a Display URL. If you want one particular headline to always show (such as one that has your target keyword in it), you can "pin it" to the ad by clicking the "pin" icon to the right of a headline. Here's a screenshot:

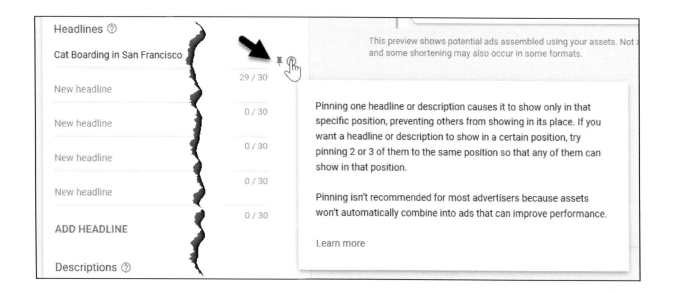

You can read about Responsive Search Ads at **http://jmlinks.com/49k**. I'm excited about this new format as it seems to be a productive hybrid between "man or woman and machine," with you as the person writing some great ad copy and Google as the AI robot mixing and matching it to achieve good results. As you create this ad type, just remember to measure your results by click-thru and conversion rate.

» USE AD EXTENSIONS

In addition to the headline, description, and path, ads on Google can also have "extensions." Google will often prompt you to write extensions as you write your ads, but I do not like that workflow. I ignore that prompt, and instead write my extensions all at once.

I especially like the "Call extension" because if someone just calls right off the ad, you do not pay for that click! Ad extensions can be viewed or added by clicking into an Ad Group and then clicking Ads and extensions on blue on the left. Next, click Extensions in the middle tab. Here's a screenshot:

When you click on that, you should see a running list of all the ad extensions that are enabled for that Ad Group. It's a little confusing because when you click on the pencil to edit one extension, Google reminds you that by editing it, you will be editing it on all other Ad Groups or Campaigns that share this extension. (While ads live at the Ad Group level, extensions can live at the Account, Campaign, and/or Ad Group level).

To add a new Ad Extension, just click the white plus sign in the blue circle, and you'll get to choose what type to add:

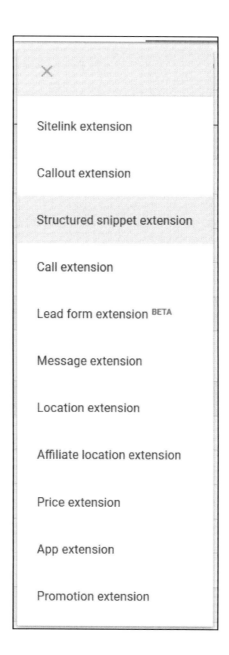

We'll overview what each means in a moment, but for now, just click on Sitelink Extension, which is the most common type. You can select which level – Account, Campaign, or Ad Group to add the extension to. Here's a screenshot:

Next, create your Sitelink extension (or other extension) by filling out the required field. Here's a screenshot:

Add sitelink extension

Add to

Account ▾

Extension

◉ Create new   ◯ Use existing

Sitelink text

0 / 25

Description line 1 (optional)

0 / 35

Description line 2 (optional)

0 / 35

Final URL   ⑦

⌄ Sitelink URL options

⌄ Advanced options

Just to be clear, remember that Ad Extensions do not always show, but if you do some highly competitive searches like *auto insurance* or *car insurance*, you can usually see them in action. Here's a sample ad for hair transplant that has extensions:

$6/Graft ARTAS Hair Transplant - Special Valid This Month Only
[Ad] www.precisionmdca.com/Hair-Transplant ▾   (916) 340-8914
No Scarring & Natural Results. Free Consultation. Call Now to Claim This Rate!
New ARTAS Hair Transplant · Doctor Owned & Operated · State-of-the-art Lasers
Services: Acne Scar Removal, Botox, Juvederm, Hair Transplants, Liposuction, Brazilian Butt Lift, Tattoo...
Meet Dr. Khattab · Why Precision MD?

The ad extensions are things like the phone number *(916) 340-8914*, the non-clickable text underneath the ad such as *State-of-the-art Lasers*, and the sitelinks (clickable) extensions such as *Meet Dr. Khattab*.

Available extensions are:

Sitelinks – these are blue-highlighted bits of text that can appear below an ad, and link to specific subsections of your website such as "contact us" or "cat grooming," etc.

Callouts – these are non-clickable text elements that can appear below an ad, usually meant to "call out" something special such as "Valentine's Day Specials" or "ask about our kitty services".

Structured Snippet extension – you select a predefined header like "Product" or "Service category" and then add callouts to specific subsections of your website. See **http://jmlinks.com/49f**.

Call extensions – these allow your phone number to appear in ads.

Lead form extension – allows you to gather data right on Google via a form.

Message extensions – these appear on mobile phone ads, and allow customers to text message you directly from the ad.

Location extension – this extension type allows users to see your store's physical address.

Affiliate location extension – similar to the above.

Price extension – allow users to browse products and prices in an ad, and then click directly to them on your website.

App extension – allow you to link from your ad to your mobile app for download and installation.

Promotion extension – this extension allows you to enter a "sale" or "promotion" such as a $ off an item.

To read the official Google help file on ad extensions, visit **http://jmlinks.com/23q**.

Here's another screenshot of an ad with clickable sitelink extensions:

The phrases, *Get a Quote* and *BIG Savings,* go to unique URLs on Geico.com, plus they have their 888 number in the ad, too. And here's a screenshot of an ad with a location extension:

```
┌─────────────────────────────────────────────────────────────────┐
│  PetSmart® PetsHotel | Overnight Boarding For Cats                 │
│  [Ad]  services.petsmart.com/PetsHotel  ▾                          │
│  Your Pet Can Stay & Play At Our Place While You're On Vacation. Book Online Now! │
│  ♥ 315 Gellert Blvd, Daly City, CA - Open today · 9:00 AM – 9:00 PM ▾ │
└─────────────────────────────────────────────────────────────────┘
```

Notice how this ad has a display URL that contains a keyword (*PetsHotel*). As always, try various keyword queries relevant to your business and see what the competition is doing. Also try very competitive search queries like "car insurance," "personal injury lawyer," or "home mortgage" to see what the Big Boys and Big Girls are doing as ads. Imitation is the highest form of flattery and a great way to learn.

Automated Extensions

Finally, Google has rolled out a new type of extension called *Automated Extensions* which are, automatically, generated by Google. You can read about them at **http://jmlinks.com/39t**. Automated Extensions are part of Google's push into AI, and I am not a fan. The problem is that Google is motivated to "get the click" and not "get the conversion," so it's AI tends to optimize these extensions with "free pizza and beer" type of content… leading into frivolous clicks. If you're neurotic and a control-freak like I am, I strongly recommend you **turn them off**.

To opt out of Automated Extensions, clicking into a Campaign, and then click "Ads & extensions" on the left. Find "Automated Extensions" at the top and click into that. Click the three dots at the top right, then "Advanced Options."

You then have to go through each type and opt out. Here's a screenshot:

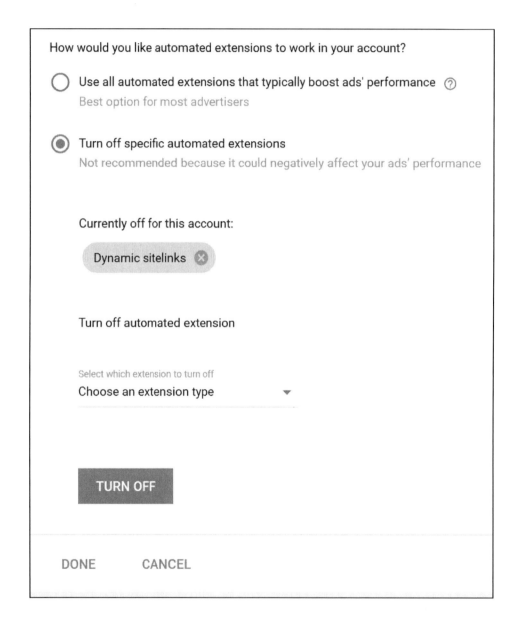

Check your Automated Extensions periodically and see if you think they are working for you. The most common types are:

Dynamic sitelinks

Structured snippets

Ad Suggestions: Turn These Off, Too

Google Ads also has a feature called "ad suggestions" which are ads that Google will write via AI and then automatically apply to your account. Again, because Google's motivation is to "get clicks," I recommend you opt out of this feature. To do so, log in to your Google Ads account, on the left click "Settings," then "Account Settings" at the top of the page, then the arrow next to "Ad suggestions," and choose "Don't automatically apply ad suggestions." Google will ask for some feedback as to why you are opting out. I often type in something like, "It's my money and I'd like to control how I spend it, thank you very much" or something snarky like that. I doubt anyone reads the suggestions at Google, so you might type in "Bing rules!" or "One troll to rule them all!" as it really doesn't matter. It's Google's world, and we just live in it. You can read the help file on Ad Suggestions at **http://jmlinks.com/49g**.

Attract / Repel on Ads and Extensions

In summary, I do recommend that you set up relevant ad extensions to your ads but also have an attract / repel frame of mind. You might not want to emphasize a *free consult* if *free consult* is likely to attract poor people or those who are not likely to convert! You might not want an ad extension that emphasizes your *cat grooming* services if those services are likely to generate clicks but are not strong revenue-generators for your company. And generally speaking, I don't trust Google's Artificial Intelligence enough to write my own extensions, so I disable the Automated Extensions feature.

» FOLLOW C/E/A ON LANDING PAGES

What happens after the click? Well, they "land" on your website. There are some best practices when it comes to landing pages for Google Ads, starting with a tight match between the keyword query and the landing page.

Accordingly,

keyword group = Ad Group on Google Ads = specific landing page

So, we'd have:

cat boarding = Ad Group on cat boarding = specific landing page on cat boarding

vs.

cat grooming = Ad Group on cat grooming = specific landing page on cat grooming

vs.

pet boarding = Ad Group on pet boarding = specific landing page on pet boarding

Note how we aren't lazy, and we don't let reality confuse us! We have a tight match between keywords and landing pages. The more specific you make the relationship among keyword, Ad Group, and landing pages, the better you'll do.

Don't Make Customers (or Google) Think!

We have a page specific to **cat boarding** even though, technically speaking, we could send the *cat boarding* people to our *pet boarding* page or our home page since "in reality" that's the same thing. But we don't want to "make our customers think" – we want the *cat boarding* people to see immediately that we board cats, and the *pet boarding* people to see, first, yes we board pets, and secondly, we focus on cats. We also want the reward to our Quality Score by having a tight focus <u>at the keyword level</u> between the keyword query and the landing page. Don't make Google think, either!

It's not generally a good idea to send everyone to your homepage, and certainly not a good idea to make users hunt for information. They'll click, and bounce, rather than click, and convert. In fact, Google strongly emphasizes that one element of Quality Score is a keyword-matching landing page.

Generally speaking, therefore, your **TO-DO** is to map out your Keywords to your Ad Groups and your Ad Groups to your landing pages and build a one-to-one correlation between *Core Keywords* to *Ad Groups* to *landing pages*.

C/E/A Methodology for Landing Pages

In terms of landing page design, you want to use the C/E/A methodology, which stands for Confirm / Engage / Act. Basically, if the search query is *cat boarding*, then when the user lands on your landing page in the top left corner, she should see an image of a happy cat being boarded, and the phrase she just entered ("cat boarding). That's your "**C**" for Confirmation Zone.

Next, moving from left to right, top to bottom, she should read some content that explains why your establishment is the best place to board a cat in San Francisco. Awards, user reviews, statistics, etc., are great here. This is your "**E**" for "Engagement" zone.

Finally, to the right, but above the fold, the desired action should be apparent. This is your "**A**" for Action zone. A common action is "free consult" or "request a quote" or something like that. Note that in contrast to writing the ad, here you want to convert EVERYONE who lands on your website into an email inquiry (or e-Commerce transaction), as you have already paid for the click, so you want to grab each and every lead.

Attract / repel refers ONLY to ad copy, not to the landing page experience.

Here's a screenshot with the three zones for C/confirm, E/ngage, and A/ct outlined on the landing page for ZOHO for the search query *CRM Software* into Google:

And here's the Geico landing page for the search query, *motorcycle insurance*, again with the C/, E/, and A/ zones clearly marked for you.

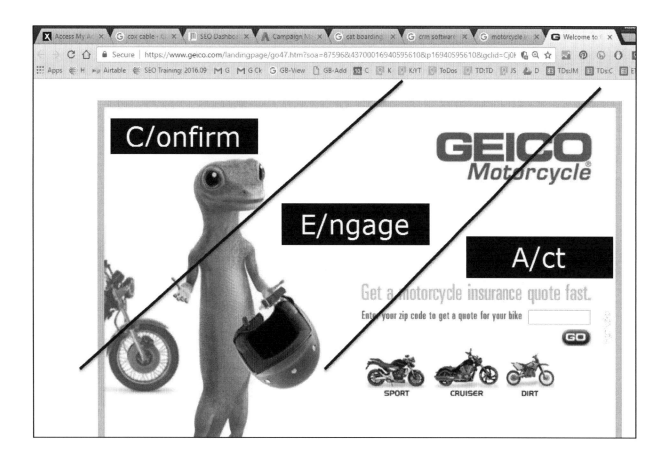

Your **TO-DOS** here are to a) do relevant search queries in your industry and evaluate competitor landing pages using this C/E/A methodology, and b) look at your own landing pages with an eye to C/E/A.

1. Does the **top left** corner **confirm** that the customer who just clicked from Google has landed on a relevant website that offers what he wants?
2. Does the **middle engage** the customer by explaining the offer and validating that you are a company that can be trusted?
3. Does the **right** have a defined **action** such as request a free consultation, download a software demo, or buy something on an e-commerce site?

And, is all the human-critical information "above the fold?" Don't make them think. Don't make them hunt. Don't make them nervous. Confirm you have what they want, you're a fantastic choice, and make it easy for them to see the next step.

To Lock In or Not?

As for allowing navigation to your homepage, and other web pages, some people advocate "locking in" the customer and others say you should at least allow navigation to the home page. My advice is to allow navigation to your home page, and website. Many customers will want to "check you out" and will want to browse your site, even if they land on a clear landing page.

Thus, while I recommend using the C/E/A methodology for your Google Ads landing pages, I realize that many customers will nonetheless browse your website. We can use Google Analytics to track user behavior and view the conversion rates of any customers who come from Google Ads. The bottom line is that each landing page, and your website as a whole, should clearly

- **CONFIRM** that users have landed on a website the offers what they just searched for
- **ENGAGE** them with information, facts, reviews, and other trust indicators that validate your company, products, and services as trustworthy and high quality, and
- have an **ACTION** such as an e-Commerce purchase or free consult / free download that makes the next step easy to see and find.

» SET YOUR BIDS

Advertisers pay by click on Google Ads. In Google Ads, you set your bid strategy at the Campaign Level. Click on your *Campaign* and then the *Settings* tab on the left. Find Bidding in the center of the screen and click the down chevron to view it.

Here's a screenshot:

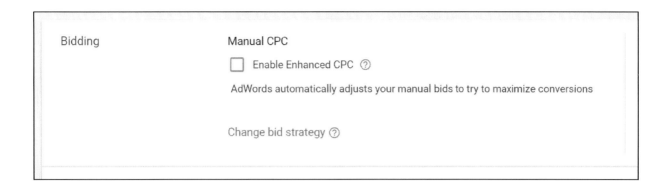

Click on Change bid strategy, and Google Ads will show you your options:

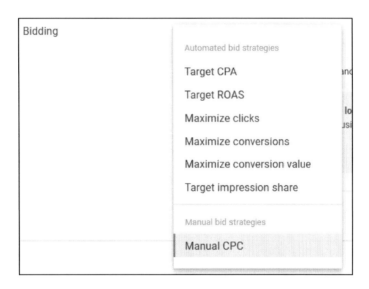

Below, I explain what each means, and indicate in italics my opinion of each option:

Target CPA. Use this if you have an e-commerce site and have enabled conversion tracking. This allows you to set a target Cost Per Acquisition. If for example, you know that you make $1.00 per widget, you can set a target CPA of $1.00 and Google Ads will do the calculations for you of how many clicks vs. how many bounces and what your best CPC is (which will be lower than $1.00 because not everyone converts). *Recommended for e-Commerce websites that have a sufficient spend and have sufficient sales per click.*

Target ROAS. This is similar to CPA but works across an entire account to attempt to maximize your ROAS (Return on Ad Spend). *Not recommended for small advertisers, and works only if you have conversion tracking running well.*

Maximize clicks. Here you provide Google your budget, and Google attempts to maximize your bids within that budget. You can also set a "bid max" to set a maximum CPC you are willing to run. *Not recommended, as I find better results with Manual CPC, but OK if you set a "bid max."*

Maximize conversions. If you have enabled conversion tracking, and have a robust e-commerce site, this option allows Google to attempt to predict which clicks will convert. It's a pretty good option, but only if you have a lot of data.

Maximize conversion value. If you have enabled conversion tracking, and have a robust e-commerce site, this option allows Google to attempt to predict which clicks will convert into a high-value conversion. It's a pretty good option, but only if you have a lot of data.

Target Impression share. Here, you target a specific number of ad impressions (times you want your ad to show) at the top of Google Search Results. *Not recommended as it's better to focus on clicks on the Search Network.*

Manual CPC. Here, you manually set your bids as the maximum you are willing to pay for a click. *Recommended strategy.*

There is also a box that says "Help increase conversions with Enhanced CPC." This bids up clicks that are likely to end in a conversion. It works if, and only if, you have enough conversion data in your Google Analytics / Google Ads account for Google AI to understand conversions.

You can read the official Google help file at **http://jmlinks.com/23x**, but it's not very clear and mixes bidding on the Search Network with bidding on the Display Network. You can read about Google's new "Smart Bidding" at **http://jmlinks.com/52c**.

VIDEO. Watch a video from Google on bid strategies in Google Ads at **http://jmlinks.com/26y**.

Smart bidding uses AI to predict clicks that are likely to lead to conversions. It works if, and only if, you have a) a lot of data flowing through your account, b) conversion-tracking is turned on, and c) you can easily monetize the conversion value. Essentially, you need to be an e-commerce website selling stuff directly on the Internet and providing that data to Google via Google Analytics. If that's you, try it out. If that's not you, don't try it. The problem is that Google propaganda acts as if everyone is running huge e-commerce stores with tons of data, tons of sales, and efficient tracking. But that's not true. In my experience, turning these options on results in much higher cost-per-clicks than manual bidding.

Bidding Strategy

Google Ads clearly offers you many bid options. Which one should you pick? Let's examine the two most basic scenarios.

Scenario #1: e-Commerce. In this scenario, you sell something online and you know how much it sells for (the "price") and how much you make per sale ("the profit"). In this case, I strongly recommend you enable conversion tracking so that Google Ads can see how many conversions you get per click, and what the true value is of those conversions. Here, essentially you want your bid to increase up to the point where you spend $1 to make one $1. You might also want to take into consideration multiple purchases and the lifetime value of a customer. If these factors apply and you enable conversion tracking, Google's eCPC and smart bidding options can work very well. Google Ads isn't bad at conversion tracking and conversion optimization.

Scenario #2: Everyone else. Most companies don't know the true value of a conversion, as they are companies like law firms or hairdressers, accountants or plumbers, and they want leads from their website via phone calls, emails, or feedback forms. You can guess at the value of a conversion, but it's a very rough estimate at best. In this scenario, while you can enable conversion tracking, you usually have too few conversions and too vague an idea of their value, so conversion value is loosey-goosey. Here, I do not find Google's Smart Bidding options to work very well and can result in massive overpayment. I recommend **manual bidding** for these types of companies. **Enhanced CPC** can also be a good option because here Google bids up your bid when it thinks it's likely to end in a conversion.

Some of the other options such as "Impression Share," or "Target Impression Share" seem to be stupid choices for stupid people who just want to throw money away via Google Ads, so I would stay away from those options.

Let's dive deeper into how to set your bids.

Bidding at the Ad Group Level

While the bid *strategy* is set at the Campaign level, the actual *bid per click* is set at the Ad Group level or at the Keyword level. We'll assume you've built out your Campaign and have at least one Group in it and have written ads in that group. Google Ads will have forced you to enter a bid at the beginning, but now go back and edit this bid.

The easiest way to set your bids is to click into the bid on the Default Max CPC column at the Group level. Here's a screenshot:

AD GROUPS	AUCTION INSIGHTS		

		Ad group	Status	Default max. CPC
☐ ●		Plumber	Eligible	$10.01 (enhanced) ☑
☐ ●		Plumbing	Eligible	$9.01 (enhanced) ☑
☐ ●		Emergency	Eligible	$12.01 (enhanced) ☑

Whatever you set as the maximum CPC bid here controls the dependent bid at the keyword level. Therefore, all keywords in the "Plumber" Ad Group will be set at $10.01 CPC maximum bid. The theory is that if you bid $10.00 and someone bids $9.00, then you don't pay $10, but rather just $9.01 to get the click (with Quality Score of course intervening).

That's the theory, but not necessarily the reality. Google isn't very forthcoming with data on the actual auction so it's a "trust us" model, and we've all seen how "trust us" has been working with Silicon Valley's tech companies. Not very well.

What to Bid at First?

When starting a new *Campaign > Ad Group*, I recommend you bid on the high side, higher than you'd expect or be willing to pay in the long run. To estimate a good starting bid, go to the **Keyword Planner** under the **Tools** menu in Google Ads, enter your keyword, and bid at least as high as the suggested "top of page (high range)" bid. Here's a screenshot

Keyword (by relevance) ↓	Avg. monthly searches	Competition	Top of page bid (high range)
cat boarding	12,100	Medium	$5.02
cat hotel	5,400	Medium	$3.66
pet boarding	27,100	Medium	$7.67

So you'd need to bid at least $5.02 for cat boarding, $3.66 for cat hotel, and $7.67 for pet boarding to start.

When you're starting a brand-new Ad Group, **bid high** as you must get the ads actually to run. Then **monitor closely** and notch down your bids slowly until you get the ads to show at least 85% of the time (as expressed by the Search Impression Share) and you have Search Top IS of > 70%. (More on **ratcheting down** your bids in a moment).

You can also use the KWFinder.com keyword research tool at **http://jmlinks.com/49j** to get CPC / bid estimates. Here's a screenshot:

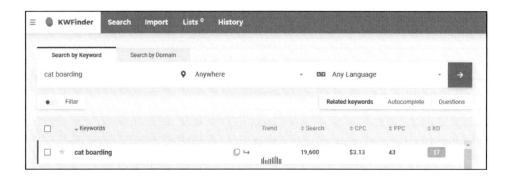

At $3.13, this free third-party tool seems to give a better estimate at the actual bid required than the official Google Ads Keyword Planner. Go figure. At any rate, set your bid on the high side at first and make sure your ads are showing. You have to get your ads running to get data before you can ratchet your bids downwards to save money.

Set Bids at the Keyword Level

You can also set your bids at the keyword level if there are certain phrases that you want to bid higher than for the Ad Group as a whole. To do this, click on the keywords tab, scroll down to a keyword, and then enter a bid.

Here's a screenshot, showing how I have bid up my bid on "best plumber" at $12.01:

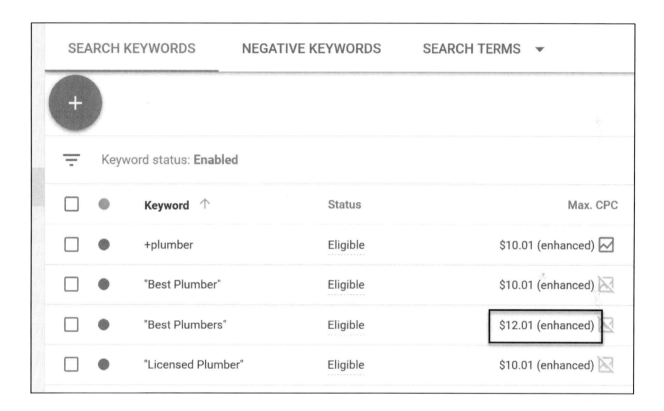

If you set a bid at the keyword level, remember that this overrides the Ad Group level. If you increase your Ad Group bid, then the bid at the keyword group stays in charge, even it's a lower amount.

Here's a tip to track who set which bids. If you're working as a team, or with a client, have one person bid as a .01, another as a .02, and a third as a .03, or even / odd. This way, you can see who bid what. So, I always bid .01, so I can tell that the bid of $5.01 was set by me, vs. the client bid which might be $5.00 and a bid by Gloria, who works for me, that would be $5.02. These pennies don't do anything to the bids in any serious sense; they just tell us who set the bids on a team project.

We'll return to bids after we jump over to Campaigns, as after a few days or a week, you want to go back and monitor your bids, bidding them up or reducing them down until you find the best bid per click for return on investment.

» SET LOGICAL CAMPAIGN SETTINGS

Because Google Ads is an interrelated "whole" and yet composed of hierarchical "parts," it's useful to zig and zag between the parts. So, return to your Campaign Settings, and review them by clicking on the *Settings* tab, with an eye to whether your Campaign settings reflect aspects of the real world such as geotargets, budget, etc.

Here are the basic settings for each Campaign in your Google Ads account that are relevant on the Search Network:

- **Goal**. If you select a Goal, Google Ads will give you suggestions based on the Goal as you work through the process. I never enable this, as I find the suggestions useless, misleading, or just annoying, but it doesn't hurt to enable a goal.
- **Networks**. Here you select Search Network (pre-selected by the above choice). If you want to run on sites like Yelp, Xfinity, Earthlink, etc., then choose Google search partners. If you want to run only on Google, then uncheck the Search Partners box. Again, never mix a Display Network and a Search Network campaign!
- **Locations**. Here is where you set the geotarget or location target for your Campaign. We'll discuss this in a moment; but just realize that you can Geotarget everyone who lives, for example, within a 10-mile radius of Tulsa, Oklahoma, or in Zipcode 94111.
  - o **Location Options**. Generally, the default is fine. I'll explain in a moment what these mean in special circumstances.
- **Languages**. You can select the desired language (e.g., English).
- **Budget**. Set your daily maximum budget here. Again, this is controlled at the Campaign level and controls the budget for all dependent Ad Groups.

- **Bidding**. As explained above, you can set a bid strategy ranging from a fully automated strategy to manual CPC. For most advertisers, I recommend *Manual CPC, Manual CPC + Enhanced CPC*, or *Enhanced CPC* as the best bid strategies.

- **Start and End Dates**. Use this feature if you want to start and stop your advertising around specific dates.

- **Additional Settings**
  - **Campaign URL options.** Use this if you have special parameters in your URLs (as may occur in e-Commerce).
  - **Dynamic Search Ads Setting.** This is an AI-based feature where Google *automatically* creates your ads for you, based on your website. Turn this off unless you are a Zillionaire who wants to waste money frivolously on Google Ads.
  - **IP Exclusions.** Use this if you know certain IP's are bad (e.g., those of competitors). Rarely used as it is too difficult to maintain manually.

» CHOOSE YOUR GEOTARGET SETTINGS WISELY

You can show your ads only to people searching in or about a specific location (e.g., Tulsa, Bixby, Oklahoma City or Zip 68716 in Nebraska). This is called *location targeting* or *geotargeting*. It's one of the most powerful advantages of Google Ads over SEO (Search Engine Optimization).

To set up or adjust your location targeting, go to *Campaigns* and click on *Settings* and then open up the *Locations* tab in the center. (It's confusing. Do not click on Locations on the left menu as that is only a report as to where your clicks are coming from. Be sure to select the Locations tab in the Center.). Here's a screenshot:

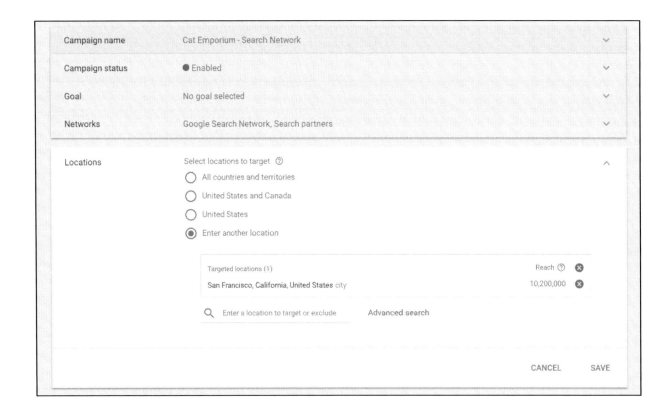

This means that the Campaign "Cat Emporium – Search Network" will show ads only to people physically in San Francisco or who append the phrase "San Francisco" to their search.

Let's review geotargeting in detail.

The best way to set or revisit your geotargeting settings is to click on **Advanced Search** as indicated in blue above. This pops up a map. Next, you have two ways to go about setting location targeting. If you select the circle "Location," then you can just enter states, cities, or even zip codes to target. Here's a screenshot showing zip code 74135:

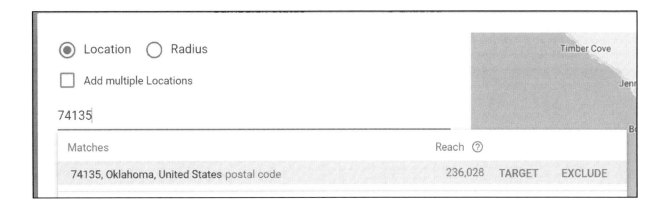

If you select TARGET that means show your ad to people in that zip code. If you select EXCLUDE, that means do not show your ad to people in that zip code. In this method, you can manually enter cities, states, and zip codes to target or exclude for a given Campaign.

The second method is to select "Radius" in the circle. This is useful if you want to target people who are within, say, a 20-mile radius of San Francisco, California. Here's a screenshot:

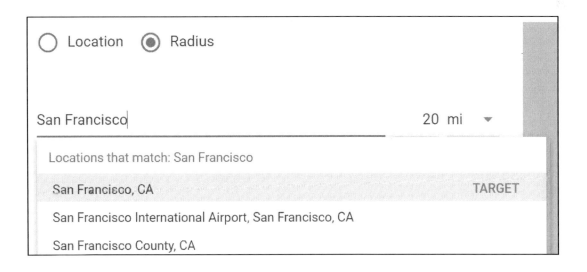

And here's a screenshot of what the map looks like with a 10-mile radius around San Francisco:

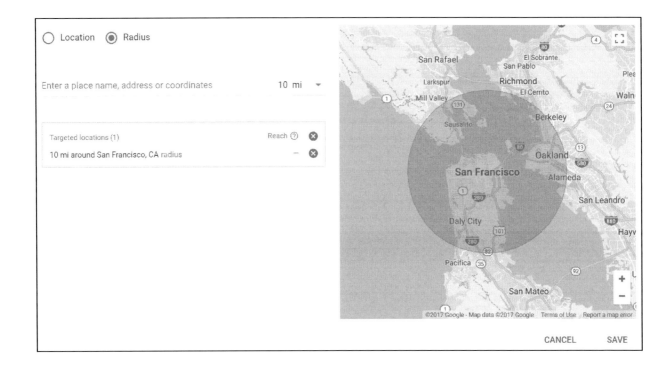

You can see that we'd reach some people across the Bay in Oakland, and Alameda, as well as north into Marin County. You can click into a city you've set like San Francisco, and then adjust up or down the geographic radius. The default is 20 miles, but you can set it to 1 mile or 100 miles, etc.

Excluding Geographic Areas like Cities, States, or ZIP Codes

Let's discuss *exclusions*. You can use the geotarget feature to include "in" cities, states, zip codes, etc., but you can also use them exclude "out" cities, states, ZIP codes, etc. These function like *negative keywords* and block your ads from showing at all.

Why might you do this? For example, consider a scenario where you are a Napa Valley, California, vineyard that sells wine over the Internet, across the entire United States. You want to use Google Ads to reach people searching for "buy wine online,' or "best cabernets from Napa Valley," etc. Google Ads is a fantastic choice to reach these wine connoisseurs who want to buy California Napa Valley wines over the Internet. However, it is illegal to buy wine online in Utah, Oklahoma, Arkansas, Mississippi, Delaware, Rhode Island, and Alabama.

By using the geotarget / exclude feature, you can exclude showing ads to people in these states. Simply go to *Advanced Search >Search*, and enter the state names, then select *exclude.* Here's a screenshot, showing a search for Oklahoma. If you look closely, you'll see Alabama has been grayed out, as I already excluded it:

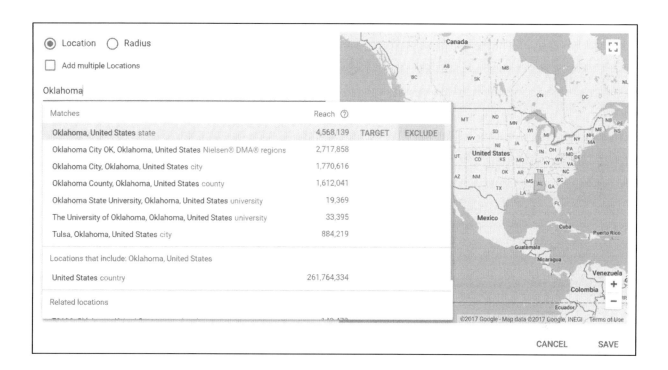

In this way, you'd set your Geotarget to United States, and then exclude states like Oklahoma and Alabama which do not allow wine shipments. There's no point in paying for someone in these states to click on your ad only to find out that they can't use your service.

Poor vs. Rich People by Geography

You can think "out of the box" when it comes to geotargeting. So, if for example, your target customers tend to live in one ZIP code, and your non-customers live in another, you can include "in" your target customers and exclude "out" your non-target customers. It may be politically incorrect to point this out but (unfortunately) in our great capitalist nation, it is often true that poor people tend to live in certain zip codes and rich people in others. By using geotargeting in Google Ads, you can include "in" rich people and exclude "out" poor people based on geotargets.

Geotarget "In" or "Out"

Rich people tend to live in certain ZIP codes and poor people in others. (You can check USA incomes by zip codes out at **http://jmlinks.com/23z**). By using geotargeting, we could exclude the poor zip codes and target only people in rich zip codes. Other ways to use geotargeting can be including "in" people in a commute zone (e.g., from Oakland to San Francisco), and including "out" people outside of a commute zone (e.g., the more difficult commute from Marin County into San Francisco).

Your **TO-DO** here is to identify communities you want to geotarget "in" and any you want to geotarget "out," and then map those to your individual Campaigns.

Advanced Location Options

Finally, click back up to your Campaign settings, find Additional Settings, and just below that click on *Location options*. Here's a screenshot:

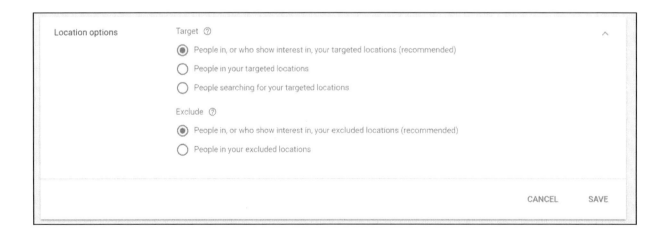

Here you will find the following cryptic language from Google:

People in, who show interest in, your targeted locations (recommended)

People in your targeted locations

People searching for your targeted locations

The way to think about this is by asking where the person is who is your target. A person physically in San Francisco who types in "cat boarding" is definitely a target, but so is a person who works across the Bay in Oakland who types in "San Francisco cat boarding." That's why the default setting includes "interest in" your target location. That is, two scenarios:

1. A person physically in San Francisco who types in "cat boarding" vs.
2. A person physically NOT in San Francisco who types in "cat boarding San Francisco," that is by appending the city name he tells Google that the city of San Francisco is important.

The *default* is for Google to interpret and run your ads on both scenarios if you geotarget San Francisco.

You'd only override these settings if, for some reason, you want to physically constrict it to people physically in the target but exclude those who include it by typing in the city name. A scenario might be a San Francisco bike rental company that only wants to target people who are truly in San Francisco and ready to bike vs. people in Milwaukee who might be planning a trip and are just looking around (but not yet physically in the City). They would thus select "People in your targeted location," and the ads would show if, and only if, the person is physically in the City of San Francisco.

For most of us, the default setting is fine, however. To be on the safe side, you could also enter the keyword *+cat +boarding +san +francisco* into Google Ads to be sure to capture search queries that are clearly looking for cat boarding in the city of San

Francisco. If cities are important to your search patterns, I recommend entering them using the plus marks. It seems to achieve better results; a little redundancy in Google Ads is a good thing.

> **VIDEO.** Watch a video from Google on how to set location targeting in Google Ads at **http://jmlinks.com/26k**.

» MONITOR YOUR KEYWORDS, BIDS, CONVERSIONS, AND PERFORMANCE

Chapter 8 goes into more detail on how to monitor Google Ads for return on investment, but for now, let's overview the basics of monitoring your performance. We'll leave aside *conversion tracking*, but if you can, you should connect Google Analytics to Google Ads, and make sure that it is tracking conversions (e.g., purchases at an e-Commerce website, or completed website feedback forms) as soon as possible.

When you're just getting started, I'd recommend keeping a very close eye on Google Ads, on at least a daily basis at first. Then, after a week or ten days of data, it's time to analyze your performance.

Account Level

Select the Campaigns Tab to compare Campaigns to each other. Note: essentially here you are at the Account "level," and looking "down" to your Campaigns. Here's a screenshot:

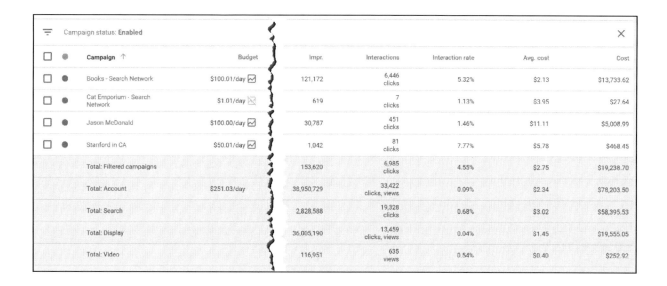

On the top right, select the time period (e.g., last month, last week, etc.). Google Ads will then give you an organized look at your Campaigns. You can select "All enabled Campaigns" to see just the Campaigns that are running by clicking the filter icon on the right (it looks like an upside-down triangle).

Here's what the **default** columns mean:

Campaign. This is the name of your campaign.

Budget. This is your budget maximum per day.

Impressions. These are the number of times your ads were shown.

Interactions. For most of us, this is just clicks.

Interaction Rate (Click thru rate). This is the number of clicks divided by the number of impressions expressed as a percentage. Generally speaking, anything 1% or higher is good.

Avg Cost. This is your average cost-per-click (CPC). Lower is better, of course.

Cost. This is your total cost spent during the time period.

Unfortunately, Google has goofed this all up in the New Interface, so I recommend you drill into columns and disable some of the goofy ones and enable ones that make more sense. Click on the columns icon on the middle right. It is three black bars, like this:

That then opens up a "Modify columns for campaigns" box. Open up each of these, and I recommend you enable the following columns:

Campaign = your campaign name.

Budget = your daily budget.

Status = whether your campaign is running or not.

Impr. = impressions, or how many times your ad displayed on Google.

Search impr. share = a measurement of how many times your ad showed / how many total times it was eligible to show as a percentage. If this is 80% for example, then it means your ad showed 80% of the time vs. relevant searches.

Search top IS = how many times your ad showed in the top position (above organic results). If this is 75% for example, it means your ad was on the top 75% of the time in positions 1, 2, 3, or 4.

Clicks = how many clicks your ads received.

CTR = your click-thru rate, or how many clicks you received over impressions. Thus a 10% CTR means your ad got clicked 10% of the time.

Avg. CPC = the average cost per click; how much you spent for a click.

Cost = how much you spent.

Bid Strategy = what type of bid strategy you used, such as "manual" or "CPA."

On the far right, you can drag up or down each column and order them in any way you like. I usually think of it as a process from showing on Google to getting the conversion, so I order them:

Campaign, Budget, Status, Impressions, Search Impression Share, Search Top Impression Share, Clicks, CTR, Average CPC, Cost, and Bid Strategy.

Once you've checked all the ones you want, click "Save your column set," and give it a name such as My Columns. Hit SAVE & APPLY and Google will apply this column set. Note: you have to do this at both the Campaign and Ad Group level, but once you save a column set you can turn it on / off by clicking on the Column icon.

Bids and SIS Scores

Return to the Campaign Level, where you're looking down at your Ad Groups, by clicking on the top breadcrumb trail navigation. You want to get back "up" to the Campaign level, so you can see your multiple Ad Groups. Enable the same columns as indicated above and save them as "My Columns." Here's a screenshot:

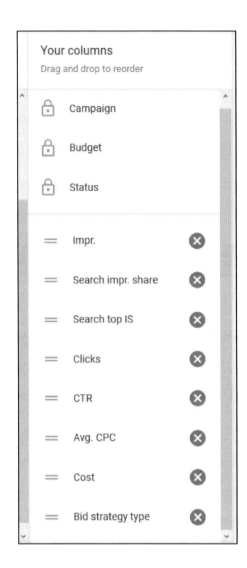

This then outputs at the Campaign level as:

Budget	Status	Impr.	Search impr. share	Search top IS	Clicks	CTR	Avg. CPC	↓ Cost	Bid strategy type
$150.01/d...	Eligible	17,654	26.59%	21.36%	920	5.21%	$1.57	$1,443.49	Manual CPC
$100.00/d...	Eligible	132	72.16%	39.66%	6	4.55%	$16.24	$97.45	Manual CPC

I recommend you set up similar columns at both the Campaign and Ad Group level. Here's a screenshot looking "down" at the Ad Group level:

		Ad group	Status	Default max. CPC	Impr.	Clicks	Search impr. share	Search top IS	CTR	Avg. CPC	↓ Cost	Conversions
☐	●	Social Media - Marketing	Eligible	$2.01 ☑	7,473	598	54.29%	49.15%	8.00%	$1.26	$754.26	4.00

Let's go over what this all means. Again, remember, we are in a Campaign and looking "down" at the Ad Groups that "live" inside a Campaign. Google Ads is a hierarchy.

Ad Group. This is the name you give to each Ad Group. I usually give it a name to reflect the core keyword such as *plumber*, or *emergency* for *emergency plumbing* in the above example.

Status. This tells you whether or not the Ad Group is running.

Default Max CPC. This tells you your bid per click.

Impr. These are the impressions for the time period, i.e., how many times your ad was shown. 7,473 means that that Ad Group's ads were shown 7,473 times during the time period.

Clicks. This tells you how many clicks your ad group received.

Search impr. share (SIS). This is a very useful metric. This shows the percent time your ad was shown vs. the eligible impressions. If, for instance, it was 100%, your ad showed all the time; if it was 69%, it showed 69% of the time and was not showing 31% of the time. You want this to be > 85% to be running "full blast."

Search top IS. This shows you how frequently your ad ran at the top vs. all eligible impressions. A 49.15% Search Top IS mean that your ad showed at the top 49.15% of the time, and did not show 51.85% of the time in the top positions. (*More on this in a moment*).

CTR. This is your click-thru rate, calculated by impressions/clicks. Higher is better, and you want this to be > 2% in general. Anything > 2% is good, >5% is very good. It speaks to how exciting and "on target" your ad headline and copy was vs. the search query.

Avg. CPC. This is the average price you paid per click. Lower is obviously better.

Cost. This is the total cost for the time period that you spent.

Conversions. If you have conversion tracking on, you can see the number of conversions and the conversion rate. This tells you that they not only clicked through but actually "converted," meaning they did what you identified as a goal such as an e-Commerce purchase or a registration or a sales lead.

Threading the Needle

Google Ads is full of trade-offs. So, assuming you did a good job on identifying high value, transactional keywords and you matched those keywords to Ad Groups, let's discuss threading the needle. You want to maximize your return on ad investment by getting the most qualified clicks to your website to generate the most conversions at the lowest cost per conversion.

A perfect Ad Group would hit approximately:

An **SIS** or **Search Impression Share** of > 85%, meaning your ads were showing nearly all the time.

A **Search Top SIS** of < 70%, meaning your ad showed in the top three or four positions, preferably three or four more than 70% of the time.

A **CTR** of > 2%, meaning people liked your ads and clicked through on them.

A **good conversion rate** and **cost per conversion**. This varies greatly based on what you are selling, but you want not only clicks but ads that convert. You can't make a blanket statement as what percent is a good one, as a conversion rate for a cheap purse may be very different from an expensive purse and even more different from a cruise to Italy.

Adjusting if Your Ads Are Not Showing

What do you do if your ads aren't showing? For example, you have an SIS that's 25%, or a Search top IS that's 10%? What are your mechanisms to improve things?

Focus. If you haven't tightly focused your Ad Groups to a specific core keyword, that will show up as poor performance. Tighten your focus.

Bids. You can bid up your bid per click until you get the SIS to be > 85%, as nothing works if your ads don't show.

Ad Copy. If your ads are not showing (i.e., they have a poor quality score), rewrite them to include the keywords in the ad headline and text. Give them some pizzazz and promise something like a "free consult" or "free download." (This will improve the CTR and improve the ad being shown).

Geotarget. If you are running out of budget, it's better to narrow your geotarget and get the SIS > 85% than to spread yourself too thin and be SIS < 85%. Google penalizes ads that run haphazardly, so I always strive to get the SIS > 85% by tuning things up.

Poor Conversions. Here your problem isn't with Google, but rather with your landing page. You're getting clicks, but they're not converting. Assuming your keyword patterns are tight (i.e., transactional, relevant searches), then work on your landing page experience. What will get users to convert to your desired goal once they land on your website? What's fouling it up?

Returning to Bid Strategy: Google's Official Explanation

Now that we have all the pieces in place, let's return to bid strategy. To learn Google's historical explanation of how bidding works, check out this **video** by Chief Economist Hal Varian at **http://jmlinks.com/39u**.

With all due respect to Hal Varian, I would like to argue that this is just so much rubbish. (Interestingly, this video has since been removed from the official Google Ads channel). This is not my experience with Google over many years and many different clients. You can't and shouldn't just leave Google Ads on autopilot, trusting you'll only pay .01 more than the advertiser below you.

If you bid too high, Google just takes your extra money despite what you read in the official help files.

In my experience, it seems that you can often get *more* clicks and certainly *more* clicks at *cheaper* cost by gradually reducing your bid and keeping an eye on your SIS to be greater than 85% and Search top IS at > 70%. It's sort of like throttling an airplane, as you're trying to reduce your bid to discover the "real" cost per click yet maintaining an 85% SIS and a Search top IS > 70%.

Let's dive into this strategy, which I call "Bid Ratcheting."

Bid Ratcheting if Your Ads are Showing

If your ads are performing well, meaning your SIS is greater than 85%, your CTR is greater than 2%, and your Search Top IS is <70%, then I recommend **bid ratcheting**, which is to gradually decrease your manual bid until your SIS falls below 85%, and/or your Search Top IS falls below 70% (meaning you are showing at the bottom of the page).

I have very good success with manual bidding and bid ratcheting. Here's my theory, substantiated by experience but not at all proven:

1. Google is somewhat **dishonest** (?) in how the auction works. Despite what Hal Varian and the official propaganda say, if you bid too high (e.g., you bid $10 and the next guy or gal bids $9), you do not actually pay just one cent more. *You pay a lot more.*

2. As you **ratchet your bids down**, you force Google to reveal the true threshold of the lowest bid you can submit to get your ads to show at SIS > 85% and a Search Top IS of >70%. *Lower bids can result in more impressions, more clicks, and even more conversions.*

3. If you bid too low, Google refuses to show your ads, indicating that there is a **"minimum bid"** threshold for all keywords. *Google puts a hidden floor into bids in Google Ads.*

Let's look at the big picture of Tech and Silicon Valley. Throughout 2016, 2017, 2018, 2019, and now 2020, what have we learned as a society? From Facebook to Twitter, Patreon to PayPal, Google to Apple, we've learned that the tech companies are quite literally *foxes guarding the henhouses*. Privacy scandal has followed privacy scandal, Russian bot has followed Russian bot, class action lawsuit has followed class action. I think I'm not alone in being increasingly skeptical about Tech Companies and whether they have anything other than profit as motivation.

Now, I'm not a socialist. I support capitalism, and I love Google. Nothing the world has ever seen has outdone capitalism for creating innovation and broad prosperity. I lived in the Soviet Union in 1983 as an exchange student, and let me tell you, it was not a pretty society nor a moral society. Don't think I'm a groovy Bay Area socialist. I'm not.

I am a hard-nosed, practical businessperson who respects Google yet realizes that their interests are not fully in alignment with mine. Go in eyes wide open. Don't blindly trust Google (or any corporation). Trust AND verify that you are getting the lowest and most effective bid by ratcheting down your bids until your ads stop and then ratcheting them back up.

Minimum Bids

Let's talk for a moment about minimum bids. As an advertiser, you should always be on the lookout for lucrative, high value, niche keywords. You may bid for something really nichey like "waterproof iPhone headphones" or "grease-resistant batteries," etc., a keyword or phrase for which you are the ONLY bidder. Guess what? You don't get to just bid one penny. There is a hidden, secret "minimum bid" inside of Google Ads, and you should start your bids high so that your ads show, then ratchet down your bids until the SIS falls below 85% (your position will be #1 as you are all alone on this pattern). Presto! You've found the minimum bid on Google Ads for that keyword.

Nowhere in the official documentation does Google talk about or explain minimum bids, but I have had many clients, students, and readers of this book who have discovered that – like the Loch Ness Monster or Big Foot – minimum bids exist.

Force Google Ads to Work

One final weird phenomenon in Google Ads. The official help files claim that if you INCREASE your bids, you'll get MORE clicks and MORE impressions. There's even a tool called "Bid Simulator" inside of Google Ads. To find it, click into an Ad Group and then onto Keywords. Find a keyword that has sufficient data and click the squiggly arrow. Here's a screenshot:

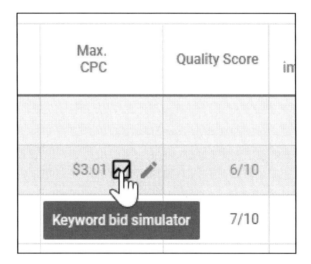

After you click, you'll see a graph that indicates if you increase your bid, you'll get more clicks. Here's a screenshot of that:

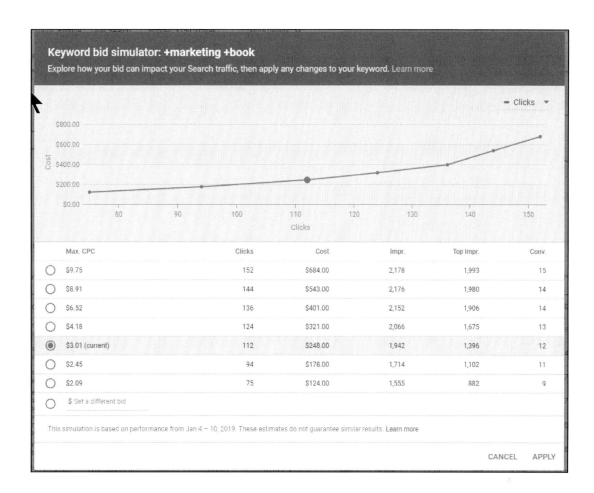

Keyword bid simulator: +marketing +book
Explore how your bid can impact your Search traffic, then apply any changes to your keyword. Learn more

Max. CPC	Clicks	Cost	Impr.	Top Impr.	Conv.
$9.75	152	$684.00	2,178	1,993	15
$8.91	144	$543.00	2,176	1,980	14
$6.52	136	$401.00	2,152	1,906	14
$4.18	124	$321.00	2,066	1,675	13
$3.01 (current)	112	$248.00	1,942	1,396	12
$2.45	94	$178.00	1,714	1,102	11
$2.09	75	$124.00	1,555	882	9
$ Set a different bid					

This simulation is based on performance from Jan 4 – 10, 2019. These estimates do not guarantee similar results. Learn more

CANCEL   APPLY

This graph is saying that if we increase our bid to $9.75, we'll get 152 clicks vs. the 112 we're getting at the current $3.01 bid. But, to be fair, look closely at the far right "Conv" or "Conversions" column, and you'll see that we only get three more conversions for a cost per additional conversion of (684-248)/3 or $162. Not a good deal! As I have said repeatedly, you get paid by the conversion and Google gets paid by the click so this type of "tool" attempts to misleading you into focusing on clicks and not conversions.

Furthermore, I have experienced many times the following. Keep your Campaign Budget the same yet *decrease* your bid. Your clicks actually increase (not decrease)! Why might this be so? My theory is that the Google Ads algorithm has to work harder to get you to spend 100% of your budget, and so it places your ads on more impressions and on better auctions. Behind the scenes, my guess is that the Google Ads engineers optimize the system to maximize the budget spend of everyone. If you bid too high, they can easily suck out all your budget. If you bid too low, they refuse to run your ads. But if you ratchet your bids down to the sweet spot, they have to work hard to maximize your budget spend, while giving you the most clicks for your money. Oh, and to be completely cynical, the AI-based bidding and ad- or extension-generating work more to Google's favor than to yours.

MANUAL OPTIONS GENERALLY OUTPERFORM AI

Experiment with budgets and bids to find what gives you the most clicks for your money, the most conversion for your money, and the best return-on-investment or ROI. It won't necessarily be what the official Google Ads help files will tell you. "Trust but verify," as President Reagan said of the old Soviet Union.

> **TO-DO.** Gradually reduce your bid per click, until you fall below SIS > 85%, a Search Top IS of >70%, and a decent click-through rate. If you SIS goes below 85%, you're bidding too low, so raise your bid If Search Top IS goes below 70%, you're probably bidding too high. Raise and lower your bid until you find the "sweet spot" where you run at the cheapest cost but show all the time.

It's hard to hit the perfect "sweet spot" here, but it's very important to realize that – despite what Google tells you – you want to bid *down* over time.

Spot Checking Your Ads

Another check I recommend is spot-checking your ads periodically to verify that they're running and to see what they actually look like.

Here's **method #1**. Click into a *Campaign > Ad Group > Keywords*. Hover your mouse over where it says a Keyword is "Eligible," and you should see a pop-up box with a green "An ad is showing now" sentence that tells you whether your ad is currently showing or not for that keyword. If you're not running, you get a red warning.

Here's a screenshot:

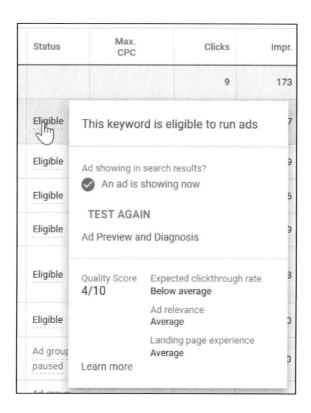

Now, ironically, on all of these three methods Google may tell you that your ad is NOT running when it actually IS running. The tools are very buggy.

Here's method #2. Click up to the *Tools* menu (under the wrench icon) and select *Ad Preview and Diagnosis*. Enter relevant search queries, set your location to a city in your target area, and "spot check" to verify that your ads are actually running. Here's a screenshot:

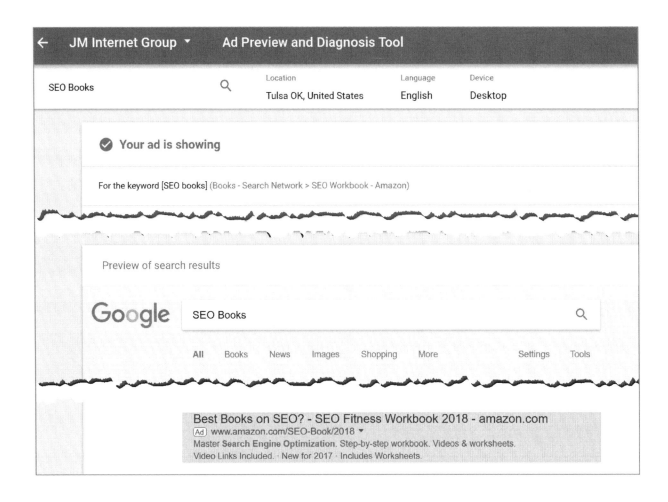

This means that my ad for my *SEO Fitness Workbook* ad is showing for the search query *SEO books* with location set to Tulsa, Oklahoma. If you click on "Device" on the top menu, you can also toggle to mobile device and tablet, to see if your ad is showing on the mobile phone and/or tablet.

Here's **method #3**. I recommend opening up a Chrome browser in incognito mode and going to the SERPS.com location tool at **http://jmlinks.com/26z**. This tool is nice because it allows you to vary your city / location, and often it is more accurate than the Google tool. (You can use it both on your desktop and on your phone). Just do NOT click on your ad in the results, of course, as you'll get charged. If location doesn't matter to you, you can just check in the Chrome incognito browser directly.

TRUST BUT VERIFY

Between checking using these tools, monitoring your impressions, and verifying that your SIS is > 85% and spot-checking, you can reassure yourself that your ads are running on Google.

Also be aware that if you just pop out your phone or check on your browser, and obviously do not click on your own ads (for fear that Google will charge you), Google will stop showing you your ads. You'll mistakenly think that you are not running. This is because Google doesn't keep showing users ads that they don't click on. The only reliable way to verify ads are running is to use one of the three methods I have explained, or at a macro level to verify you have an SIS score > 85%.

What to Do If Your Ads Are Not Showing

If your ads are not showing, you have these options:

1. **Raise your bids.** It's an auction, and your ads are not showing because you're bidding too low.
2. **Tighten the ads** by rewriting them to include keywords, or refocus your Ad Groups into very tight, nichey keyword clusters.
3. **Reduce your geotarget**.
4. **Improve your Quality Score** by offering "free stuff" in your ad copy and/or improving your landing page. Rewrite your ad headlines and text to be more enticing!

Do your spot checking *before* making any changes, as it takes about 3-5 hours for Google to adjust to new bids. In fact, if you change your bids or your ad copy, and then attempt to preview your ads, they'll often go offline. Your process is first to log in to Google Ads, check your SIS, spot check your ads using the Preview Tool, and then adjust your bids upwards or downwards.

Between spot-checking your ads and using the SIS score of > 85% and Search Top IS of >70%, you can verify that your ads are running on desktop, on mobile phones, and on tablets as well as city-by-city if you are geotargeting. In this way, you are sure your ads are running, and you can work in a more focused way on raising your click-thru rate, lowering your bids as much as possible, and increasing your conversion rates once people land on your website.

What you're trying to do is to **tune your ads** by tightening the relationship between the Ad Group, the target keywords (and negative keywords), the ad copy, and the bid per click to get an SIS > 85%, a Search Top IS of >70%, and the lowest possible CPC you can get away with, always with an eye to your conversions.

» Shoot Your Dogs and Let Your Winners Run

Once you're up and running, you want to check your ad copy as well. You're looking to write ads that get strong Click Thru Rates (CTRs) and good conversion rates by applying the "attract / repel" ad strategy.

To monitor your ads, click into a Campaign. Next, click up or over to the Ads tab from within an Ad Group. This will show you the ads that are running in each Ad Group. I recommend running at least three ads simultaneously. Compare the ads, especially their CTR or Click Thru Rate, and conversion rates if you're tracking conversions.

> **Run at least three ads per Ad Group.** Then "kill" (or at least pause) the lower performing ad as measured by CTR, and replace it with a new ad. Over time, you can thus optimize your ad performance by constantly "killing" the bad ads, and "running" the better ads. In fact, I find the best performance when I run multiple ads in an Ad Group and make sure that the different variations contain various permutations of the keyword targets.

I recommend that you "kill" your lower-performing ads on at least a monthly basis, and rewrite them. Then, over time, compare your ads against each other, and run / select ads with the higher click-thru rate, and ultimately higher conversion rate. Google does this to some extent automatically, but by writing and re-writing your ads, you can improve your CTR.

Remember, however, to use the **Attract / Repel** strategy in writing your ads so as to not fall into the trap of writing ads with words like "free" or "cheap" that will get you a lot of clicks, but few valuable conversions. If at all possible, look for ads have both a good click-thru rate and a good conversion rate.

Similarly, at the Ad Group level and Keyword level, look for high-performing keywords and Ad Groups. "Kill" your lower-performing Ad Groups and/or Keywords, but first write / re-write your ads to make sure that the ad content isn't the problem.

Over time, you are looking to "shoot your dogs" and "let your winners run" by deleting low-performing keywords, Ad Groups, and even Campaigns and running / enhancing those that are performing. In the long term, performance is measured not by *clicks* or even *click-thru rates*, but by *conversions* and money made!

»» DELIVERABLE: SEARCH NETWORK WORKSHEET

The **DELIVERABLE** for this Chapter is a completed worksheet on the Search Network. This is a deep dive into your Keyword Patterns, Campaigns, Ad Groups, Ads, and Keywords, so that you end up with a well-organized Google Ads account, and -over time – are able to identify winning keywords and terminate non-winning keywords.

For the **worksheet**, go to **http://jmlinks.com/adw2020**, then re-enter the password, "adw2020," and click on the link to the "Search Network Worksheet."

5

DISPLAY NETWORK

Ads on Google's **Display Network** or **GDN** don't appear on Google, but rather on blogs, news sites, videos, apps, Gmail, user forums, and other websites that participate in Google's network of content websites. For example, if your customers are reading *People Magazine, Chicago Tribune,* some esoteric blog on cats, or watching *Saturday Night Live*'s latest political spoof on *YouTube*, they can see your Google Ads populated via the GDN. If they're checking email via Gmail or interacting with Apps on their phone, they can see ads as well, and so on and so forth. Through remarketing, you can "follow them around" as they browse the Internet. The GDN can be a goldmine or a disaster; it all depends on how well you manage your advertising efforts.

Let's get started!

TO-DO LIST:

>> Review the Basics of the GDN

>> Set Up a Basic GDN Campaign

>> Ad Group Organization on the Display Network

>> Create Winning Ads on the Display Network

>> Target Your Ad Group: Keywords

>> Target Your Ad Group: Audiences & Remarketing

>> Target Your Ad Group: Placements

>> Target Your Ad Group: Other Targeting Methods

>> Target Your Ad Group: Apps

>> Target Your Ad Group: Gmail

» Target Your Ad Group: Combining Methods

» Monitor Your Placements to Exclude the Naughty

» Understand Bidding & Quality Score on the GDN

» Monitoring Your GDN Campaigns

»» Deliverable: Display Network Worksheet

» REVIEW THE BASICS OF THE GDN

Remember that Google advertising is really two distinct networks:

1. the **Search Network** (primarily Google but also search-driven sites like Yelp, YouTube search, or Comcast), and
2. the **Display Network** (a network of sites such as YouTube and Gmail but also blogs, parked domains, apps, web portals and many low quality and even fraudulent sites).

Remember that – rather nefariously – Google's "default" setting on Search Network campaigns is to INCLUDE the Display Network. Here's a screenshot:

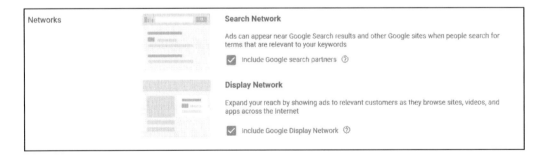

Do not fall for this Google gotcha! Turn OFF the Display Network for your search campaigns by unchecking the box "Include Google Display Network."

To verify which networks you are on, click into any Campaign, then click on Settings on the left, and then you should see a tab in the center that says "Networks." It should say "Google Search Network" and nothing else, if it's a Search Campaign; if it's a Display Network only, you'll see it in the "Type" bar at the top. Here's a screenshot:

If the center line says "Google Search Network" and "Display Network," you've mixed the networks. Play with these settings until you get all your Campaigns to run on either the Search Network or the Display Network, but never both. You want your Search Campaigns only on the Search Network, and your Display Campaigns only on the Display Network. With that in hand, you can proceed in this Chapter to learn how to manage the Display Network.

VIDEO. Watch an (overly cheerful) video from Google on the Display Network at **http://jmlinks.com/27b**.

Search vs. Browse

Conceptually, the easiest way to grasp the difference between the two networks is to understand *browse* vs. *search*. Whereas in *search*, the target customer goes to Google and *pro-actively searches* for your product or service by keyword, in *browse*, he doesn't go to Google at all nor does he pro-actively enter in search keywords. Rather he's reading a blog or newspaper site, checking his email on Gmail or watching a YouTube video, and as he's browsing, he just *happens to see your ad* somewhere on the web page. *Search* is all about pro-active searching, and *browse* is about getting your ad "adjacent" to what the customer is actually paying attention to.

Three big points to remember about the Display Network are:

1. Ads on the GDN are competing in a **"browse"** environment, so they have a much harder time getting the user's attention (i.e., lower click-thru rate) and then making the sale (i.e., lower conversion rate). This is because you are hijacking the user from something he *is* doing (i.e., reading a blog on cats) to something he *is not* doing (i.e., reviewing his cat boarding options).
2. The GDN has **many poor quality sites** up to and including fraudulent sites, so ads on the GDN often generate many clicks but few conversions because the websites on the network itself are often very low quality.
3. Google is motivated to get you to advertise everywhere to get clicks, so official Google information on the GDN tends to be **overly optimistic**. Google propaganda misleads you into thinking the GDN is a great opportunity when it is very much the poor stepchild of the Search Network.

In general, the click-thru rate (CTR) and the conversion rate on ads on the Display Network are many factors of ten lower than on the Search Network. This is because a) people are in "browse mode" on the GDN, so less likely to be primed to click or convert into a purchase and b) there is a lot of noise and even fraud on the GDN, so many clicks are purely frivolous and hence do not convert. For example, a common problem is game apps used by children; ads are placed on them, and kids wildly click here and there on the games as they play, mistakenly clicking on your ads (costing you money and making Google money) but there is little to no chance they'll actually buy your product. **The GDN has its uses, but deploy it with extreme caution!**

Google's Contradictions on the GDN

Remember, again, the incentive structure among Google, the user, and you as the advertiser;

Google gets *paid by the click* and is incentivized to maximize ad clicks on the GDN.

AdSense partners (i.e., websites and apps that participate in the Display Network) also get *paid by the click* (they share revenue with Google for each ad click) and are also incentivized to maximize ad clicks on the network.

You, as the advertiser, however, get *paid by the conversion* and are incentivized to minimize low-quality clicks (those that do not convert, or that yield low-value revenue).

Most problematically, Google has a conflict of interest in that it simultaneously benefits from clicks on the network but is also supposed to police out fraudulent clicks. We, as advertisers, are required to "trust Google" and its "partners" that they are not engaging in click fraud at the worst, or poor policing at best. To read a shocking account of the problem visit **http://jmlinks.com/25f**. To read up-to-date information on "click fraud," visit **http://jmlinks.com/49m**. It's a huge problem and not just for Google; Facebook, Twitter, Instagram, and LinkedIn all have issues as to how "real" clicks are on their networks.

Why Advertise on the Display Network?

If the GDN is so problematic, why advertise on it? Here are a few important reasons:

- **Browse over search**. While the Search Network is fantastic if, and only if, people are pro-actively searching for keywords that relate to your product or service, the GDN can get you in front of potential customers across a plethora of websites (adjacent to their interests), thereby getting you in front of customers who might not be pro-actively searching for a product or service like yours.
- **Niche Targeting**. The GDN can identify blogs and other websites in an industry niche and place your ad precisely on these niche venues. In this way, a company that sells high-end biking supplies can "build its brand" by advertising specifically on high-value cyclist websites on a recurring basis.
- **Repeating your message**. For items with long sales cycles and high values, like Caribbean cruises or life insurance, remarketing on the GDN allows an advertiser to reach potential customers not just at the moment of search but to "follow them" around the Internet over the days, weeks, or even months that they toy with a big purchase decision.

- **Brand and Awareness Building**. By combining the GDN with the Search Network, you can constantly remind your target audience of your company and brand. Brand-building – the constant repetition of a company's message – is now available to even small, nichey companies via the GDN.

The GDN is a tool that has its uses. But if you choose to advertise on the GDN, just be aware of its contradictions and commit to regularly monitoring your placements and performance for fraud and low-value placements.

How the Display Network Works

At its simplest level, the Display Network works as follows:

- **Publishers** with websites or apps join AdSense (**http://jmlinks.com/24a**) and become part of Google's **Display Network**. They agree to allow Google to place ads on their websites and/or apps.
- **Advertisers** set up Display Network campaigns in Google Ads and tell Google where to place their ads via targeting methods such as *keywords, placements,* or *remarketing* (discussed in detail, below).
- As **users** browse websites and apps, Google places ads on the websites or apps (called "placements" in GDN lingo). Users see these ads as they browse websites, apps, YouTube, and Gmail.
- Advertisers *compete* to get their ads on placements (websites and/or apps) in the Google Display Network by bidding per click and/or by impression.
- When a **user clicks on an ad**, Google makes money off the click and splits this with the publisher of the website and/or app.
- The **user** then leaves the website, and **lands** on the **advertiser landing page**, where he either converts or does not.

Publishers get paid by the click. Advertisers compete in the auction by the click. Google makes money, the publishers make money, and you as the advertiser *spend* money to get traffic to your website. If you've done your homework, you can get high-quality traffic to your website that actually converts and makes you money. If you haven't done your homework, you'll just spend money on frivolous placements and even fake / bot clicks.

VIDEO. Watch a video from Google on the basics of the Display Network at **http://jmlinks.com/52f**.

» SET UP A BASIC GDN CAMPAIGN

In order to understand how the GDN works, you'll need a basic GDN campaign if you don't have one running already. Here's how. If you already have a GDN Campaign, you can skip this section.

First, log in to your Google Ads account, and click into Campaigns, and then click the blue circle to start creating a new Campaign. Choose a goal such as "Website traffic," and then Select "Display." Here's a screenshot:

Under that, select "Standard display campaign. You then have three options: "standard," "smart display," or "Gmail." Here's a screenshot:

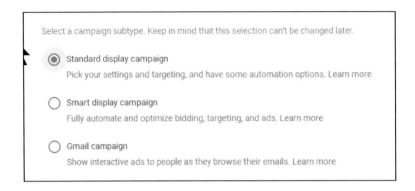

We'll discuss each option below, but for now choose "Standard." Give your Campaign a name (*I recommend naming it with the suffix – Display or GDN so you know it's a GDN Campaign*), select the Geotarget (e.g., Stamford, Connecticut, or 25 miles from Stamford, CT, for example). Select a bidding strategy such as Manual CPC and a budget.

Click Additional Settings in blue to open up the additional settings. Here you can set up very specific things. Importantly, I recommend you always use **frequency capping** so that a person does not see your ad over and over and over and over again. A good limit is three times per day per Campaign. Here's a screenshot:

Next, create and name at least one Ad Group, and give it a budget and bids. You may be forced to choose among a bunch of other confusing options; just do the best you can for now, and then we'll circle back and go over these steps one by one.

Unfortunately, the first set up is a supremely annoying set of steps. But once you've gotten to the Ad Group, you can skip to the bottom and click "Create Campaign." In fact, I recommend you do so (rather than set up everything at once as Google recommends), as it is easier to manage everything once you have the "shell" of at least one Campaign and one Ad Group. Ignore the warning messages, and then once you've gotten a Campaign created, **pause** it so you don't waste any money.

It's very important to pause your Campaign until you are 100% ready as Google has a new "feature" that will run your ads with no targeting at all, just to make Google money. The whole set up process from scratch is extremely annoying and difficult as they throw too many questions at you too quickly. Just set up a Campaign with an Ad Group that is set to run on the GDN, and pause it. Now, you're ready to dig into your first Campaign.

Two Key Settings: just as on the Search Network you can geotarget your ads, and opt in or opt out of desktop, mobile, and/or tablet traffic by adjusting your settings on the Campaign Settings tab. Therefore:

1. Select a **geotarget** for your campaign. For example, if you are a hair salon in Stamford, CT, then choose a radius of 10 miles from your salon. This means, for example, that someone browsing a website in the GDN or watching a YouTube video who is also within 10 miles of your shop is eligible to see your ad, while someone outside of 10 miles is not.
2. Select your **device targeting** of phones, tablets, and/or desktop. Make at least an educated guess as to which platform(s) will convert best for you, and set the device targeting accordingly.

» AD GROUP ORGANIZATION ON THE DISPLAY NETWORK

We will get to targeting settings in a moment, but first, let's review the basics of how to organize your Ad Groups on the GDN. First and foremost, your Ad Groups should reflect your product / service lines or your core keywords from your search campaigns. For example, for Jason's Cat Emporium, we might have the following three Ad Groups:

Cat Boarding, targeting people who need to board their cat for vacation;

Cat Grooming, targeting people who want to get their cat professionally groomed; and

Cat Toys, targeting people who want to buy luxury toys for their cat.

Keywords are very loose on the Display Network, so think of these as thematically connected one to each Ad Group. Each group is more a way to help you organize your ads thematically than a tight match between keyword and ad as on the Search Network.

Targeting Lives at the Ad Group Level for Display Campaigns

Secondarily, targeting (as we shall discuss in a moment) "lives" at the Ad Group level on a Display Campaign (vs. at the Campaign level in a Search Campaign), so if you want to target in different ways you would do best not to mix and match targeting methods in one single group. For example, you might have an Ad Group that uses *remarketing* (re-showing your ads to people who have visited your website), another one that uses *keyword targeting*, and still another that targets persons who are "in the market" for cat-related stuff. Even if each were promoting only your "cat boarding" service line, each "buyer persona" or "buyer situation" should have its own unique Ad Group in your GDN campaign.

Your **TO-DO** here is to outline your Ad Groups, starting with your product / service lines (or core keywords) and splitting them, if necessary, if you will be using different targeting methods. (You might want to read this whole Chapter first, so you understand targeting options if you're not sure.)

≫ CREATE WINNING ADS ON THE GDN

Now let's dive into how to create ads for the GDN. While ads on the Search Network (e.g., Google) are limited to text, ads on the Display Network can be images as well as text. Indeed, they can even be interactive and engaging to the mouse!

Inside one of your Ad Groups, click on the blue button to create an ad, and you'll see two options:

Responsive Display Ad (recommended option) – this is a combination of both graphic and text ads and is the most common and most useful option. When you click on this, Google will guide you through scanning your target website, uploading images or choosing from stock images, writing up to five headlines, one or two long headlines, five descriptions, your Business name, and a Partridge in a Pear tree. OK, I'm kidding about the Partridge in a Pear Tree, but the point is that you input the graphical and text elements and Google will use AI to combine them into attractive text and image ads across the Display Network.

Upload display ads. This option allows you to upload your own graphics. It's useful if you are a larger company and want to control the look and feel of your ads tightly. Click through and then click on the blue "Supported sizes and formats" to learn the specifications. You should **upload all available formats**, as you do not know which format will match which placement on the network. In addition, you should also create the first option as it allows text-only ads, which appear on some unique sites on the network.

Think Billboard Advertising.

While ads on the Search Network (i.e., Google itself) are more like ads in the old-fashioned yellow pages, where a user is pro-actively searching for a service (like a plumber or a roofer), very likely to look at ads, and primed to buy after the click, ads on the Display Network are more like billboards on the side of a highway. Users are zipping along, on their way to other destinations, and your job is to attract the attention of relevant customers and get them to shift from "what they're doing" to "hey, I want to visit that website."

- For fun, browse funny billboards and ponder how they make you take notice at **http://jmlinks.com/27c**. Now, return to your own ads and brainstorm how to make them visually "pop" as users are browsing sites on the Internet.

In terms of the technical ad production, Google Ads' "scan website" feature makes it very easy to quickly create ads for all available formats on the Display Network. Just enter your "Final URL" and follow the step-by-step instructions. Google does a great job of pulling graphics from your website and giving you options to configure your ads. Here's a screenshot:

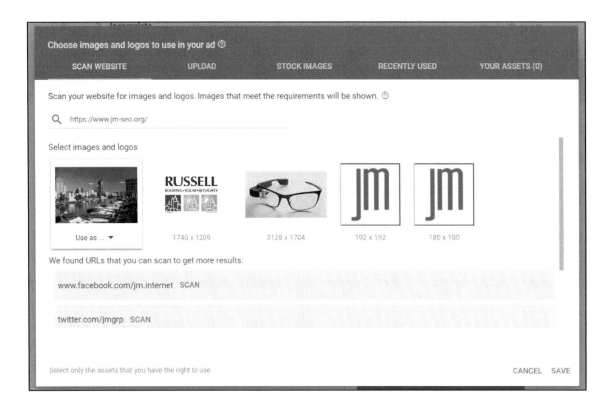

Once your ad is created, you can preview it and even email the preview to other people on your team.

Attract / Repel Ad Copy

Similar to the Search Network, remember that your best ad strategy is **attract / repel**. You don't want zillions of clicks but rather clicks from highly qualified buyers who ultimately convert to sales. Accordingly, think of ads that will "attract" your best customers but "repel" those who are not likely to buy, or likely to spend just a little money. Don't be afraid to scare off cheap people, or persons who are unlikely actually to buy your product or service. A good ad on the Display Network –

- is *available in all image sizes*, including the text-only option;
- clearly conveys your *business value proposition*, including what is unique and attractive about your product or service;
- contains a *call to action* such as "free download" or "call for consultation"; and
- *attracts* your target customers while *repelling* those who might click but not convert.

Populate at least one Ad Group with all relevant ad formats with clever "attract / repel" ads, and you're ready to dive into how to **target** or **trigger** your ads, which is where the complexity and power of the Display Network truly lies.

Smart Campaigns

Google Ads has a new feature called "Smart Campaigns." It relies on Artificial Intelligence to automate bidding, targeting, and even ad creation. To use this option, start at the beginning by creating a Campaign and selecting Display. Then select "Smart display campaign." Here's a screenshot:

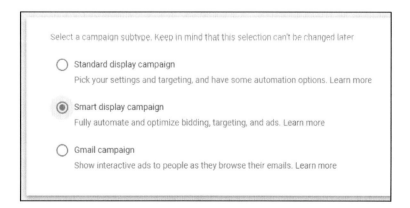

Alternatively, you can also create what is called a "Smart" Campaign, which is a blend of Search and Display by selecting the "Smart" option prior to selecting the Display Network. Here's a screenshot:

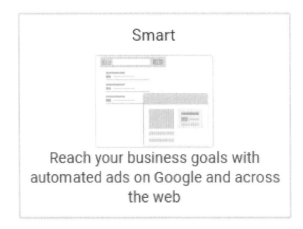

Smart Campaigns give Google the option of showing your ads on either the Search and/or the Display Network at any given moment. Whether you choose the generic Smart option or the Smart Display Option, they work in more or less the same fashion, letting Google AI build out everything for you.

Regardless of which type you choose, you next set the geotarget, language, and bidding strategy. You need to be able to use **conversion-tracking** so that Google AI can attempt to optimize on conversions; it doesn't work very well with click-based options. So be sure to enable conversion-tracking in Google Ads and Google Analytics.

In terms of ad creation, you then input a final URL where you want to send traffic, images and logos pulled from your website or Google's stock art gallery, five headlines of 30 characters, one long headline of 90 characters, and your business name. Google then targets your ads on the fly, creates your ads on the fly, and sets your bids on the fly.

I am **not a fan** of Smart Campaigns for several reasons:

1. Google has a fundamental **conflict of interest**, encouraging it to maximize clicks and not conversions;
2. The Google Display Network is full of **nefarious if not fraudulent websites and apps**, pro-actively set up to fleece advertisers out of their money (and Google does a terrible job at policing this problem);
3. For most advertisers outside of high-volume e-commerce, **conversions are insufficient** to allow AI to fully optimize the advertising;
4. You, as the advertiser, are **ceding fundamental control** to Google over what your ads say, where they appear, and the conversion-tracking aspects.

I have tried Smart Campaigns for myself and my own clients, and the results have been abysmal. But try them for yourself and your company. Just monitor their performance. If they work for you, use them. If they don't, don't. You can learn more about Smart Campaigns at **http://jmlinks.com/49q**.

A Google Display Network Gotcha

Let's return to targeting on the GDN. The Google Ads interface will tempt you into mixing several targeting methods into one Ad Group. Do not fall for this "gotcha," as you will waste a lot of money and get poor results. Instead:

Set **ONE** and **ONLY ONE** *targeting* option per Ad Group.

If you mix targeting options, Google may combine them as "or" statements and not "and" statements. For example, if you put in keywords like "cat boarding," "pet boarding," and "cats," and also target remarketing (people who've hit your website), and also target people by demographics, i.e., those who are aged 25-30, it will tend to use the broadest match possible (i.e., people aged 25-30) and ignore your more focused targeting.

GOOGLE LOOKS FOR THE BROADEST TARGETING METHOD

You'll end up with lots of spurious clicks because the targeting is too broad. Instead, have a focused Ad Group around a specific targeting method such as keywords like "cat boarding," another one on "remarketing," and still another targeting "young people," and you'll be able to see what's happening more clearly and focus your efforts on those targeting methods that yield the best ROI.

Targeting Options

Inside of an Ad Group, you can access the targeting options by clicking on the left column, where you'll see:

Keywords

Audiences

Demographics

Topics

Placements

Each of these refer to "ad **targets**," which is how you tell Google to **trigger** your ad to be displayed on the GDN. (Like Google, I will use *target* and *trigger* interchangeably to mean the same thing: how you communicate to Google as to when to show your ad). Just as on the Search Network, ads are shown based on your *bid per click* in the ad auction (you have to outbid your competition to run your ad, based on what you're willing to pay per click), plus your *Quality Score* (the higher the click-thru rate, the more relevant the ad, and the more relevant your landing page, the more likely your ad is to run), plus your *trigger* or *target*. On the Search Network, the only trigger is the *keyword*; on the Google Display Network, it's more complicated.

*Let's go through each option one-by-one, starting with **keywords**.*

» TARGET YOUR AD GROUP: KEYWORDS

Keywords as a trigger mechanism exist in both the Search Network and the Display Network but function in very different ways.

Keyword matching is **tight** on the Search Network. (*Exact, phrase, modified broad, and broad*).

Keyword matching is **loosey-goosey** on the Display Network!

Google doesn't explain this clearly, but here's what I mean. On the Search Network, the user pro-actively types keywords into Google, such as *cat boarding, cat kennel*, or *cat grooming* (or keywords such as *dog boarding, iguana boarding*, or *exotic bird grooming*). Google knows user intent because after all, a person who types in *dog boarding* isn't looking for *iguana boarding* and a person who types in *cat grooming* isn't looking for an *exotic bird hotel!* Some keywords are problematic (e.g., *cheap cat boarding, pet boarding*), but we as advertisers manage those through negative keywords and through writing attract / repel ad copy.

KEYWORD MATCHING IS LOOSEY-GOOSEY ON THE GDN

Not so on the Display Network. A user doesn't type anything in when he visits the Chicago Tribune's article on *Cats at the Westminster Kennel club dog show? Sort of, in a first* (**http://jmlinks.com/24c**), or when he's reading a Gmail from his Aunt Nancy on best recipes for Chicken Pot Pies for their weekend family reunion in Nebraska, or when he's on an App for how to de-stress. Google can spider the content and take a guess at what's important, but is the *Chicago Tribune* article more about cats or about dogs? Is the user a cat lover or a dog lover, or just a Chicago resident? As for the Gmail on Aunt Nancy and Chicken pot pies, is it about chicken, about Nebraska, about a family reunion, or about pot? As for apps, they're also all over the place.

Accordingly, keyword matching between the desires of the advertiser and the intent / interests of the user is loosey-goosey on the GDN!

Google also looks at the recent search history by the user; if Aunt Nancy has Googled "Chicken pot pie recipes," that's a clue to show recipe articles. But if she's now browsing a blog on things to do in Omaha, perhaps "Omaha museums" is a more relevant search?

Despite Google's façade as an "all-knowing" tech company, on the Google Display Network, it simply makes its best guess at what it calls "contextual targeting" (**http://jmlinks.com/24d**), meaning it attempts to match the content of the article on the Web, video on YouTube, email on Gmail, or app (plus recent search history or remarketing tags), with the keywords entered by advertisers.

Here's a screenshot of how Google views keywords and targeting on the GDN:

About contextual targeting

Contextual targeting is one of a few different methods that you can use to get your display ads on sites, apps, and webpages that are part of the Display Network. This method of targeting uses the keywords or topics you've chosen to match your ads to relevant sites. Note: This only applies to keywords with "Content" selected for the keyword setting.

1. You choose keywords and topics ⌄

2. Our system analyzes webpages that make up the Display Network ⌄

3. Your ad gets placed ⌄

They make it sound as easy as one, two, three. But it isn't. In short, the keywords you enter as triggers for a Display Network Campaign only match the keywords of the article in what I call a "loosey-goosey" fashion, meaning not very much and certainly not with the laser precision available on the Search Network. Accordingly, you want to think of a GDN Campaign as attempting to reach people who are *browsing* on themes and topics related to your products in a very broad way.

While on the Search Network, I recommend you think in a very focused and detailed way about your keywords, on the Display Network, I recommend you relax and think more broadly about keywords, including ones adjacent to your product or service area.

Input Your Keywords

An easy way to get started on the GDN is to copy the structure of your search campaigns. Take a Campaign that is running on the Search Network, and then duplicate its Ad Groups on the GDN. If you don't have your keyword list handy, you can export your keywords from a Search Network Ad Group. Just click into an Ad Group, click on Keywords on the left, and then find the downward arrow on the top right. Here's a screenshot:

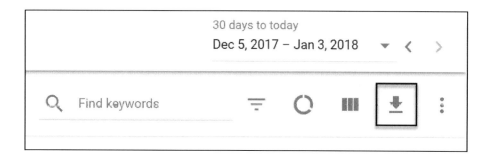

Export them into a CSV or Excel file, and remove all the "+" signs, "quote" marks or brackets as well as any duplicates. You just want the keywords with no markers for the Display Network.

With your keyword list in hand, click over to your Display Network Campaign, and then the matching Ad Group.

Next, at the Ad Group level, click into an Ad Group (or create a new one) for keyword-targeting. Click into that Ad Group and click on Keywords on the left. Click on the white cross in the blue circle and copy/paste over your keywords. Here's a screenshot:

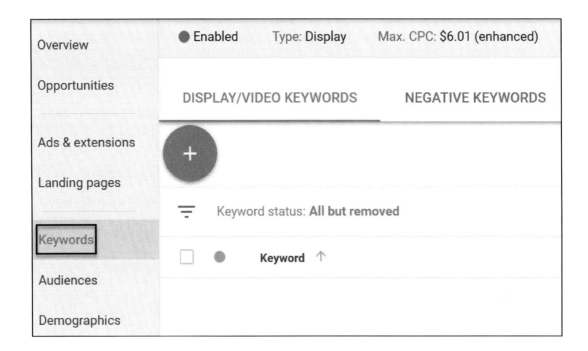

As you input keywords, step back and consider what Google means by "Keyword setting" which is visible at the bottom as you input keywords. Here's a screenshot:

The default setting at the bottom is "Audience," which means Google will do its best to match your keywords to the user profile as people are browsing the network. If you want to be tighter, matching only web pages that contain these keywords select

"Content." The former means Google is looking at user clues and at website clues; the latter means it is only looking at website clues.

Remember: do not mix targeting methods! Once you've set your keywords for this Ad Group, you're done. Don't be tempted by the left column to go into Audiences, Demographics, etc., and choose those options as these would be "or" statements and destroy the focus of your keywords. If you want to try different targeting methods, I recommend that you fill out the first Ad Group with ads, and then use the Copy / Paste feature to duplicate the Ad Group. Then, remove the Keywords from the duplicate Ad Group and create a different targeting method.

Name each Ad Group in your GDN campaign to clearly indicate the target method. Here's a screenshot of Ad Groups promoting my SEO Book on the Display Network, with each name clearly indicating the target method. The Ad Group, "SEO Book – Keywords," for instance, is using the keyword targeting method while the Ad Group, "SEO Book – Remarketing," is using the remarketing targeting method.

		Ad group ↑	Status	Default max. CPC
☐	●	SEO Book - Audiences	Paused	$4.01
☐	●	SEO Book - Keywords	Eligible	$4.01
☐	●	SEO Book - Placements	Eligible	$4.01
☐	●	SEO Book - Remarketing	Eligible	$4.01

» TARGET YOUR AD GROUP: AUDIENCES & REMARKETING

Let's examine the next type of targeting on the Display Network: Audiences. You've probably had the experience of visiting a website, such as Progressive.com or Zappos.com, clicking around, perhaps even adding a product or two to your shopping cart, and then, the next thing you know, you start seeing **recurring ads** for that vendor over and over and over and over and over again as you browse other sites on the Internet such as YouTube, Chicago Tribune, People Magazine, etc. What's going on?

It's called **remarketing**, and it's the next type of trigger available on the GDN, listed under "audiences." Remarketing is far and away the *best* and *most important* targeting method on the GDN. Here's how it works.

As you first visit sites on the Internet, such as Progressive.com or ChicagoTribune.com, for example, each website places a cookie or "tag" on your browser, and then through the magic of Google Ads remarketing, you can be shown "relevant" ads by that vendor as you browse other sites that participate in Google's Display Network.

> **Remarketing** allows you a "second chance" to convert a customer by allowing you to show / reshow ads to him as he surfs other websites on the Internet after first visiting your website. That's why it's called **RE**marketing.

Remarketing vs. Retargeting: Conceptually Different

Remarketing is a little different than *retargeting*, and Google participates in the former as well as the latter. *Retargeting* is when you reach people who have not first visited your website but who are matched as "similar" to your target customers by a third-party service, whether that be Google or true third party retargeting vendors such as AdRoll (**https://adroll.com**). Indeed, you can use remarketing and retargeting on Facebook as well (Facebook's system is probably #2 to Google's for remarketing / retargeting).

Let's return to Google Ads, and think of it this way:

> *Remarketing* is reaching people who have touched your website at least once.

> *Retargeting* is reaching "similar audiences" who have not yet touched your website for the first time.

Unfortunately, the blogosphere uses the two terms interchangeably, but they are conceptually distinct. Just ask yourself whether you want to reach people who have already visited your website (remarketing), or new people who might be similar but have not yet visited your website (retargeting).

Remarket High-Value Products or Services

Remarketing works best for a high-value product or service that has a long sales cycle. An example would be a Caribbean cruise. It's expensive and a big commitment to take your family on a Caribbean cruise, so you'll probably do some research, check out a few of the big vendors such as Disney Cruise Lines, Carnival Cruise Lines, and Norwegian Cruise Lines and discuss the options and expenses with your spouse and family. It's expensive, and it has a long cycle from interest to purchase.

REMARKETING WORKS BEST FOR HIGH-VALUE PRODUCTS

Cruise line marketing is an excellent choice for remarketing, because you might first search "Caribbean cruises" on Google (Search Network), visit a few sites like Disney Cruises or Carnival Cruises, and then go watch videos on YouTube about Jamaica, Cuba, Barbados and other destinations (Display Network). You might research snorkeling, things to do in Kingston, Jamaica, etc., and only then return to vendor sites to select your cruise line. There's a lot of back and forth, many websites that get visited, a long time between interest and purchase, and a high-value purchase.

This makes it ideal for remarketing.

By using remarketing, Carnival Cruise Line can transform that *first* visit you make to their website into a *continuous remarketing effort* as you visit site after site after site in the Google Display Network. Remarketing extends that opportunity for Carnival Cruise Lines to sell to you from the short-time interaction on their website to the long-time interaction as you browse many sites as you research every aspect of planning your perfect family vacation to the Caribbean.

Note: remarketing is not available in sensitive categories such as healthcare, pharmaceuticals, gun purchases, etc. If your website category is not eligible, you're remarketing code will be invalidated after installation. And **note**: remarketing is generally not effective for *low-value products* as the cost per click can be quite expensive.

Setting up Remarketing

To enable remarketing, you have to install a little Google Javascript tracking code on your website. *Yes, you, too, can participate in Google's massive invasion of our privacy across the Internet by participating in remarketing and installing the tracking code!* (If you'd like to see what Google thinks your personal preferences are, make sure you're signed in to your Gmail or Google account, and visit **http://jmlinks.com/24q**; if you'd like to see what Google knows about the websites you've visited, go to **http://jmlinks.com/24r**. The point is that *remarketing* is how Google, in cooperation with sites on the Display Network and advertisers, uses what it knows about you (and others) to show you relevant ads as you visit sites in the GDN).

Create a Remarketing List

In order to use remarketing, you have to create a remarketing list. The most common way to do this is to "tag" everyone who visits your website. Your first step is to set up and enable the Google Ads remarketing tag on your website. Here's how.

First, log in to Google Ads and click on the tools menu at the top. Select Audience manager. Here's a screenshot:

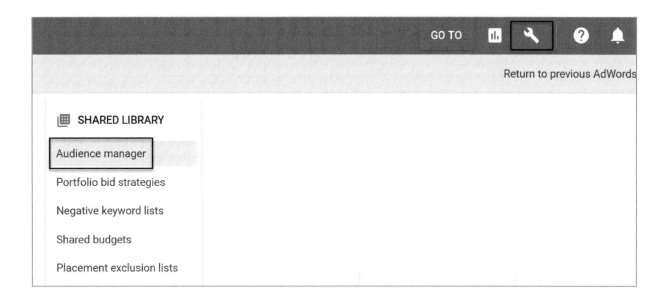

Next, click *Audience sources* and follow the steps there. The easiest way to do it is to enable Google Analytics via Google Tag Manager and cross-link Google Ads to Google Tag Manager / Analytics. You can read the step-by-step instructions on Google at **http://jmlinks.com/39y** as well as how to link Google Analytics and Google Ads at **http://jmlinks.com/39z**. I recommend you use the new Google Tag Manager (**http://jmlinks.com/41b**) and follow the instructions at **http://jmlinks.com/41a**. It's a little complicated, so you may need to bring in your resident computer nerd. Or go to Fiverr.com and search for "Google remarketing." Or click the *Question Mark* icon on the top right and reach out to Google Ads technical support by phone. They'll lead you through it.

Note that you can have a list of everyone who has hit your website as well as smaller lists such as people who did not convert, or people who hit the *cat boarding* landing page vs. the *cat toys* landing page. Remarketing can be very focused – from everyone who hit your website, to just folks who did not convert, to people who clicked into the *cat boarding* page and made a purchase, etc.

Using Tag Assistant to Verify Your Installation

Google has, unfortunately, done a very bad job of explaining how to set up and install the remarketing tag. It can be pretty confusing! Like Google Analytics, the remarketing tag is a little Javascript code that you MUST get installed on each and every page of your website.

Fortunately, as you play around with the required code in Google Ads, Google Analytics, and Google Tag Manager, there is a Chrome plugin that will test your remarketing code installation. It's called **Tag Assistant** by Google (**http://jmlinks.com/24h**). Install it, visit your website, and then at the top right of your browser, you can test your installation. Here's a screenshot of Tag Assistant confirming that the remarketing tag is activated on JasonMcDonald.org:

You can also use Tag Assistant on other websites (e.g., competitors) to see if they are using remarketing.

Once you've set up an audience, give it a few weeks and then check the audience in Google Ads to verify that there are "people" in it. Login to Google Ads, click on the *Tools Menu > Audience Manager*. You should then see your list, and it should have numeric values for the *Size:Display* column. Here's a screenshot:

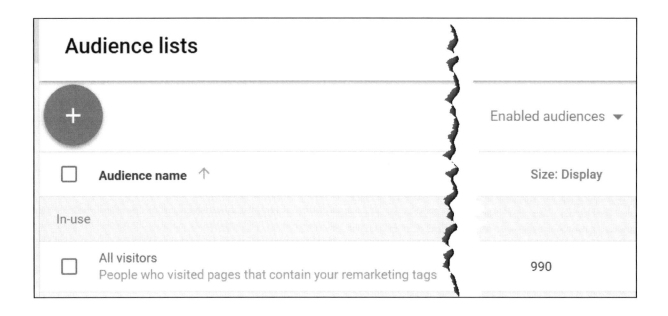

If you show a positive, growing number to your list, then it's working. You are now "tagging" people as they visit your website, and you can remarket (i.e., show your ads to them), wherever they are on the Display Network.

Attach Your Remarketing Audience to an Ad Group

With your list in hand, return to the Ad Group that you want to target using remarketing. Click into the Ad Group, and then click *Audiences*. It gets a little confusing, so bear with me. First, you'll see two options – *Targeting* (*recommended*), and *Observation*. *Targeting* essentially means that you want to use these parameters to target ads at a group; *observation* just means that you want Google to supply information on that aspect. Start with *Targeting*.

Next, you should see three options across the top, "Search," "Browse," and "Ideas." Click into *Browse > How they have interacted with your business > Website visitors*. You should see one or more of your remarketing lists there. Here's a screenshot:

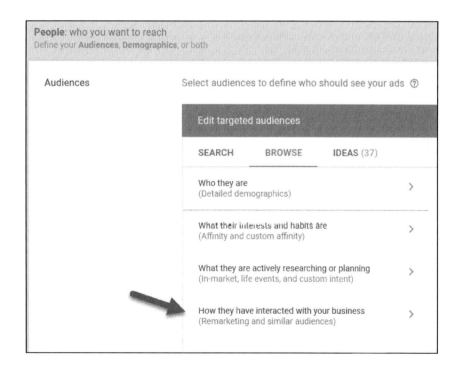

Click into "Website visitors." This, and only this option, gets you people who have interacted with your business by hitting your website. Generally speaking, the easiest is to select "All visitors," which means anyone who has hit your website.

Voila! Your ads will now show to someone who is "on" the list anywhere that they are on the GDN. Be aware that they don't necessarily realize that they've been "remarketed to." Many people are mystified at how ads "follow them" around the Internet, and this is how.

Once you've set up a remarketing list, you can attach it to any Ad Group you set up. For example, you can attach it to one Ad Group focused on the Display Network, another focused on Gmail, and still another focused on YouTube. Remarketing, after all, is a "targeting method," not an Ad Group nor an Ad.

Expanding Your Audience

If you want to be more aggressive, you can use *retargeting*, by selecting *Similar audiences*, for example. Look just above "Website visitors," and you should see "Similar audience." Here's a screenshot:

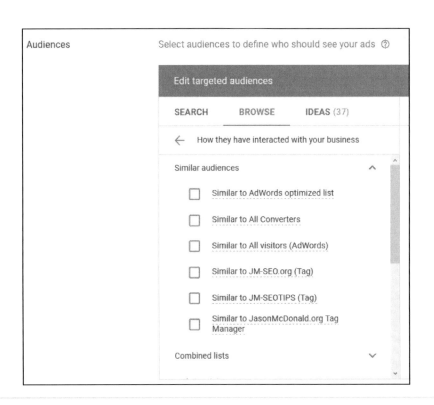

Google Ads will attempt to match "your list" to "their lists." If your customers are cat people, Google will attempt to go out and find cat people; if your customers are dog people, Google will attempt to go out and find dog people, and so on and so forth. That's what "similar" means. Just be clear in your own head that *remarketing* (people who have ALREADY hit your website) tends to be much higher ROI than *retargeting* (similar audiences who have NOT hit your website).

For this reason, I recommend keeping the two targeting methods separate. Create a NEW Ad Group using "similar audiences" vs. your other Ad Group using your own remarketing list. Then, you could compare two Ad Groups:

1. One that targets people who have hit your website, that is, "remarketing" vs.
2. One that targets similar people as identified by Google AI, that is "retargeting."

Verify Your Targeting Method

Once you've set up an Ad Group or if you want to verify that you have the correct targeting method, here's how you can drill into what Google calls the "Automated targeting" settings. First, click into your Ad Group. Next, click "Audiences" on the left. Click the Blue Circle, and then "Edit Audiences." Click "Edit All Targeting" on the top right. You should then see a screen showing ALL the targeting options that are in play vis-à-vis this Ad Group. We'll return to these in a moment.

In this way, you'll be able to measure which performs better as well as to bid higher or lower accordingly. To read the official Google help file on remarketing, visit **http://jmlinks.com/41c**.

RLSA Ads

In a special twist, there are even what are called "Remarketing Lists for Search" or RLSA ads. In this way, you "remarket" to people who are searching Google. That is, someone who is "on" your list can be "remarketed to" when he or she returns to Google and does a search. An example of this would be when someone searches for a vacation, hits the Disney.com website (and gets "tagged" for remarketing), and then returns to Google to search for things such as airline tickets, hotels, travel information about Anaheim or Orlando, etc. The ads on Google Search are thus triggered not directly by the search keywords but rather by the remarketing list. It's a hybrid! Read more about RLSA ads at **http://jmlinks.com/41d**.

Ad Groups and Remarketing Lists

Remember this is a targeting method, only, and that the targeting method or trigger "lives" at the Ad Group level in Google Ads. Accordingly, the best practice is to match a targeting method to an Ad Group. For example, you might set up:

> Persons who clicked the Jamaica cruise page > Jamaica targeting group > Ads on Jamaica cruises.
>
> Persons who clicked the Cabo San Lucas cruise page > Cabo San Lucas targeting group > Ads on Cabo San Lucas cruises.

And remember, at the end of the day, they'll see the ads NOT on your website but on other sites such as People.com, ChicagoTribune.com, YouTube, Gmail, and other participating sites in the Display Network (except for RLSA ads, if you set those up, as those appear on Google).

As you create your ads, upload highly relevant text and image ads, or use the "Scan Your Website" tools in Google Ads to create a series of ads. As the person browses sites on the Internet, then she'll see your ads again and again (until she clicks and converts).

The process is:

Remarketing List (e.g., *all website visitors, visitors to the cat boarding page who did not convert, visitors to the cat grooming page who did not convert,* etc.) > **targeting method** in Google Ads > **show ads** to these people as they browse various sites on the Internet that participate in the Google Display Network.

The beauty of remarketing is that you know these people are highly qualified (*why else would they have visited your website?*), and you don't have to worry about placements on the GDN – Google will automatically follow them around the Internet! Remarketing as a targeting method is less vulnerable to nefarious or fraudulent sites, which is another plus. Indeed, the sky's the limit, and you can even create *dynamic remarketing ads*, showing people very specific ads relating to the very specific products or services that they have visited (but not purchased) on your website. To watch a Google video on dynamic remarketing ads, visit **http://jmlinks.com/24m**.

Setting a Frequency Cap

Because people get annoyed at seeing an ad over and over and over again, one tip is to set a "frequency cap" so that they might see your ad just two or three times. To do this, go to the Campaign level, click on *Settings* on the left, and then *Additional Settings* in the middle. Then click "Frequency capping." Set a limit such as three per day. This means that no individual will see your ads more than three times in one day, which helps reduce the annoyance factor. Here's a screenshot:

In fact, setting a frequency cap is a good idea across the all your Display Network campaigns as it also helps fight click fraud, so I recommend you do this for every GDN campaign.

Note, of course, that you pay by click so, at some level, you don't need to be too concerned about showing your remarketing ads pretty frequently. For this reason, I recommend pretty high-frequency caps like three times a day or ten times a week.

Bids on Remarketing

Finally, whatever type of remarketing / retargeting you may decide to do, be aware that you will generally have to bid pretty high to get your ads to run because many, many advertisers are using remarketing and you are competing against a very large universe to get your remarketing ads to run. Just as on the Search Network, bids on the Display Network are set at the Ad Group level. Often times, however, focused ads on the Google Search Network are, ironically, often cheaper than remarketing ads because of the intense competition for remarketing by big brands.

» TARGET YOUR AD GROUP: PLACEMENTS

While most of us will use the keyword or remarketing targeting methods, there are other targeting methods to consider. Next up is the "Placement" methodology. Let's say that you really like specific websites in your industry, or you'd like to pre-select the websites onto which Google will put your ads. You can be much more in control by choosing *placements*.

At the Ad Group level, click *Placements* on the left. Click the blue circle and then click Add Placements. Here's a screenshot:

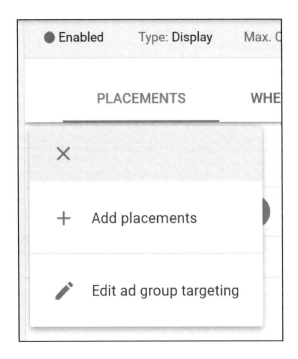

Here's where it gets a little tricky. If you know the placements you want to run on and you are sure that they are in the Google Display Network, then you can add them as URLs (domains). For example, both CNN.com and Entrepreneur.com run Google ads, so you can click *Enter multiple placements* at the bottom and then add them. Here's a screenshot:

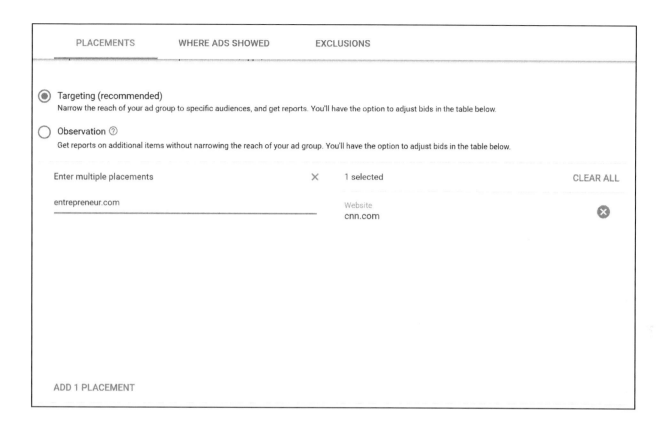

If you're not sure whether a placement is (or is not) in the Google Display Network, you can do some research. (**Note**: even though you can enter any website domain into *Placements*, that doesn't mean your ads will show on that website. *JM-SEO.org* or *Facebook.com*, for example, can be entered but because neither site participates in AdSense, these are moot entries).

There are two possible scenarios here:

1. **You know the placement already**. You already know that *thecatsite.com*, for example, is awesome to reach cat-oriented people, so you enter each domain manually to build out your targeting list.
2. **You do not know individual websites**. Here you enter a keyword such as "cats" or "cat boarding," click "Websites," and browse individual websites.

Returning to your process of identifying possible placements, you want to build a placement list. A good method is NOT to add website domains one by one as you find them, but rather use the built-in tool to discover them and build a list on a Notepad or Excel spreadsheet outside of Google Ads first. Then copy / paste your list of desired placements into targeting. In this way, you can also re-use this list if you want to use the same placements for a different Ad Group later.

Here are the steps.

First, at the Ad Group level, click on *Placements* on the left. Click the blue circle and then *Add placements*. Second, where it says in gray *Search by word, phrase, URL, or video ID*, enter a relevant keyword such as *cat boarding*. Here's a screenshot:

PLACEMENTS	WHERE ADS SHOWED	EXCLUSIONS

⦿ Targeting (recommended)
Narrow the reach of your ad group to specific audiences, and get reports. You'll have the option to a

◯ Observation ⓘ
Get reports on additional items without narrowing the reach of your ad group. You'll have the option

cat boarding	⊗	None selected
Websites (1K+)	›	Your ad can ap
YouTube channels (308)	›	match your oth
YouTube videos (1K+)	›	targeting.
Apps (182)	›	
App categories	›	

Third, click on Websites and Google Ads will open up a list of "relevant" websites. Here's a screenshot:

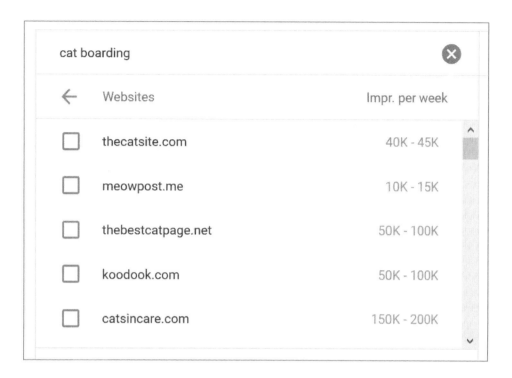

Fourth, do not add them at this time! Rather, copy paste the URL / domain of each one, such as *thecatsite.com*, or *meowpost.me*, into a new tab on your website. Check out the website and decide if you think it is relevant to your target customer. If so, add it to your list of desired sites on Notepad or Excel. If not, do not add it. In this way, you can build up a list of high volume, relevant websites on which to run your ads and avoid the problem of nefarious sites or poor matches.

Once you have a list of your domains (e.g., *thecatsite.com*, *catsincare.com*), then copy / paste this list from your Notepad or Excel by clicking *Enter multiple placements*. Finally, note (as I will explain below) that you can **combine** placements and keywords as a targeting method. For example, you could then run on *thecatsite.com* PLUS keyword = *boarding* to show ONLY on articles on the site that talked about *boarding*, or you could run on *CNN.com* and ONLY on articles on the site that talked about *marketing* if you were selling marketing services, for example. In this way, you can vastly tighten the focus of a Display Network Ad Group.

» TARGET YOUR AD GROUP: OTHER TARGETING METHODS

There are a few other targeting methods that are worth mentioning. We've looked at the big three – keywords, remarketing, and placements. Most advertisers need not go beyond these big three. However, there are other targeting methods.

Here is a summary:

Audiences. We've discussed remarketing, which is the most important Audience targeting option. However, there are other options within Audiences that bear mentioning. Go into an Ad Group, and click on Audiences on the left. You should see SEARCH | BROWSE | IDEAS. Click on **Search** and you can drill down into –

1. *Who they are* – this options gives you attributes such as "Parental status" or "Education."
2. *What their interests and habits are* – this option gives you "affinity audiences" such as people who are interested in Home & Garden, or Media & Entertainment.
3. *What they are actively researching or planning* – this is probably the best option as it gives you so-called "In-market Audiences," as in people who are "in the market" for a new car.
4. *How they have interacted with your business* – this gives you remarketing and similar audiences as discussed above.

Click on *Ideas* and Google AI will attempt to analyze your search campaigns or other advertising and make suggestions. The AI is not very smart, so I strongly do not recommend using this option.

Demographics. Click into this option and you can not only see who has clicked on your ads, but you can increase or decrease your bids accordingly.

Topics. This type of targeting is similar to keyword-targeting, but broader. For instance, if you click "Arts and Entertainment," you are asking Google to target people who are browsing blogs, apps, and video sites that deal with "Arts and Entertainment." This is a very loose way to target, so should be used with caution.

In my experience, none of these are very good except for **in-market audiences**. If there is an in-market audience that specifically matches your target customer (e.g., business loans, credit cards or employment, accounting & finance jobs, or dating services), it can be a pretty good choice. (This makes sense because Google knows the most about us based on what we search for (a.k.a., "intent"), which tracks pretty closely with being "in the market" for such-and-such product or service). Regardless, experiment, track your conversions, and you may find something that works for you. What works for one advertiser / product / service will not work for another and vice-versa, so deploy and test, deploy and test, rinse and repeat, etc.!

» TARGET YOUR AD GROUP: APPS

One novel feature of the Display Network is **app advertising**. You can advertise to people who are using apps that participate in the GDN to promote your own app. To show ads to people using apps, create a new Campaign and select "App." Next you find your App in either the Android (Google Play) or iOS (Apple) app stores and follow the steps. You then follow the steps and can advertiser your app to other app users to encourage installs. This setting is now heavily AI-based, so you have few options other than "trust in Google" to make the ads run. If you are an App-based company, it can be a good option to quick-start your App installs. But most of us are not App-based companies, so I would ignore it. If you're marketing an App, you can learn more about App ads on the GDN at **http://jmlinks.com/52h**.

» TARGET YOUR AD GROUP: GMAIL

Gmail is Google's free email service and is used by millions of people. You can target Gmail as a "placement" on the Google Display Network and get your ads to show on

Gmail. It's one of the better opportunities. As Gmail is directly owned by Google, it seems to be less prone to the fraud and problems that plague the wider Google Display Network.

> **VIDEO.** Watch a video from Google on how to advertise on Gmail at **http://jmlinks.com/27d**.

If you think that customers will be emailing back and forth with friends, families, and colleagues on a topic that's related to your business, it's worth trying out ads on Gmail. A cruise / family vacation, for example, will often generate a lot of emails and is a good candidate for Gmail ads.

To create a *Campaign > Ad Group* for Gmail ads, follow these steps:

1. Click the white cross in the blue circle to create a new campaign.
2. Choose a goal, or just choose "Create a campaign without a goal's guidance."
3. Select "Display," as Gmail ads are technically part of the Display Network.
4. Select "Gmail campaign" as your option.
5. Click "Continue."

At this point, the steps are essentially the same as any Google Display Network campaign, so select your Location Target, Bidding Options (such as conversions or clicks), and enter a Budget. The targeting options are also the same as on a traditional Display Network campaign, so choose among:

> **Keywords**. Target your ads by keywords; these are based on the content of emails people are sending back and forth on Gmail.

> **Audiences**. You can remarket to people who have already hit your website or choose among Google's targeting options. You can also expand your audiences by letting Google use automated targeting options.

Demographics. You can target your ads by demographic options based on what Gmail knows about its users.

Below these options you will see "Automated Targeting." Click into this and you will see three options: "No automated targeting," "Conservative automation," and "Aggressive automation." Here, again, Google is pushing AI on you. I recommend you select "No automated targeting" as the best option as in my experience Google tends to be far too loose with when and where your ads will run. Remember, Google has every incentive to maximize clicks and be overly aggressive with your ads and budgets.

Here's a screenshot:

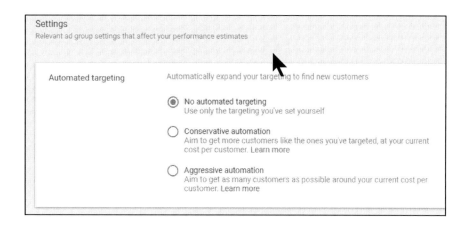

If you're a gambler, try "conservative" or "aggressive" automation and experiment with Google's AI-based systems. As always, pay attention to your clicks, your cost per click, and conversions to see what works best for you.

Returning to Gmail, you'll need to create your ads. Go back to *Ad Group > Ads & extensions* to create a Gmail ad. Here again as on ads on the Display Network, you can upload images and add in text to create the text and image variations that will combine to form your Gmail ads. Follow the general principles of "attract / repel" as you write ad copy (and upload images) that attempt to *attract* your best customers and *repel* those who are not relevant and/or not likely to buy. You may not see the "scan website" feature until you follow the annoying step-by-step instructions. It's hidden under "Ad assets" when you create a new ad. Here's a screenshot:

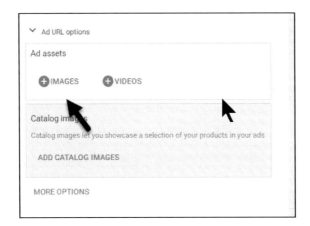

Google has an excellent step-by-step help file on how to set up ads on Gmail at **http://jmlinks.com/25g**. In summary, Gmail ads can be a powerful way to reach people in emails, though you must choose your targeting options carefully to avoid non-relevant matches.

» TARGET YOUR AD GROUP: COMBINING METHODS

Remember that you can mix and match features in Google Ads. So, for example, you could have an Ad Group using remarketing for people who are interested in Caribbean cruises who live in Chicago, by having a Campaign that is geotargeted at people who live in Chicago and have an in-market audience of cruises, or people who are using their mobile phones to target consumers who skew young.

It's a good idea to sit down with a spreadsheet and draft out your parameters, as for example:

> **Search**. People who are searching for Caribbean cruises using keywords like "Caribbean cruises" or "Cruises to Jamaica."
>
> **Remarketing**. People who landed on your website, but did not convert, so you show / reshow them your ads for a Jamaica Cruise as they visit sites like Chicago Tribune, YouTube, People Magazine, etc.

Retargeting. Let Google think for you, and find people similar to your remarketing list, and show them ads on the Display Network.

Mobile. Show specific ads to people using their phones vs. their desktop computers.

Geotarget. Show ads to people in specific areas (e.g., Chicago vs. Miami).

Schedule. Show ads during specific days, or times of the day.

Etc.

You can, in summary, mix and match features in Google Ads – the sky's the limit!

As for **targeting methods**, you can also mix and match targeting methods on the GDN, but I would generally advise against it. I recommend you think of scenarios, first, and targeting methods, second. For example, for a cruise line, moving down from the "most likely" to convert to the "least likely," you'd have:

Best choices -

Search. People pro-actively searching for Caribbean cruises. (Best choice: Google Search Network, targeting method: **keywords**).

Search: People pro-actively searching adjacent searches (e.g., "Things to do in Jamaica) who have hit your website but did not convert. (Best choice: Google Search Network, targeting method: **RLSA**).

Then second-best choice -

Browse. People who have landed on your website but did not convert. (Best choice: Google Display Network, targeting method: **remarketing**).

Then third-level choices -

Browse. People who are browsing sites on the Caribbean, on cruises, even on Jamaica. (Best choice: Google Display Network, targeting method: **placements**).

Browse. People who are browsing sites on the Caribbean, on cruises, even on Jamaica. (Best choice: Google Display Network, targeting method: **keywords**).

Browse. People who are browsing sites on the Caribbean, on cruises, even on Jamaica. (Best choice: Google Display Network, targeting method: **in-market audiences**).

Browse. People who are browsing sites on the Caribbean, on cruises, even on Jamaica. (Best choice: Google Display Network, targeting method: **similar to remarketing lists)**

Browse. People who are browsing sites on the Caribbean, on cruises, even on Jamaica. (Best choice: Google Display Network, targeting method: **affinity**).

Remember, you can see your choice options by going to a **Display Network Campaign > Ad Group**, scrolling along the left column. It's confusing because Google Ads mixes two very different concepts:

1. The *targeting method* you are using such as "keywords" or "Audiences"
2. *Data* from what actually happened, that is whether a particular keyword generated a click or impression, or whether a particular audience led to an impression or click.

For this reason, it's best to be very organized when you first set up a campaign and use one, and ONLY one, targeting method. Do not mix targeting methods because a) Google is likely to interpret this as an "or" statement, and you'll get a very broad result, and b) mixing targeting method makes it hard to figure out which one is working better than the other.

Google Ads doesn't make it easy to see which ones are "on" and which ones are "off," so I recommend naming your Ad Groups to clearly mark their targeting method such as naming your GDN Ad Groups something like:

GDN: Cat boarding: keywords

GDN: Cat boarding: remarketing

GDN: Cat boarding: in-market audience

etc.

Targeting vs. Observation

With the exclusion of the Search Network, you can combine targeting settings. Generally, I would NOT recommend that you do this. It's easier to manage if you have ONE Ad Group have ONE targeting setting, as in ONE Ad Group that uses keywords and ONE Ad Group that uses remarketing. Technically speaking, however, you can combine them into "and" statements, as in "OK Google, show my ad to a remarketing customer who you also think is relevant because the keyword is 'Jamaica vacation,'" but because targeting is loosey-goosey on the GDN, I wouldn't recommend overthinking this.

Confusingly, Google uses rather strange terminology to discuss targeting settings:

Targeting. This means Google is actually using this data to decide whether or not to show your ad.

Observation. This means that Google isn't using this data to decide whether or not to show your ad. You can, however, see data for this targeting setting AND increase or decrease your bid accordingly.

In certain situations, however, you can use targeting settings to be MORE restrictive, that is, to be an "AND" statement rather than an "OR" statement. One example where you might want to combine methods is PLACEMENTS and KEYWORDS. So, you might want people who are on CNN.com AND using keywords "Caribbean cruise," because CNN.com is a huge site with many irrelevant areas. You can read a detailed explanation on combining targeting methods at **http://jmlinks.com/24n**. Again, for most of us, I would do, at most, the Search Network and then perhaps remarketing and/or placement targeting and leave it at that.

Don't overthink it. The GDN is loosey-goosey, so be prepared to cast a wide net!

» UNDERSTAND BIDDING & QUALITY SCORE ON THE GDN

In general, you bid per click (and pay per click) on the GDN just as you do on the Search Network. Bids are set at the Ad Group level. If you like, however, you can mix and match targeting methods and raise or lower your bids. Similar to the Search Network, you have these bidding options:

> **Focus**. You can focus on clicks or on conversions. Focusing on conversions is better but you must enable conversion tracking and, ideally, have a dollar value for the value of a conversion.

> **Get Clicks**. You can set this to "Automatically maximize clicks" or "Manually set bids."

If you click at the bottom on "Select a bid strategy directly," you'll see your full bid options, which are:

> **Target CPA.** Target a "Cost per acquisition," which works best if you are e-commerce and know the true value of a sale. You're telling Google to attempt to find impressions and clicks that will result in a cost of acquisition of less than your target.

Maximize Clicks. Let Google use AI to attempt to maximize your clicks at the cheapest CPC. You're telling Google to get the most clicks at the cheapest total cost.

Viewable CPM. This is a bid strategy unique to the GDN, meaning you pay only for impressions (not clicks). This is good if you want to target branding or stay top of mind with customers and are not as interested in clicks and results. It's called "viewable" because you only pay when 50% of your ad shows on screen for 1 second or longer.

Manual CPC. Here you manually set your bid maximum. You can also let Google use "Enhanced CPC" to raise your bids when it thinks a conversion is more likely. This is the option I most frequently use.

You can review bidding options on the Display Network at **http://jmlinks.com/49n**.

Quality Score on the Display Network suffers from the same contradiction as it does on the Search Network. Google and the AdSense sites on the GDN get paid by the click, and you get paid by the conversion. Accordingly, Google will try to push you to run on lots of sites and write ads that promise "free, free, free" to generate lots of clicks. You want to be very choosy as to which sites you run on, however, and you want to write ads the attract your best customers and repel tire-kickers and others who are not likely to convert, nor likely to buy high-profit items.

You also have to worry about **click fraud** on the Display Network. On Google itself, Google alone is making money by clicks, but on the Display Network, there are third parties who create apps or websites, then create "bot armies" to generate clicks on ads on them and make money off of this scam. I do not believe Google does a very good job of policing this problem on the Display Network, so you can have a fake Quality Score that means nothing other than spurious clicks!

Thus, while there is a lot of discussion on the blogosphere about Quality Score on the GDN, I recommend you focus on impressions, CPC, conversions, cost per conversion and ROI, that is whether your spend is ultimately less than the profit you make from advertising on the Display Network. Be very careful to monitor your placements and look for nefarious websites or apps that are generating lots and lots of impressions and clicks but few conversions. These are likely scams. Quality Score nice "in theory," but the only metric that matters for you is whether a click becomes a sale or not.

⟫ Monitor Your Placements and Exclude the Naughty

Even before you activate a Display Network campaign, you should exclude various "naughty" websites and apps. The Display Network is full of junk and nefarious websites, so to use it, you must be careful. I recommend that at the account level, therefore, you disable many of the most problematic websites at the very beginning. Once you're running, you also want to check your placements on a regular basis and identify "naughty" websites and apps to exclude them.

Excluding Content Types

Here's how to set universal settings to (hopefully) exclude your ads from being shown next to nefarious and inappropriate content. First, click up to your account level at the "Overview" level. Next, on the left column, click *Settings*. Then in the middle click *Account Settings*. Find *Excluded Content* in the middle and click the down arrow to open the dialogue box. Here's a screenshot:

Check the most problematic boxes, which are **everything** under "Sensitive content."

Next, return to the previous screen, and open up "Excluded types and labels." Here the really bad one is "Parked domains," which are empty domains that run Google ads. You can also filter your ad against general vs. PG vs. teen audiences (similar to the ratings at the movies), and block ads from appearing on games, YouTube live, embedded videos, and below-the-fold. The safest thing to do is to exclude against all content types listed, but you need to at least allow "general audiences" as unchecked on the left-hand side.

You can also do this at the Campaign level by clicking into a Campaign, and then clicking *Settings > Additional settings*. Again, find Content exclusions in the middle and check the boxes for types you don't like. Just remember if you set it at the Campaign level that you have to reset it for each and every Campaign you create. That's why I generally do this at the Account level.

Identify Naughty Placements

On an on-going basis – and at least monthly – you want to identify and exclude "naughty" placements. Some of these appear to be fraudulent websites that live in the Display Network for no purpose other than generating fake clicks, and others are just junk. No one knows for certain, and Google certainly isn't talking. After you've run your Campaign(s) for at least a week, or perhaps a month, you can explore where your ads were placed (called "placements") and block ones that are either inappropriate, have expensive costs per clicks, or poor or expensive conversion rates or any of these problems. Here's how.

Click into a Display Network Campaign that has sufficient data. Click *Placements* on the left column. Click *Where Ads Showed* in the middle. You should then see a running table of where your ads are being shown vis-à-vis the time horizon you indicate at the top right (e.g., last month, last thirty days, all time, etc.). *All time* is probably the best choice as a time horizon. Next, click and sort by column; I recommend sorting by Cost first. Here's a screenshot:

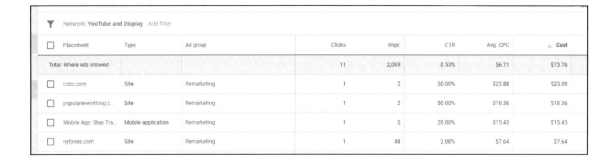

You can also enable columns, including a column for conversions and cost per conversion. Identify websites or apps that are a) costing a lot of money and/or b) have a high cost per click and/or cost per conversion. To block a website or app, just click the checkbox and then *Edit > Exclude* from Campaign. Here's a screenshot:

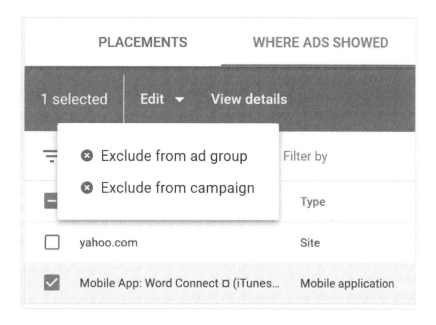

You can also download your placements into Excel, identify the bad / nefarious placements, and then upload a master list into the Shared library. This is located under *Tools > Shared Library > Placement Exclusions* list. Here's a screenshot:

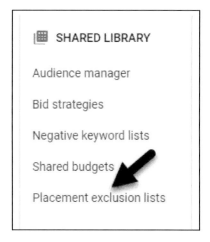

If I am working with a client that is heavily using the Display Network, I build up a "Naughty list" of apps and placements in this way and then link the "Naughty list" to all my Display Network campaigns. In this way, you can "inherit" the intelligence from the "Naughty list" from an old campaign to a new one and avoid the painful and expensive learning curve of finding out the naughty placements.

Apps are particularly nefarious. They show up as "Mobile App" in the list, and you can manually exclude them one by one. Ads that show on Apps are complicated, so to learn more about this problem visit **http://jmlinks.com/52g**. Another way to exclude Apps is to go into *Devices* and put a bid adjustment of negative 100%, but this will exclude your advertising from all mobile phones, not just apps.

Once you are running ads, I recommend checking your Placements at least monthly and then aggregating them into your "Naughty list." This is very important because you will be refining the Display Network to weed out the bad / nefarious websites and over time, you can be much more effective with your Display Network campaigns. As to why Google doesn't do a better job policing its own network, well, I suppose we can wait for a World Communist Revolution against greedy corporations or just do it ourselves in the meantime.

» MONITORING YOUR GDN CAMPAIGNS

The most important monitoring you'll do is to weed out nefarious placements. In addition, you want to have conversion tracking enabled between Google Ads and Google Analytics. In this way, you can see what placements are not just getting clicks but also getting conversions. "Kill your dogs, and let your winners run" is as relevant to the Display Network as to the Search Network. You are constantly looking to identify strong performers (to keep) and weak performers (to terminate). To learn more about conversion tracking in Google Ads, see this official Google Ads video at **http://jmlinks.com/41q**.

Other Metrics

While conversions are the Holy Grail of all advertising on Google Ads, you want to be aware that in many cases you won't get immediate conversions. In fact, Display Network campaigns are often run for branding or awareness issues. To that end you want to measure on at least a monthly basis:

Placements by Impressions. Which placements are generating the most impressions? Are they relevant?

Placements by Clicks. Which placements are generating the most clicks? Are they relevant?

Placements by Cost. Which placements are the most expensive? In total, by CPC, and by cost per conversion? Why? Are they worth it?

Placements by Click Thru Rates. Which placements are generating the highest CTRs? Why? Can you increase the impressions on these placements? How?

Placements by Conversions / Conversion Rates. Which placements are generating the highest conversions and conversion rates? Why? Can you increase the impressions on these placements? How?

Consider evaluating your Campaigns by **targeting method** according to the metrics above as well. For example, which targeting method (e.g., Keywords vs. In-market audiences) is generating the highest impressions, clicks, CTR, conversion rate, etc.? As you experiment with your GDN Campaigns look for placements and/or targeting methods that seem to be "working" and expand them and look for placements and/or targeting methods that do not seem to be "working" and kill them. Another metric that's valuable is the bounce rate on your website. Since a lot of Display Network advertising is about brand-building, look not only at the conversions generated but at the bounce rate and time on site as shown in Google Analytics. If people are clicking through on your GDN ads and checking out your website, then this is indicative of brand-building.

"Let your winners run and kill your dogs" is as valid on the Display Network as it is on the Search Network. Nurture your winners in terms of targeting methods, placements, and ads. Kill your dogs. Be merciless.

In addition, remember to consider alternatives to the Display Network such as advertising on Facebook, LinkedIn, Twitter, or YouTube and compare results on those "browse" systems against those on the GDN. Identify the best performers and put your money there, and abandon those that do not perform – the GDN may (or may not) be your best venue. If you're interested in learning more about social media marketing, check out my *Social Media Marketing Workbook* at **http://jmlinks.com/smm**.

For each network, you can also browse their "advertising" site such as:

Facebook Advertising at **https://www.facebook.com/business/**

LinkedIn Advertising at **https://business.linkedin.com/**

Twitter Advertising at **https://ads.twitter.com/**

Pinterest Advertising at **https://ads.pinterest.com/**

YouTube Advertising at **https://www.youtube.com/yt/advertise/**

We'll consider YouTube Advertising in Chapter 7, but be aware that really any one of these networks is far larger than any single website or app in the Google Display Network, and all of them (except for YouTube) exclude Google placements. For this reason, if you think that "browse" is a good way to reach potential customers, be sure to consider advertising on one or all of the competitive social media platforms. There's more out there than just the Google Display Network, as massive as it is.

»» DELIVERABLE: DISPLAY NETWORK WORKSHEET

The **DELIVERABLE** for this chapter is a completed worksheet on the Google Display Network. You'll investigate whether you want to run on the GDN, at all, and if so, in which ways (especially which targeting method(s) and placements make the most sense).

For the **worksheet**, go to **http://jmlinks.com/adw2020**, then re-enter the password, "adw2020," and click on the link to the "Google Display Network Worksheet."

6

SHOPPING CAMPAIGNS

Customers buy stuff online, a lot of stuff online. Fewer and fewer people go to brick-and-mortar stores, especially for standardized products. When Joe or Jane Consumer wants to buy a new dog toy, yoga pants for that upcoming workout, or even retinol cream to take care of their crow's feet, they go online. In this Chapter, we'll review the two big networks for selling products online: Google Shopping Campaigns and Amazon. The reality is that Google is the #2 player for products, so I would not ignore Amazon as part of your strategy! You can also set up a shopping campaign on Bing (which runs essentially like Google), though Bing is a very distant #3.

Let's get started!

TO-DO LIST:

» Understand Shopping Campaigns

» Set up Shopping Campaigns

» Bid Effectively for Shopping Campaigns

» Consider Alternatives to Google Shopping: SEO & Amazon

»» Deliverable: A Shopping Campaigns Worksheet

» UNDERSTAND SHOPPING CAMPAIGNS

Shopping ads, or shopping "campaigns" as they are officially called, refer to product ads that appear on Google. (Note: they used to be referred to as PLAs or "Product Listing Ads"). These ads refer only to physical products, so if you do not sell a physical product, you can ignore this Chapter. But if you do sell physical products, especially online but also in a brick-and-mortar store, shopping campaigns are yet another way to get your product in front of people as they search Google. Take an example. Search Google for "cat toys." You should see pictures of products on the right of the screen. Here's a screenshot:

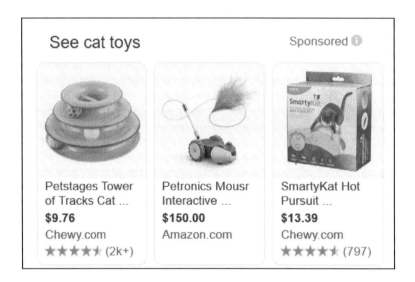

If you click on an ad, you then click from Google to the vendor website, which is usually an e-commerce website where you can buy the product online. It can also be an ad for a local store that has this item in inventory.

For example, if you click on the "Petstages Tower of Tracks," you end up on Chewy.com and see the full product plus how to purchase it. Here's a screenshot:

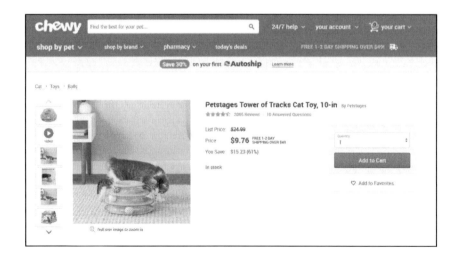

In this way, Shopping Ads are a great strategy to get traffic from Google to your e-commerce store. And who's to say that a person who lands on Chewy.com will only buy the "Tower of Tracks Cat Toy?" He might buy not just this toy but several others, sign up for email alerts, and become a long-term customer. One simple click from Google on a Shopping Ad can be worth far more than just the individual product sale; it can be worth the "lifetime value" of a loyal customer.

SHOPPING ADS ARE ABOUT PRODUCT SEARCH

Shopping Ads are different than other ads on the Google Search Network. They have these elements:

Product Image. They show a thumbnail of the product itself (hence, high-quality product images are a must to succeed on Google Shopping Campaigns).

Product Title / Name. Shopping Campaigns do not use keywords, but rather product names and descriptions as triggers, so you ideally have product titles / names that contain relevant keywords.

A Price. Especially for products that are standardized, Shopping Ads allow consumers to quickly look for the cheapest price.

A Domain. Chewy.com is the domain in the example above, but all Shopping Ads must show the domain of your e-commerce website.

Product Reviews. A one to five-star system by which customers can review products; these live on your e-commerce store and are transmitted to Google.

Keywords. Shopping Ads do NOT use keywords like regular Google Ads, so as you build out your Shopping Campaigns, you'll need to work with a Data Feed that comes from Merchant Center. It's a more automated process; more about this in a moment.

Note also that a consumer can click on the category headline designated here as "See cat toys" to browse Google's database of product ads. Here's a screenshot:

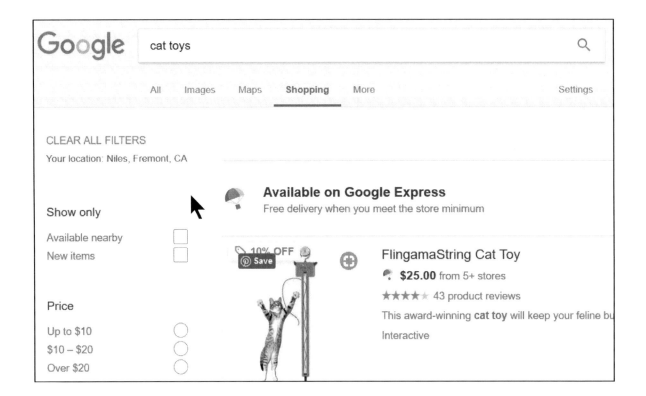

In this way, Google is going head-to-head against Amazon (the market leader) by consolidating products from participating vendors into an easy shopping system on Google.com. (We'll return to Amazon in a moment). Notice as well that a consumer can click on "Available nearby" on the left, to locate products in nearby brick-and-mortar stores. Shopping Ads are not only for online websites but are also for local merchants who want to use Google to drive traffic to real-world stores,

There are three types of Shopping Ads:

1. **Product Shopping Ads.** These ads highlight individual products in your inventory as submitted via an XML feed and Google Merchant Center.

2. **Showcase Shopping Ads.** These ads allow you to showcase a group of related products; you create these directly in Google Ads by grouping similar products together.
3. **Local Catalog Ads.** These ads use feed data from a local brick-and-mortar store to drive traffic in the real world to your real store.

Most of us will focus on #1, product shopping ads. This is the most common and most effective type, as it drives traffic from Google to your e-commerce store online. #2 is similar, in that you are taking folks who are doing Google product searches and bringing them into your online store by showcasing more than just one product in a "showcase" ad. #3 is the unique scenario when you are targeting local customers and highlighting that you have such-and-such product for sale, right now, in a nearby local store.

Are Shopping Campaigns Relevant for You?

To find out if Google Shopping Ads are relevant to your business, try searches for your keywords and pay attention to whether you see product ads appearing on the right of Google. They're easy to spot because they have images (unlike regular Google ads which are text only). Shopping Ads generally appear on Google, Search Partners, YouTube, Image Search and on the Google Display Network in limited ways for what are called "local catalog ads." They also, of course, appear on the desktop, tablet, and mobile phone.

To access a written tutorial on Shopping Ads, visit **http://jmlinks.com/48k**. To watch quick videos on how Shopping Ads work, visit **http://jmlinks.com/48m** and **http://jmlinks.com/48n**.

Bing Shopping Campaigns are essentially modeled after Google Shopping; to learn about Bing options, visit **http://jmlinks.com/49b**.

» SET UP SHOPPING CAMPAIGNS

Setting up Shopping Campaigns is a four-step process:

1. You need an e-commerce-enabled website, that is a website that can sell products in an automated way. The big e-commerce platforms such as Shopify or BigCommerce make it easy to run an e-commerce store; both also work well with Google Merchant Center.
2. You need to set up a Google Merchant Center Account at **http://jmlinks.com/52k**.
3. You need to connect your Merchant Center Account to your Google Ads account at **http://jmlinks.com/52m**.
4. Finally, you need to set up Campaigns and Ad Groups in Google Ads.

Once you have a "data feed" coming in from Merchant Center to Google Ads, you then return to pretty familiar territory as Shopping Ads are then managed directly in Google Ads. The one strange thing is that you do not manage keywords or bids directly.

Let's review your steps. First, we'll assume you've set up an **e-commerce website** and populated it with products. All your products need keyword-focused titles, nice-looking thumbnail images, price information, availability, shipping, and review capability. It's a bit of a catch-22 with respect to reviews, as you can't get reviews without sales and you often won't get sales until you get reviews. Try to pro-actively ask existing customers to review products after each purchase. Slowly but steadily, you should start to get reviews on your products as they sell.

> *Be sure to populate your product titles with* **keywords** *as this is the primary way Google "knows" how to match your product with relevant searches.*

Next, you need a **Google Merchant Center** account. You can learn about Merchant Center at **http://jmlinks.com/48p**. They have a robust help center at **http://jmlinks.com/48q** and you can even "talk to a human" by calling 855-290-0348. Google is very keen on getting products into its system, as they recognize that they are far behind Amazon on product search and e-commerce! They even have a robust YouTube Channel at **http://jmlinks.com/48r** with good introductory videos.

You may need to consult with your webmaster or other resident "computer nerd" to make sure that data flows from your e-commerce site to Google Merchant Center. However, the big vendors like Shopify and BigCommerce have help files on integrating their systems with Google Merchant Center. For Shopify, see **http://jmlinks.com/48s** and for BigCommerce see **http://jmlinks.com/48t**. If you're using another vendor, ask their tech support or just Google, "{your e-commerce platform} Merchant Center" and you can often go right to the help file. (Note: you can also create a Google Spreadsheet if you want to manually enter product information for Shopping Ads; this is explained in the Google Ads / Merchant Center help files and YouTube videos).

Third, you need to connect your Merchant Center to your Google Ads account. Check out the Google help file on this at **http://jmlinks.com/48u**. You can also search YouTube to find a cornucopia of video tutorials on how to use Merchant Center and Google Ads for Shopping Campaigns.

Set up a Google Shopping Campaign

Finally, now that you've linked your Merchant Center to your Google Ads campaigns, you're ready to set up Campaigns and Groups in Google Ads. Log in to your Google Ads account and click on the blue *Campaign button* > *New Campaign*.

Next, select *Sales* > *Shopping* to get you into the Shopping Campaigns. Follow the steps to create your first Campaign. As with regular Google Ads, you can focus on a specific country, state, or even city. The trick is to organize your Merchant Center by lists or feeds and match these to Ad Groups in Google Ads. This will be necessary for bid management.

> **VIDEO.** Watch a quick video tutorial on how to set up Google Shopping Campaigns at **http://jmlinks.com/48v**.

You can also access a written step-by-step tutorial from Google at **http://jmlinks.com/48w**. You'll generally start with an "all products" group, but it's recommended that you filter and reorganize your Ad Groups so that you have a more focused approach. To learn more about this, visit **http://jmlinks.com/48x**.

You might focus, for example, an Ad Group around "dogs" vs. one around "cats," or one around "cat collars" vs. one around "cat food," so that you can bid more aggressively on higher profit items. You can also "tag" items in your spreadsheet or data feed and then use those "tags" to create Ad Groups so that you can bid more aggressively where there is more money to be made.

Negative Keywords

Even though you do not use keywords for Shopping Campaigns, you can (and should) use **negative keywords** such as "free," "cheap," or "Amazon," so that you are showing your ads to persons most likely to click through to your e-commerce site and actually make a purchase. You can access step-by-step instructions on negative keywords and Shopping Campaigns at **http://jmlinks.com/49d**.

» BID EFFECTIVELY FOR SHOPPING CAMPAIGNS

First and foremost, if you're running an e-commerce or Shopping Campaign, there's no excuse for not tracking all activity from the click to the sale. You should be able to estimate your ROAS (*Return on Ad Spend*) from this data. Just be aware that one person might click through from Google for just one item and then buy more, and that a "new customer" brought from Google might become a "long term customer," so you have to look at the lifetime value of a customer when measuring your return on investment.

FOCUS ON LIFETIME CUSTOMER VALUE

Bid options in Shopping include:

Manual Bidding. You manually set your maximum bid.

Maximize Clicks. Google automatically attempts to maximize your clicks.

eCPC / enhanced Cost-per-click. Google looks at your conversions and attempts to bid up / bid down when you are most likely to get a conversion. This is the most common bid strategy.

Target Return on Ad Spend (ROAS). Google automatically sets your bids to maximize your conversion value, while reaching an average return on ad spend that you choose. This requires conversion data but, if possible, this is one of the best bidding strategies.

Many vendors find the best success with a few tightly focused Ad Groups for their most profitable products (with high or aggressive bids) and a "catch-all" Ad Group for everything else. You can also prioritize your Ad Groups as high / medium / low. This is called "campaign priority" and helps Google understand which Ad Group should get first crack at a click. See **http://jmlinks.com/48y** for more information.

Throughout in your e-commerce analytics or Google Analytics, you want to monitor what Google Ads is doing and make sure that you're spending less per click than you're making per click, taking into account multiple purchases by the same customer and the lifetime value of a customer. An important concept is to motivate your customers not only to buy a single product immediately, but to sign up for your email list, follow you on social media, and bookmark your e-commerce store so that your Google Ads are not only bringing in "one-time sales" but also "long term customer relationships."

Smart Shopping Campaigns

As is true across all Google products, Google is keen to promote AI. Thus Shopping Campaigns have a subset called "Smart Shopping campaign." In this scenario, you create your product XML feed, attach it to Merchant Center, and "presto" Google creates and manages your ads for you. For it to work and work well, you need to not only enable conversion tracking but have enough conversions for Google AI to accurately predict conversions and thus manage your bids, placements, and creatives. To learn more about "Smart Shopping Campaigns," visit **http://jmlinks.com/52j**.

» CONSIDER ALTERNATIVES TO GOOGLE SHOPPING: SEO & AMAZON

There are a couple of things that Google won't tell you about Shopping Ads.

The SEO Alternative

First, if you can bring customers to your website via SEO (Search Engine Optimization), you can get traffic for free from Google. This is especially true for very nichey searches. For example, many consumer electronics have very specific batteries. When these batteries die, consumers will often pop the battery out of the device and then Google by battery type or model number to find an easy replacement to buy.

For example, *LIT0155* is a specific type of battery. If you Google *LIT0155*, you'll see product listings across the top and then Amazon prominently in the first organic or free spot (achieved via SEO). Here's a screenshot:

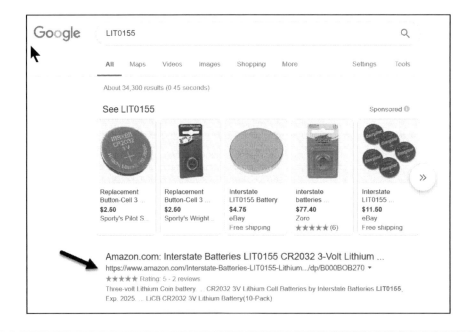

Often times, you can get your own e-commerce site to rank for these very specific, niche keyword searches and capture the click – for free – from Google. The number three organic result on this search, for instance is Zoro.com. Here's a screenshot:

Interstate Batteries CR2032, 3-Volt, Lithium Battery LIT0155 | Zoro.com
https://www.zoro.com › Lighting, Flashlights & Batteries › Batteries › Lithium Batteries ▾
Order INTERSTATE BATTERIES CR2032, 3-Volt, Lithium Battery, LIT0155 at Zoro.com. Great prices & free shipping on orders over USD50!

So, while you might not rank on Google for the generic search for "lithium batteries," you might be able to rank via SEO for the very specific search "LIT0155" or piggyback on Amazon's very strong SEO. It's easier to rank for free for these very nichey searches if you properly optimize your e-commerce website for search engine optimization.

The Amazon Alternative

Secondarily, more and more consumers go directly to Amazon for product searches. If you sell your products via Amazon, you want to be sure to give equal attention to your Amazon strategy, through SEO for Amazon and/or advertising on Amazon. Amazon is the #1 product search site, after all, and way ahead of Google for many product categories.

To sell on Amazon and/or advertise your products on Amazon, here are your steps:

1. Sign up for an **Amazon Seller Account** at **https://sellercentral.amazon.com/**.
2. **List your products** on Amazon, optimizing their product name, description, photo, and reviews.
   a. Amazon also has a new option of an Amazon Storefront, allowing you to essentially set up an e-commerce website for your business or brand directly on Amazon. Learn more at **http://jmlinks.com/49a**.

3. If desired use, use *FBA* (fulfillment by Amazon) to have Amazon manage the shipping of your products directly. To learn more about FBA, visit **http://jmlinks.com/48z**.

Once you've registered for an Amazon Seller Account and/or set you your storefront, Amazon has many advertising opportunities. Amazon is keen to sell ads (just like Google), and with its position as #1 in product search, Amazon is the fastest-growing ad platform on the Internet today. There is no doubt that it will soon rival Google, YouTube, and Facebook as one of the big boys in digital ads.

You can learn about Amazon advertising at **https://advertising.amazon.com/**. At the top left, browse "Sponsored Products," "Sponsored Brands," and "Stores" to explore opportunities. It's very similar to Google Shopping Campaigns, except that there is no need for a data feed, since that's already "inside" Amazon by design. The big issues are:

Keywords. You can advertise by keywords, similar to on regular Google Ads. Select "cat toys," "cat collars," or "cat food," for example and link that to your ads. Like Google Ads, Amazon offers broad match, phrase match, and exact match options.

Artificial Intelligence. Alternatively, you can let Amazon AI think for you, and just let it place your ads where it thinks they'll do the best. This is similar to Google's "Smart Campaigns" option.

You can run both types of ads and then compare the results to determine the best return on investment. Similar to Google, however, be aware that there are both "free" and "paid" results on Amazon, so in some instances you may already rank "for free" and be poorly served by advertising on a specific keyword or category. If you do, you might "cannibalize" your revenue, with users clicking on ads instead of the free listings.

Here's a screenshot of ads on Amazon for "cat collars:"

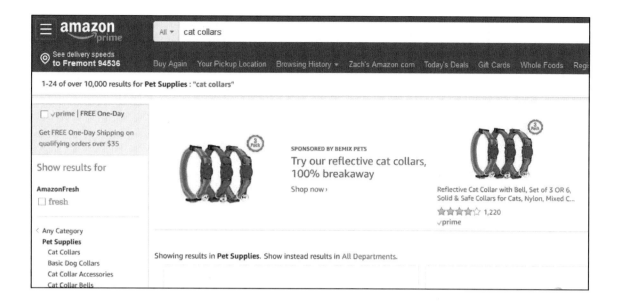

Notice how ads are designated as "sponsored." Also note how Amazon is now placing ads underneath product as for example:

I recommend you run on both Amazon as well as on Google and compare the ROI of each. You may find that Amazon has more volume than Google and a higher ROI (or not). But don't fail to consider Amazon.

»» DELIVERABLE: A SHOPPING CAMPAIGNS WORKSHEET

It's time for your **DELIVERABLE**: a completed **Shopping Campaigns Worksheet**. If your company sells product online either via e-commerce or possibly via Amazon, you need to consider Google Shopping Campaigns. Use the worksheet to outline your strategy. For the worksheet, go to **http://jmlinks.com/adw2020**, then re-enter the password, "adw2020," and click on the link to the "Shopping Campaigns Worksheet."

SURVEY OFFER

CLAIM YOUR $5 SURVEY REBATE! HERE'S HOW -

- Visit **http://jmlinks.com/survey**.
- Take a short, simple survey about the book.
- Claim your rebate.

WE WILL THEN -

- Rebate you the $5 via Amazon eGift.

~ $5 REBATE OFFER ~

~ LIMITED TO ONE PER CUSTOMER ~

SUBJECT TO CHANGE WITHOUT NOTICE

RESTRICTIONS APPLY

GOT QUESTIONS? CALL 800-298-4065

7

YOUTUBE

YouTube, owned by Google, is the #1 video site on the Internet and often touted as the #2 search engine, larger than Bing or Yahoo. Everyone – including your customers – uses YouTube in some capacity, which can make it an incredible advertising opportunity. While you can use text ads and placement targeting on the Display Network to get your text ad on YouTube, you'll do far better if you produce a short video on your product or service and then advertise that video on YouTube. This Chapter focuses on video advertising opportunities on YouTube. (Refer to my *Social Media Marketing Workbook* at **http://jmlinks.com/smm** for a full discussion of *free* opportunities on YouTube).

Let's get started!

TO-DO LIST:

» Research Your Customers on YouTube

» Set up a Channel on YouTube

» Upload a Video to Your Channel

» Enable Clickable Links in Your Video

» Set Up a YouTube Campaign in Google Ads

» Target Your Ad: Video Targeting

» Evaluate Your YouTube Advertising Performance

»» Deliverable: YouTube Advertising Worksheet

» RESEARCH YOUR CUSTOMERS ON YOUTUBE

Videos on YouTube "live" on a Channel, so to advertise on YouTube, you'll need to set up a Channel. To get started to see if YouTube could be good for you, first, do some **research** to decide whether your target customers are "on" YouTube, and, if so, what they are doing. Everyone is "on YouTube" sooner or later, but in general, you'll get the best advertising performance if one of the following criteria apply:

- **Search**. People are likely to search YouTube pro-actively. "How to" searches such as "How to get a puppy to stop biting" or "How to truss a turkey" are very popular on YouTube, so if your company produces something that explains "how to do something," or if your market is adjacent to "how to" searches, then YouTube can be good. An example would be a cooking gadget company that could advertise on "how to" cooking videos, a dog training company that can advertise on "how to" training videos for dogs, or a physical fitness supplement company that can advertise on "how to" videos for crunches or pushups

ARE YOUR CUSTOMERS ON YOUTUBE?

- **Browse**. People are going onto YouTube to watch videos on thousands of topics, and you can demographically target them. For example, let's say you marketed Donald Trump paraphernalia, you'd know that many Trump supporters and political junkies go on YouTube to keep up with politics, and watch certain kinds of videos or certain kinds of channels. (The same would go for political junkies of the Left). Or, suppose you're targeting young adults, and you know that they are big consumers of music videos. It can also be very specific such as targeting fishermen / women who watch YouTube for fishing videos (as there are TONS of fishing / outdoors videos on YouTube).

Before you decide to set up a Channel or advertise, you want to **research** whether your target customers are on YouTube, and if so, whether they are *searching* and/or *browsing* video content.

- If they're searching, what types of keywords searches are they doing?
- If they're browsing, what type of videos are they watching? Which channels on YouTube are the most relevant and popular?

As you investigate YouTube, I recommend you also browse their help file at **http://jmlinks.com/49x** and their splashy, "Why Advertise on YouTube?" site at **http://jmlinks.com/49y**.

Keyword Research

Unfortunately, there isn't a YouTube-only keyword discovery tool (like the Google Ads Keyword Planner) that focuses only on search volumes on YouTube. You have to use the generic Google Ads Keyword Planner.

Return to Google Ads, and go to *Tools > Keyword Planner*. Generally, if a search has a "how to" flavor to it and it's visual, you can bet it will be searched on YouTube. Secondly, go to YouTube, and just start typing. Also pay attention to YouTube's own autocomplete by going to YouTube and typing in relevant keywords and search queries. Here's a screenshot for "bass fishing" autocomplete on YouTube:

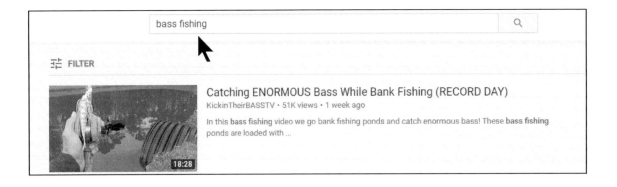

bass fishing

bass fishing **tips and techniques**
bass fishing **with frogs**
bass fishing **tournament**
bass fishing **videos**
bass fishing **tips**
bass fishing **in the winter**
bass fishing **with plastic worms**
bass fishing **challenge**
bass fishing **in ponds**
bass fishing **2017**

Revisit your Keyword Worksheet and add a tab for YouTube. Brainstorm core keywords and ad groups that reflect how people search YouTube. As you browse videos that pop up on YouTube for searches relevant to your product or service, pay attention to the **view count** of videos. For example, if you search on YouTube for *bass fishing*, you'll see this video at or near the top:

bass fishing   Q

꞉꞊ FILTER

Catching ENORMOUS Bass While Bank Fishing (RECORD DAY)
KickinTheirBASSTV • 51K views • 1 week ago
In this **bass fishing** video we go bank fishing ponds and catch enormous bass! These **bass fishing** ponds are loaded with ...

18:28

You'll notice that it has 51,000 views, which means a lot of people are searching for and watching videos on bass fishing. If you see many videos relevant to your product or service with (relatively) high view counts, you know that YouTube may be a great marketing tool for you. If not, not. "Bass fishing" is an example of the type of content in which a focused audience goes to YouTube to watch engaging content, and can thus be effectively targeted via video advertising. Thus, you have two basic scenarios on YouTube:

1. Customers pro-actively go to YouTube and **search directly**, usually for "how to" videos such as "how to bass fish at night" or "how to bass fish with frogs."
2. Customers have a passion and they go to YouTube to watch "helpful experts" and their "**community**" via video. "Bass fishing" is an example of this type of "YouTube community."

Filter YouTube Search Results

As you research whether or not your customers are on video, enter keywords and click the search icon. You can also filter YouTube search results as follows:

1. Type in a keyword and click the search icon (magnifying glass)
2. Click "Filter" on the left.
3. Select "View count" on the right to see videos with the highest views.
4. Click "Filter" on the left, again.
5. Click "This year" on the left.

In this way, you can find the highest viewed, most recent videos on YouTube for a topic. Using our "bass fishing" example, I filtered by "view count" and "this year," and came up with the following video at 6.1 million views:

Evidently, videos of hot-looking women in bikinis fishing for bass are VERY popular on YouTube! Be that as it may, you can easily see that lots of folks are watching fishing videos on YouTube and if you sell fishing tours, fishing lessons, fishing gear, etc., YouTube would be a very powerful venue to place your ads.

Finding Video Volume for Browsing

You may decide that **search** isn't that important on YouTube, but you do suspect that people are **browsing** and watching videos on YouTube. If per my example above, you see a lot of videos that are keyword-relevant that have high view counts, then you know that there's a lot of *searching* and probably *browsing* of video content going on.

BROWSE AND VIEW VIDEOS TO DETERMINE VIDEO VOLUME

Another way to research whether YouTube might be for you is to scroll down on the left column, to *Browse Channels*. (If you can't find it, visit **http://jmlinks.com/52n**, as YouTube in the infinite wisdom of Google AI hides it when you're already logged in). Via *Browse Channels*, you'll see broad categories of videos such as *Beauty & Fashion* or *Sports*. You can click into individual channels to browse popular videos and get a sense of the channel subscribers. These are much broader categories than searching by keywords, but they can give you a sense of whether or not your target customers are active on YouTube. Inside of *Browse Channels*, you can also click on "Popular on YouTube" to see the currently most popular videos. And, you can also click on *Trending* on the left column to see what's trending.

However, as you browse YouTube, don't fall into the trap of assuming that you have to be in a "mega" industry like pop music to make it work for you. Many people watch videos in very nichey ways in YouTube such as quilters who want to learn how to quilt, teenagers who want to put on eye makeup, and fishermen (and women) who want to learn how to be better anglers, so "riches are in the niches" on YouTube just as on Google.

Your research process is:

> Are my customers watching YouTube videos in a targeted way?
>
> If so, what is the target? What keywords, channels, and video topics?

Make a list of channels, videos, and keywords that identify "where your customers" hang out on YouTube. This will become your targeting strategy.

» SET UP A CHANNEL ON YOUTUBE

Assuming you've decided that, yes, your customers are on YouTube and, yes, you'd like to give YouTube advertising a go, the next required step is to set up a Channel for your company if you haven't already. The easiest way to do this is to sign up for a Google Account via Gmail. I'd recommend that you use the **same email** that you use to login to Google Ads, if at all possible. (You can and should link your YouTube and Google Ads account (see **http://jmlinks.com/41k**)). Using the same email address for both is the easiest and best, however. Alternatively, you can also create a brand-new YouTube account.

Here are your steps:

1. Go to **https://www.gmail.com/** and sign up for a Gmail account, if you don't have a Gmail you already use for corporate stuff on Google.
2. Alternatively, you can set up a Google account and link this to any email such as **yourname@company.com**. To do this, read the help file at **http://jmlinks.com/25j**.
3. Next, visit **http://jmlinks.com/25k** and follow the instructions to "Create a channel with a business or other name."

Populate your Channel with a nice-looking cover photo, icon, and fill out the contact information on the "About" tab. You now have a YouTube channel!

» UPLOAD A VIDEO TO YOUR CHANNEL

Before we five into direct video advertising, allow me to point out two "lazy man" ways of advertising on YouTube without actually creating a video. The first way is to enable "Search Partners" in a Google search campaign. This is an effective way to reach people who may be searching directly on YouTube, especially for "how to" searches such as "how to Bass fish for beginners" or "how to train your cat to do such-and-such." Inside of a Search Campaign, click on Settings on the left, and then look at Networks in the middle. If you want to run on YouTube, you should see "Google Search Network, Search Partners." Here's a screenshot:

Unfortunately, Google does not break out where your ads appear for Search Campaigns, but you can create a very focused group with key phrases such as "how to buy car insurance." Here's an example showing Google Search (Partner) ads showing on a YouTube search for "how to buy car insurance:"

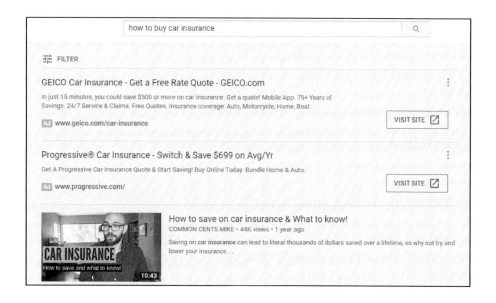

The upside is your search ads can show on YouTube if you enable "Search Partners." The downside is they will also show, by default, on second-rate search sites such as Comcast.net, Yelp.com, etc., and often generate low-quality clicks. You also get zero break-out reporting. Another upside is that Google will monitor user search behavior and sometimes show these ads on YouTube based on past search behavior on Google.

The second "lazy man" way to get your ads on YouTube is to use the Google Display Network and use "Placement targeting." Here, essentially you define YouTube as a "placement" for a Display Network Campaign. Create a specific Ad Group in a Display Network Campaign, then click into Placements, and set "youtube.com" as a target placement. Here's a screenshot:

You can then add on additional placement criteria such as keywords, audiences, etc., to get text ads to show on YouTube. Read the Google Ads help file at **http://jmlinks.com/27e**). The best ads are short and to the point, quickly explaining who you are, what you have to offer, and why a person on YouTube should care.

Creating a Video Ad for YouTube

Leaving aside these two "lazy man" ways of getting your ads on YouTube, the best way to get your advertising message on YouTube is to create a video ad. You need at least one video (posted to your Channel) to be able to take full advantage of YouTube's features. You need to shoot a short video about your company, product, or service. The best ones are less than 30 seconds, short and to the point, and lead to a desired action.

The sky's the limit on video production. You can Google "videographers" in your local area to find people to help you shoot a short video. You can use tools such as Camtasia, iMovie, and Windows Movie Maker. You can use services such as Fiverr to find video editors, and you can literally just Google "make a video ad for YouTube" and read the ads and organic results.

YouTube also has a very good mega resource on how to advertise on YouTube at **http://jmlinks.com/41f**. Of course, like all official Google information, it's pretty salesy!

Once you've created your video ad, login to your YouTube channel, and in the top right click on the upwards arrow to upload the video. Be ready with:

- A short video title.
- A short video description, including an *http://* link to your website for more information.
- Keywords to "tag" your video.

Create a "Custom Thumbnail" by clicking "Custom Thumbnail" (this may not show on a brand-new Channel). I recommend a simple, easy-to-read Video Thumbnail as this will show up as your ad on YouTube search and as a recommended video. Here's a screenshot of how a video ad looks on YouTube search:

You can read the official YouTube help on how to create custom thumbnails at **http://jmlinks.com/27f**.

Once the video is uploaded and approved by YouTube, find your video, you'll need to copy / paste the URL at the top of the page. It should look something like **https://www.youtube.com/watch?v=CRB6w4Dmjdw**.

What Makes a Good YouTube Ad?

What makes a good video ad on YouTube? They say that imitation is the highest form of flattery, so here are three video ads I recommend you add into your research. As you watch them, try to "reverse engineer" them in terms of their story arc:

1. Your Soap is Sh*t? at **http://jmlinks.com/52q**.
2. Create Photo Books from Your Phone at **http://jmlinks.com/52r**.
3. This Unicorn Changed the Way I Poop at **http://jmlinks.com/52s**.

In each case, notice:

- The first few seconds of the video aggressively catch your attention.
- The video then "tells a story" that connects a "problem" or "desire" that the viewer has with the "solution" the vendor has.
- The videos have an obvious "call to action" embedded in the video narrative, plus use YouTube features such as "video cards" (top right), and clickable links (in the video description) to make it easy for the user to take action.
- The videos use emotion, especially humor, to engage the viewer and even encourage them to like, comment, or share the video to friends and family.

The most important aspect of video creation is the aggressive "hook" at the beginning to get the viewer to agree to watch the video, the clear call to action, and the narrative story that both entertains and educates the viewer. For a more sober explanation of what makes great video ads, you can watch a short video on the "ABCD" method of planning a great video ad at **http://jmlinks.com/52p**. Only Google could make something as fun as video ads, boring, but they succeeded. Toggle between Claire Kelly's dreadfully boring but useful synopsis and the three video ads listed above to get your ideas flowing.

To succeed on YouTube, you must create short, compelling, videos.

A wise YouTuber once told me to think "street performance art" and not "movie" when making a good video for YouTube. Here's what he meant:

1. **Make the video short.** People are "in a hurry" to something else, and they aren't signing up for a long movie format. Short is better than long. I'd recommend one minute or less.
2. **Make it simple.** Use 6th grade English, not Ph.D. level English. Be very succinct and to the point. Don't beat around the bush.
3. **Make it (visually) provocative**. You have to get them to STOP and take a look. They're not signing up for the latest Meryl Streep movie in which they pay their money, get their popcorn, and are willing to sit through twenty minutes of previews and some long and pompous introduction before getting to the action. You have to get them to STOP by nearly shouting: HEY LOOK AT ME! THIS IS WEIRD, CRAZY, INCREDIBLE (without destroying your brand image).
4. **Have a defined next step or action.** What do you want them to do after they watch your video? A probate attorney, for example, wants to explain a little about probate and then get them to click FROM the video TO her website, where she wants them to register for a FREE CONSULT. She'd literally say something in the video like, "Probate is crazy complicated, so click the link in the video description to request a FREE CONSULT with my office!"

And of course, a good video is **good-looking**. But here you don't' really need a slick, professionally produced video as much as a video that is **authentic**. People want to know that you really "know your stuff" about probate law, for example, and that trust that you create gets them to take the next action. They really don't care about your hairstyle or the lighting, though, <u>good sound is a must</u>.

Go search and browse YouTube by keywords relevant to your business and watch some ads that are close to what you and your company would like to promote. Pay attention to how the ads a) grab your attention quickly, b) communicate their value proposition, and c) lead to a "next step" or "desired action."

Another good resource is Google's list of the most popular ads on YouTube, as for example at **http://jmlinks.com/41h**.

Once you have your video ad produced, you can upload your video to your Channel. Give your video a short, to-the-point headline and write a short, to-the-point description. Be sure to have a good-looking and catchy thumbnail image.

» ENABLE CLICKABLE LINKS IN YOUR VIDEO

Be sure to include a clickable link in your video description, preferably right after the first sentence, and in the format of **http://www.yourwebsite.com/**. It MUST be in the *http://* format to be clickable! You can then reference the link for "more information" in your short video ad, such as telling the viewer, "Click on the link in the video description to learn more!"

Here's a screenshot from the famous Dollar Shave Club video's description, showing the clickable link from the video description to their website:

That link - **http://dlrshv.es/b3FELr** - gets the user to the Dollar Shave website with just one easy, click, so you gotta have one in your video!

Create Cards in Your Video

"Cards" on YouTube are yet another way to drive traffic from your video to your website. Cards are clickable links in the video itself. In order to create YouTube cards that link to your website, however, you must link your YouTube account to your website, and you must join the YouTube Partners Program. (See

http://jmlinks.com/49u). This requires more than 1,000 subscribers, so it will not be available if you have a brand-new account.

To add a "card" to your video:

- Click on your logo on the top right of YouTube, when you are logged into your Channel.
- Click on Creator Studio, and then click on Video Manager on the left-hand menu. (Note: you may see "YouTube Studio" which is in beta roll out as of this writing; in that case, click to the bottom and return to "Creator Studio Classic.").
- Find your video and click edit.

"CARDS" ARE CLICKABLE LINKS IN A VIDEO

Click on "Cards" to enable YouTube's "Cards" feature, and insert text, an image, and a link to your website URL.

VIDEO. You can read the official Google help file on YouTube cards at **http://jmlinks.com/27h**.

Cards appear in the top right of a YouTube video and "pop out" when they appear. Users can click on them to learn more and then click from the card to your website. Here's a screenshot showing the card in the top right corner:

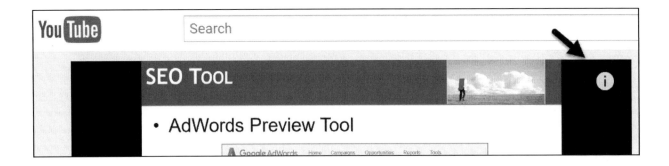

At this point, you've created a Channel, uploaded a video advertising your company or product, and inserted *http://* links in the video description, and at least one card for more information.

Just remember as you set up videos and/or video ads on YouTube to be on the lookout for where it will allow you to put clickable links: in the video description, in cards, in call-to-action overlays, and in the new call to action extension. All options are not always available, so just be aware that you may or may not see them.

» SET UP A YOUTUBE CAMPAIGN IN GOOGLE ADS

If you already have a *Campaign > Ad Group* on YouTube, you can skip this section. If not, to create a video campaign, log in to Google Ads, and click the blue circle. Select *Video* as the campaign type. Select one of the three options – *Product and brand consideration, Brand awareness and reach*, or *Without a goal*. The first two give you step-by-step instructions, while the third option is totally do-it-yourself. Follow the steps to define:

Campaign Name. Give it an easy-to-remember name such as *Cat Boarding: YouTube*. I recommend you put YouTube at the end so you can see at an instant that this is a YouTube Campaign and not a Search or Display Campaign. Note there are two formats on YouTube that are commonly used, and I recommend you create separate campaigns for each format.

Instream Ads. These are video ads that generally appear before a video. The user is forced to watch up to five seconds and then he or she can click into the ad or click "skip." Name your Campaign something like *Cat Boarding: YouTube – Instream.*

> **In-stream Ads** occur in what YouTube calls the **TrueView** ad format, meaning you pay, if and only if, a person clicks thru on your ad, watches more than 30 seconds, or half of the video ad (whichever is lesser). There is also what are called a TrueView for action or TrueView for Shopping, which are format subtypes that allows a prominent Call to Action (CTA). To learn more, visit **http://jmlinks.com/49v**.

Video Discovery Ads. These are video ads that appear when a user pro-actively searches YouTube by keyword. These are similar to ads on Google.com. Name your Campaign something like *Cat Boarding: YouTube – Discovery.* Here, you pay when someone clicks on your ad.

Other Formats. YouTube also offers other formats such as Outstream Ads (on partner sites), Non-skippable in-stream ads (ads that the user cannot skip), and Bumper ads (short six-second ads that are non-skippable), but these are generally used only by very large advertisers who want to use YouTube like television for branding purposes. See **http://jmlinks.com/49w** to learn about all available formats.

Budget. Set up a daily budget. Just as on regular Google Ads, you specify a maximum spend per day.

Networks. Here, you need to make an important choice –

> **YouTube search results.** Use this option to show your video when someone pro-actively searches on YouTube. (*Must be used in combination with the next option*).

> **YouTube videos.** Use this option more when people are in "browse" mode to show your video before, after, or along videos as people browse. (*Must be used in combination with the first option*).

> **Video Partners in the Display Network**. I <u>do not recommend</u> this option, so uncheck it. Here you have the same problem with click fraud and nefarious sites as on the Google Display Network.

Ad Group. Create an Ad Group, again reflecting your product or service (keyword) organization such as *Cat Boarding, Cat Grooming,* or *Cat Toys* and name it appropriately as for example *Cat Boarding: YouTube Discovery – Keywords,* or *Cat Boarding: YouTube Instream – Remarketing.*

Bidding. Set a bid per view. Note that on YouTube you pay by the *video view,* not by the click. YouTube uses what they call "TrueView" pricing meaning you pay if, and only if, the user watches your video for at least thirty seconds or to the end of the video, or if it's a search ad if they click on the video and/or an action. See **http://jmlinks.com/41g** for a full explanation.

Targeting. Leave these options blank for now, as we will discuss in detail. These are marked as *People who you want to reach* and *Content where you want your ads to show.*

Create your video ad. Enter the exact URL of the video you want to promote here. Select a format such as *In-stream ad* or *bumper ad* ("browse mode") or *video discovery* ("search mode") ad. Write a headline and description. Select a landing page; I recommend that you use *Your YouTube channel page.*

Again, similarly to regular Google Ads, Google stupidly makes you go through every step even if you are not ready. Once a *Campaign > Ad Group* is created, however, you can then insert new Ad Groups and Ads much more easily, adjust targeting, etc. Just go through the steps to create your first *Campaign > Ad Group > Ad* and then it will be much easier to manage. What's stupid about this is you only have to do this the very first time, and then from then on, it's much easier to manage.

At the end of this process you should have your first *Campaign > Ad Group > Ad.* Pause it so that it doesn't start running until you are completely ready.

Location Targeting in YouTube

You can geotarget on YouTube! For example, Jason's Cat Boarding Emporium could target people watching "cat videos" who also live in San Francisco. Or a pet store could target people watching videos on dog and puppy training who live in Oakland, Berkeley, or El Cerrito, California.

LOCATION TARGETING WORKS IN YOUTUBE

Geotargeting makes it easy to get your ads right to people near your local business and is one of the most exciting features in YouTube advertising. Accordingly, select your Geotarget (e.g., United States, or drill down to a specific city or state). You do this by being at the Campaign level and selecting *Locations* on the left. For example, since I am only interested in people who live in San Francisco and have cats, I could target cat videos on YouTube but by setting the geotarget to San Francisco, only people who are physically in San Francisco would see my ads. This is a fantastic feature to YouTube advertising as you can have your cake and eat it too – meaning target very broad video types (e.g., "cat videos") but to very narrow locations (e.g., "San Francisco").

Mobile Bid Adjustment

You can also control your mobile bid adjustment in YouTube, if you do / do not want to run on phones and/or tablets. Once you've created a Campaign, click on *Devices* on the left and configure your device targeting by setting bid adjustments up or down. An example here might be a probate attorney who would figure that the most serious people would be watching her videos on their computers, and so she would set a bid adjustment of negative 100% for mobile. If you think there is a strong pattern between mobile vs. desktop vs. tablet, this is yet another useful YouTube targeting refinement.

≫ TARGET YOUR AD: VIDEO TARGETING

Now that you've inputted your ad to YouTube, it's time to dive into targeting options. Targeting "lives" at the Ad Group level, just as in regular Google Ads. Click into your Ad Group on YouTube, and you'll see targeting options on the left. As with the Display Network, it's a best practice not to mix and match targeting options (though you can in some situations). Let's review targeting options.

Keywords. Here, similar to the Display Network, enter **keywords** that you think someone might be searching on YouTube and/or that might describe similar or adjacent videos. **This is the most common and most powerful way to target your videos.** In our *Cat Boarding* example, we'd enter keywords like *cats, cat boarding, cat care, kittens,* etc. Google has taken away a lot of YouTube targeting features, so I wouldn't worry about plus signs, quote marks, etc., just enter keywords and remember that, as on the Display Network, the targeting is pretty loose on YouTube. Note that Google uses how they search not only on YouTube but on Google for keyword-based targeting.

Audiences. Here you will see *Search | Browse | Ideas* at the top. Click into *Browse,* and you should see:

> **Who They Are.** This is demographic targeting based on attributes such as Parental Status, Marital Status, Education, and Homeownership.

> **What their interests and habits are.** These are "affinities," such as whether they're into Banking & Finance, Beauty & Wellness, Food & Dining, etc.

> **What they are actively researching or planning.** This refers to "in-market audiences," such as people who are "in the market" to buy a house or a car. If relevant to you, this is one of the best targeting options.

> **How they have interacted with your business.** This leverages your remarketing audience. So, for example, you can "tag" people who visit your website and then show them your video ad as they browse YouTube videos. You can also expand to "retargeting" using Google AI to expand to people "similar" to those who have already hit your website.

> **Combined Audiences.** This is a new feature that allows you to use "And" statements to combine any of the above features.

Demographics. You can see the age, gender, parental status, and household income of the people who have viewed your YouTube advertising.

Topics This is very similar to audiences and attempts to target people based on things that interest them like games, health, fitness, etc.

Placements. This is unique on YouTube. You can find videos or channels that allow advertising and then copy / paste their URLs here. However, if a channel or video is not "monetized" (meaning that the owner does not allow YouTube to place ads), this is all in vain. Double-check to see if you see ads on any relevant placements. Google doesn't enable clickable links here, so open up a new browser window and search YouTube by Channel or Video name to find out if it allows advertising. If you see ads, it does. If you don't, it doesn't.

» EVALUATE YOUR YOUTUBE ADVERTISING PERFORMANCE

Once your ads are up and running on YouTube, evaluating the performance is similar to the rest of the Display Network. Click into an Ad Group. Then, along the left column, click:

Keywords to browse the keywords the triggered your video ads. As elsewhere on Google Ads, you can create "negative keywords" to block your ad.

Audiences to learn characteristics about the audiences reached.

Demographics to see age information (if available).

Topics to see topics.

Placements and then *Where ads showed* to see which videos / channels ran your ad. As on the Display Network, you can block your ad from placements.

You can also go into Google Analytics to view clicks coming from YouTube to evaluate what happens "after the click." To do this, create a Segment by clicking on the *Segments* tab in Google Analytics, and then *Custom,* and source as *YouTube.com.*

And within your YouTube Channel, you can click into *Creator Studio > Analytics* to browse information about your videos.

VIDEO. Watch a video on how to set up Segments in Google Analytics at **http://jmlinks.com/25p**.

Returning back to your YouTube Channel (not Google Ads, and not Google Analytics), you can go to *Creator Studio > Analytics* and then drill down into an individual video to see key performance indicators such as watch time, view duration, views, geographies, genders, traffic sources, and playback locations. In summary, there is really a wealth of information in Google Ads, Analytics, and YouTube about what happens with your videos!

»» DELIVERABLE: YOUTUBE ADVERTISING WORKSHEET

The **DELIVERABLE** for this chapter is a completed worksheet on YouTube advertising. You'll investigate whether you want to run on YouTube, at all, and if so, in which ways (especially which targeting method(s) and placements make the most sense).

For the **worksheet**, go to **http://jmlinks.com/adw2020**, then re-enter the password, "adw2020," and click on the link to the "YouTube Advertising Worksheet."

8

METRICS

Making money on Google Ads is easy! *Just make $1.01 for every $1.00 you spend, and you'll make money each and every day!* It's not quite that simple, of course, as the line between "what you're spending on Google Ads" and "what you're getting in sales" can be pretty fuzzy. Even worse, Google Ads "support" is always there – *like a good bartender* – egging you on to keep spending on *clicks* and *branding*, when really you should focus on *conversions* (defined as either *sales* on an e-Commerce website or completed *sales inquiry* forms for more complicated products or services). In this Chapter, we'll dive into how to measure your performance on Google Ads, and how to use Google Ads metrics to improve your return on investment (ROI) continually and/or your *return on ad spend* or **ROAS**. Be forewarned: *you may know what you want to know but not actually be able ever to know it*, so to speak. Or *not know it fully*; you'll need to combine some hard metrics with some soft gut instinct. "Half of my advertising dollars are wasted," so the saying goes; "I just don't know which half."

Let's get started!

TO-DO LIST:

» ROI: Make $1.01 for Every $1.00 You Spend

» ROI: It Gets Complicated

» Spot Check Your Ads

» Check Your Spending Metrics

» Monitor the Display Network and/or YouTube

» Set up Goals in Google Analytics

» Set up Conversion Tracking in Google Ads or Google Analytics

» Review Your Conversion Data in Google Ads

» Identify Problems and Opportunities

»» Deliverable: A Google Ads Metrics Worksheet

» ROI: MAKE $1.01 FOR EVERY $1.00 YOU SPEND

Conceptually and in a perfect world, your **Return on Investment** (**ROI**) from Google Ads is deceptively simple:

For every $1.00 in ad spend, make at least $1.01 in profit.

But in reality, this equation is very complicated. On the **spend** side, you can certainly see how much you are paying for impressions and for clicks, and you can correlate both impressions and clicks to keyword search queries (*on the Search Network*) and placements (*on the Google Display Network*). You can very easily see what you're spending on a daily, weekly, or monthly basis for clicks and impressions and correlate that with keywords or placements. These are what I call your **Spending Metrics**. (Note: in a perfect world, you'd also calculate and include the cost of you and your employees' labor spent setting up and managing your Google Ads account, but we'll ignore those costs).

Conversion Metrics

Your profit from Google Ads, however, depends not on your *Spending Metrics* but on your **Conversion Metrics**. Here we have to move from the *what's-easy-to-measure* (your spend) to *what's-hard-to-measure* (your sales).

Let's take a simple scenario of a customer who comes back from vacation in Mexico, had a great time, picks up his cat at Jason's Cat Emporium, and wants to reward his Kitty with a brand-new cat collar. He goes to Google, searches for *cat collars*, finds our e-Commerce store and makes a purchase.

We have:

Google search query: *Cat Collars*

He sees our ad for "Amazing Cat Collars" and clicks. (Behind the scenes, we have pre-identified the search query "cat collars" and bid $2.00 for the click. We "win" the auction and pay Google $1.75 for that click, one penny more than the next highest bid for the click on Google).

He purchases the cat collar for $10.00. (Our cost is $4.00, which we pay to our Mexican cat collar partner (*as the collars are made in Mexico, where he could have bought the cat collar for just $1.00 – but that's another story; we'll also ignore shipping and other costs for this simple example*)). Our profit per collar is thus $6.00.

So, on the vendor side, we have this equation to calculate our ROI:

Revenue from the sale of the collar from the customer: **$10.00**.

Cost of collar (paid to our Mexican supplier) **$4.00**

Cost of click (paid to Google): **$1.75**

Profit = ($10.00 -$4.00) - $1.75 = $4.25.

ROI is calculated as ($10.00 - $4.00) - $1.75 / $1.75 = 2.42 = 242%

(meaning you more than DOUBLED your money).

ROI as a formula is *Profit -Advertising Cost / Advertising Cost* expressed as a percentage. You want a positive, big number!

Now, this formula assumes that, first, you can actually determine the data inputs (costs, in particular, can be hard to determine), and, second, that this is a sale you got from Google Ads and Google Ads alone (meaning, you wouldn't have gotten it if you didn't advertise). Those are assumptions that are not always easy to meet or determine in the real world.

That said, a focus on ROI tells you to keep your eye on making at least $1.01 for every $1.00 in incremental spend on Google Ads. It's a good but unrealistic goal.

Lifetime Customer Value

There's another important but hard-to-measure variable: the *lifetime value of a customer*. Suppose this is a brand-new customer, who had never heard of Jason's Cat Boarding Emporium. He discovered us through Google Ads, made a single purchase, but now that he knows we exist he keeps coming back to us in the real world and in the virtual world by directly visiting our website. He's signed up for our email alerts, and now follows us on social media. We no longer have to keep paying Google Ads to get his attention or purchases. This "one-time" visit originating via Google Ads is thus worth far, far more than that single sale. This is called the "lifetime customer value." Indeed, even if we lose money on that first transaction, we make money because of the lifetime customer value. Hard to measure? You betcha. Real? You betcha.

Calculating Your Maximum Bid

Let's return to our simple example. How much can we pay Google for a click on Google Ads and still make money?

Assuming a 100% conversion rate (that is, that EVERY click to our website leads to a purchase), then we can safely bid up to $5.99 and make a profit. For example, if the click cost $5.99 and the collar costs us $4.00, then we would make $.01 from each sale of the $10.00 Kitty collar.

> Our **ROI** is *Profit -Advertising Cost / Advertising Cost* expressed as a percentage or $6.00 (our profit per collar) - $5.99 (cost of the click)/ $5.99 (cost of the click) = .16% (return on our money). We're positive, or (barely) in the black.
>
> Once we spend MORE than $6.00 on the click, our ROI goes negative. If, for example, we spend $7.00 on the click, then our ROI is $6.00 - $7.00 / $7.00 = -14%. We're negative, or in the red.

Not All Clicks Convert

But here's where it gets complicated, even with a simple e-Commerce website. First and foremost, not every click ends in a sale!

If our conversion rate is 50%, then we can only pay half as much for a click ($5.99 / 2 = $2.95) because half our clicks fail to end up in sales, and so on and so forth. The lower our conversion rate, the less we can bid per click. And, of course, the lower our profit, the less we can bid for clicks, too. (*If our Mexican supplier raises the price of the collar to $7.00 from $4.00 then, accordingly, we have to pay less per click to break even.*)

The *Cost Per Click* must be less than the *Profit Per Click* for you to make money on Google Ads, or turning that around your *Profit Per Click* must be greater than your *Cost Per Click*:

Cost Per Click < Profit Per Click

Or

Profit Per Click > Cost Per Click

And the Profit Per Click is the *profit per sale times the conversion rate.*

Profit Per Click = Profit Per Sale X Conversion Rate

If, for example, we make $6.00 per sale of a collar, and we have a 100% conversion rate, then our profit per click is $6.00. But if we have a 50% conversion rate, then our profit per click is cut in half, becoming $6.00 x .50 = $3.00. With a 100% conversion rate, we can bid up to $5.99 to "get the click," but with a 50% conversion rate we can only bid $2.99 per click, and so on. In most cases, your conversion rate will be much, much lower than 50%, more like 2% or 3%, so with a 2% conversion rate, our profit per click is

$6.00 (the profit of each collar) x .02 (the conversion rate) = .12 or 12¢ per click!

Turning this around, if we "bought" 100 clicks on Google that would cost us 100 x .12 = $12.00, and with a 2% conversion rate those 100 clicks would have generated two sales at $6.00 each, so we would break even at any CPC < .02.

If you want to dive more deeply into these equations, I recommend that you check out Google's Chief Economist, Hal Varian, and his video that explains how your bidding strategy should intersect with your profits.

> **VIDEO.** Watch a video on ROI on Google Ads by Google's Chief Economist, Hal Varian at **http://jmlinks.com/25q**.

Mr. Varian goes way into the details on ROI and bidding strategy, but let's keep it simple and summarize what you, as an advertiser, can actually attempt to measure and then attempt to improve on in the real world:

Measure:

- Your **impressions**, **clicks**, and **click-through rate** vs. target **keywords**.
- Your **Google Ads costs** measured as cost per click vis-à-vis target keywords, landing pages, and products or services.
- The **conversion rate** as measured by how many people click through to your landing page vs. how many of them actually buy something (or complete an inquiry form).
- The **revenue** and **profit** (*revenue minus expenses*) of the related product or service; or, if you're measuring a sales lead, the imputed value of that sales lead to your ultimate product or service.

Note how this is all keyword-centric. You bid on keywords, so keywords are the foundation of success to Google Ads.

Improve on Google Ads:

- **Decrease** your cost per click via **better bidding**.
- Identify **keywords that convert** ("winners") vs. keywords that do not convert ("dogs"), and *let your winners run, and shoot your dogs.* Ditto for ads; identify high performing vs. low performing ads.
    - Pay attention not only to the **conversion rate** (i.e., *which clicks end in sales or sales leads*), but also which products or services generate **more profit** vis-à-vis your Google Ads spend, that is higher *quality* keyword patterns.
- **Write Better Ads.** Write better ads that "attract" high-value, converting customers and "repel" low-value, non-converting customers as well as ads that have a sufficiently high CTR (Click Thru Rate) to get you a better Quality Score.
- **Improve your landing page experience** and **conversion rate** so that you not only get clicks to your landing page, but a higher percentage of those clicks convert to a sale and/or sales lead.

This last point is important. You won't always get an immediate sale or sales lead, so brainstorm not only what sale / sales lead you want but also **intermediate steps** that can help you "capture" the name / email / phone of a prospect so that your sales staff can work on turning a mere *prospect* into a paying *customer*. Free downloads, free eBooks, free software, and even "sign up for our incredibly interesting email newsletter" can also be considered conversions. After all, if you nab the potential customers name, email, and phone you don't have to keep paying Google to talk to her!

ONCE YOU GET THE CLICK, GET SOMETHING FOR IT

Let me repeat this as it's incredibly foundational to your strategy:

> Once you've received the click from Google, do everything possible to capture your customers' contact information, start a relationship or conversation with them, etc.

Throughout, don't focus so much on clicks, and the click-thru rate as much as on cost-per-click, conversion rate, and the value of each conversion.

» ROI: It Gets Complicated

Just make more money per click than you're spending per click! That's in the hypothetical *Hal-Varian-Google-economist make-believe world* that Google lives in. But you and I live in the real world, and we often do not have the required data at our fingertips. If we're running an e-commerce store, we may have a good idea of the profit per sale, and we can get the conversion rate from Google Analytics or our e-Commerce platform. We're in the strongest position to really know how much we can pay per click.

Some Clicks Convert (Just Not Immediately)

However, even at the best e-Commerce store, not every click will immediately end in a sale; some visitors may leave the website, and come back days or even weeks later, and then purchase. What looks like a failure (no conversion) may actually be a conversion. Google Analytics and Google Ads do attempt to track customers for 30 days giving you some conversion data in a 30-day window, but it is far from perfect.

Lifetime Customer Value (LCV) and Gut Instinct

In addition, a customer may "find you" one time through Google Ads and then become a "customer for life." The lifetime customer value (LCV) may be far, far more than the simple value from that immediate click to sale conversion on Google Ads. You need to pay attention to this metric, and you can't expect an immediate click to sale behavior, especially for complicated or expensive products like Disney Cruises or Toyota Camrys. On the negative side, it may be that the customer already found you via SEO / organic reach on Google or perhaps word of mouth (first), and then clicked on your ad. In this case, Google is falsely attributing to Google Ads a sale that you "would have gotten anyway" from this customer.

> Some factors (e.g., some clicks convert not at first but after a period of back-and-forth) indicate that your *revenue from Google Ads is higher* than actually reported in the data.

> And some factors (e.g., Google Ads falsely takes credit for sales you would have gotten anyway through SEO or word of mouth) indicate that your *revenue from Google Ads is lower* than actually reported in the data.

My feeling, therefore, is to *take the data seriously* but to *take it also with a grain of salt* (yes, I know that's a contradiction!). Your "gut instinct" as to whether Google Ads is working is as important as any "hard" data that your data wonks and Hal Varian can come up with.

ROAS: Return on Ad Spend

Another metric that people like to use is called *ROAS* or *Return on Ad Spend*. This is a simpler, "back of the napkin," way to measure your Google Ads performance. The formula to calculate ROAS is:

> **ROAS** = revenue from ad campaign / cost of ad campaign

If, for example, your ad campaign generates $10,000 in revenue and costs your $1,000 you have:

$$\textbf{ROAS} = \$10{,}000/\$1{,}000 = 10 \text{ or } 1000\%.$$

For a quick, online ROAS calculator visit **http://jmlinks.com/41m**. The problem with ROAS, however, is that it ignores cost. You can generate revenue with Google Ads yet still lose money if you don't calculate the costs that go into getting those clicks (i.e., Google Ads costs) as well as your own costs of production. So, while the industry often focuses on ROAS, I recommend you focus on ROI instead (at least conceptually).

And, throughout, realize that you often can do no better than "back of the napkin" calculations as to whether you are making money, or not, with your Google Ads investment. Those that run very tight and easy e-commerce stores are in the best position to calculate their ROI, but most of us (even in e-commerce) will have some "variables" that we do not know for certain. Do your best.

Beyond e-Commerce: Feedback Forms and Sales Leads

Many of us will not be running e-Commerce sites. We will measure the performance of our websites in terms of completed feedback forms or sales inquiries. A law firm, for example, will want to use Google Ads to generate clicks for the search query "Personal Injury Lawyer Tulsa" and measure the performance by incoming sales leads off of a web form. Ditto for a Kansas City plumber, who would want his ads on Google to generate inbound web forms or telephone calls.

How much is a completed web form worth? Well, in an ideal world, you'd know the value of the potential lawsuit (or potential plumbing project) plus the probability that your firm is going to win, and you'd deflate all that by your conversion rate (as the client could potentially take his or her lawsuit or plumbing project somewhere else). There's little to no probability in the "real world" that you'll be able to do anything much better than guestimate these numbers. So, sorry, Hal Varian, the equations don't work because we don't have the necessary data, and we never will!

You may never have all the required data. Get over it, and use gut instinct

The best you can do is decide how much you're willing to pay for a completed feedback form via Google Ads and calculate your conversion rate based on the clicks that come from Google Ads to your website.

Sales Leads Are Valuable: Do Not Undervalue Them!

For businesses that depend on feedback forms, I'd recommend setting a ballpark figure as to the value of each completed feedback form and judging Google Ads vs. this figure. However, in my experience, most companies VASTLY devalue the cost that they should pay for a lead.

DON'T UNDERESTIMATE THE VALUE OF A "SALES LEAD"

Companies will say (with no data to back them up), "we're willing to pay $10.00 for a feedback form," when the value of that "lead" can be $1,000 or $10,000, so please try to get your team to be reasonable about the true value of a completed feedback form. In fact, I'd recommend multiplying that value by 2x or even 12x as, in my experience, most companies vastly underestimate the true value of leads!

Compare Google Ads, for example, with other forms of advertising like participation at industry trade shows. To go to a trade show, you have the cost of the booth space, the cost of the booth set up, employees' time and travel, etc., and you might get just a few hundred (if that) inquiries from your trade show expense. Each "lead" at the trade show might be costing you literally hundreds or thousands of dollars, compared with a "lead" form Google Ads that might just cost you $25.00 or $75.00 or something like that. So, be fair to Google Ads, and recognize just how expensive (and how valuable) sales inquiries can be to your business across different advertising and marketing venues.

Visits, Bounces, and Telephone Calls

Another big problem is **call tracking**. In many industries such as plumbers, lawyers, and roofing companies, the person is most likely to do a Google search, land on your website, check your reviews, and then call you on the phone. That phone call "originated" from Google Ads, but it isn't easy to track. Google has call-tracking inside of Google Ads (if you enable call extensions or click to call on mobile), but realistically, very few people will call right off of an ad. They want first to visit your website. Companies like CallRail (**http://www.callrail.com**) and CallTrackingMetrics (**http://www.calltrackingmetrics.com**), can enable call tracking on your website and feed that data into Google Ads. Even so, you have the problem that many people will do a Google search, click, visit your site, leave, come back days or weeks later, and then engage. The visits, bounces, and call tracking problems can make it "seem" like you have fewer conversions from Google Ads than you really have had.

Time on Site, Branding, and Other Metrics

After e-Commerce sales and completed feedback forms, other valuable goals for your website can be signups to your email lists, engagements on social media (e.g., "liking" your company Facebook page), or even time on site. Some companies, especially big ones, look at advertising as a branding experience and aren't that interested in clicks. You might measure impressions (especially on the Google Display Network) as a KPI (Key Performance Indicator) of brand awareness. Just be careful as only the very biggest companies can afford to throw their money away on "brand awareness" advertising; most medium to small businesses need to show some ROI more significant than impressions.

Google Ads is expensive, so I would be very skeptical of these "soft" metrics, with the possible exception of **email sign-ups**.

In summary, be aware that, conceptually, you want a positive ROAS / ROI but, in the real world, you will probably have to follow your gut instinct in combination with some very loosey-goosey data from both Google Ads and Google Analytics.

» SPOT CHECK YOUR ADS

One of the easiest yet most important metrics to measure is whether your ads are running at all, and how frequently. I recommend you "spot check" your ads manually one a week at first, and then at least twice a month once you're up and running. Sometimes Google will say they're running (*and they're not*) or will say that they're not running (*and they are*). For these weekly or monthly checkups, also pay attention to other variables such as whether you are running on good keywords, actual search queries, clicks, costs, click-thru rates, cost per click, conversions, etc.

DON'T JUST SET IT AND FORGET IT!

Here are two easy ways to verify your ads are running, especially by changing your location if you are using geotargeting. Have your keywords handy, as you want to spot check your ads against your most valuable keywords.

Method #1. Enable an "incognito session" on your browser. Then, use the SERPS.com location tool at **http://jmlinks.com/25r**. Input your keyword, set a location by city or zip code, and hit search. DO NOT CLICK ON YOUR AD as it will cost you. Just check as indicated below. Unfortunately, sometimes Google won't show any ads in an incognito session. In that case, clear your cookies, go to Google and try searching for your ad using the SERPS.com tool; I often use the Microsoft Edge browser for this purpose, as I regularly use Chrome and Microsoft Edge has a wonderful feature to clear cookies with each session. It's ironic to use the Microsoft Edge browser to check whether Google Ads are running, but it's a good solution!

Method #2. Use the Google Ads Ad Preview and Diagnosis Tool. Log in to Google Ads, and click on *Tools > Ad Preview and Diagnosis*. On the right-hand side, enter a city, select Desktop or Mobile, and make sure it's Google.com (Google.ca for Canada).

In both methods, you should see your ad displayed most of the time. Note: vary your city location if you are using geotargeting to confirm that your ad is showing in various cities.

Here's a screenshot showing my ad for *Social Media Expert Witness* with the city set to Tulsa, Oklahoma, and device site to Mobile:

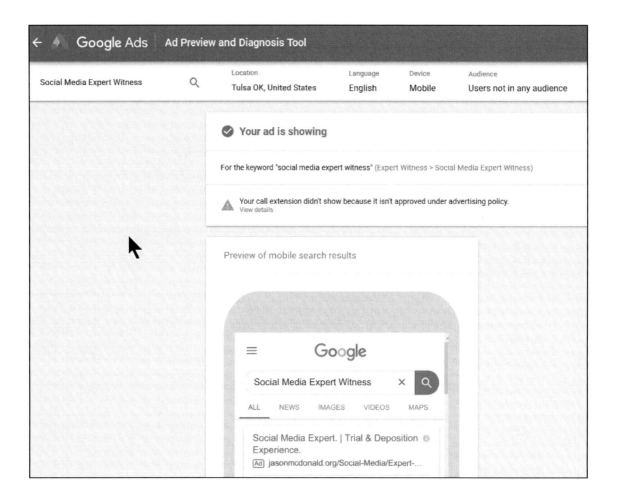

Google will highlight your ad in green to make it easy to find. Generally, you want your ads to be showing in the top positions, which are #1, #2, #3, and #4. If your ad is at the bottom, your bid and/or quality score is too low; if your ad is not showing at all, your bid and/or quality score is even worse. Either up your bid or rewrite your ad / keyword / landing page to improve your quality score, until your ad shows consistently.

Method #3. Finally, inside of Google Ads, you can see if an ad is showing by doing an analysis at the **keyword** level. Drill into an *Ad Group* > *Keyword*. Hover your mouse over "Eligible" in the "Status" column, and you should see a pop up indicating whether your ad is currently running for that keyword. Here's a screenshot:

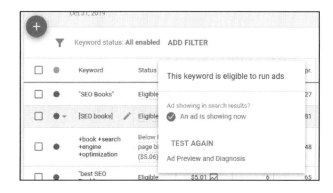

This method may falsely indicate you are (or are not) running, so take these metrics with a grain of salt.

You must use a combination of manual searches, the SERPS.com tool, the Google Ads Preview Tool, and keyword eligibility to spot check – just be aware that none of these tools is 100% reliable.

Search Impression Share or SIS

Beyond spot-checking, how can you measure whether your ads are running on a day in, day out basis? Fortunately, inside of Google Ads, there is a valuable metric called "**SIS**" for "**Search Impression Share**." Your SIS score measured as a percentage shows how frequently your ad was shown vs. how frequently it was eligible to run. For example, let's say that there are 1,000 searches per month for *cat collars* in the USA and you want to know what percentage of time your ad was actually showing, that is:

Available Impressions Per Month: **1000**

Your ad appears on **800** of these impressions (for example).

Your SIS is **80%**, meaning your ad ran 80% of the time it was eligible to run.

SIS tells you the percentage of the time your ad was actually showing. It exists at the Campaign, Ad Group, and Keyword levels.

I recommend you shoot for an SIS score of 85% or more, meaning your ad shows at least 85% of the time. If your ad is running less than about 85% of the time, something is wrong – either your bid is too low, you're hitting your budget constraint, or your quality score is too low. If you're hitting the budget constraint, you'll get a notice "Limited by Budget" in Google Ads. It's not a good idea to be limited by budget; if our ROAS /ROI is positive, we want to run "full blast," so either reconfigure to tighter keywords (or placements if you're on the GDN) or increase your budget. (You can also get a notice that says, "Below first-page bid," and again either increase your bid or improve your quality score. Spot check your ads in both cases to verify that they are / are not / running).

AIM FOR AN SIS > 85%

To figure out the universe of available impressions, divide your impressions by your SIS. So, if your Google Ads Campaign shows 800 impressions with an SIS of .80 (or 80%), then the total universe of available impressions was 800/.80 = 1000. Once you're running ads, in other words, you can do a little math to determine the available universe of ad inventory and then multiply that by your click-thru rate to get your clicks, and then multiply those clicks by the average CPC to get your budget spend if you were to run "full blast" at 100%, or at least close to it.

To blow your mind further, this data is *more accurate* than the data reported in the Google Ads Keyword Planner!

Enable SIS

The SIS score is available for Campaigns, Ad Groups, and Keywords, but you must "enable" it as a column. To enable SIS, at the Campaign level, go to Campaigns, and then click on Columns, then Modify Columns. Next, find "Competitive Metrics" and select "Search Impr. Share." I usually then save this set of columns by giving it a name like "SIS," so I can re-enable it each time I log in.

You have to go through the same procedure at the Ad Group and Keyword levels to be able to view SIS there.

Here's a screenshot of SIS at the Campaign level:

CAMPAIGNS	AUCTION		Impr.	Search impr. share
+				
≡ Campaign status: **All enabled**				
☐ ●	**Campaign** ↑		Impr.	Search impr. share
☐ ●	Books - Search Network		6,593	67.20%
☐ ●	Jason McDonald		166	86.53%
☐ ●	Stanford in CA		858	90.95%
	Total: Filtered campaigns		7,617	69.59%

This means that for my "Jason McDonald" campaign (which focuses on high-value expert witness work), I am running at 86.53%. The goal is to run > 85%, which means "full blast." Thus, for my books, you can see I am at 67.20%, meaning they are not running full blast. I thus need to increase my budget or bids, improve my quality score, or otherwise configure this Campaign better. The trick is to do this in such a way that you still generate a positive ROI.

You can check your SIS at every level: Campaign, Ad Group, and Keyword. Thus, for a high-value keyword, you can and should check that your SIS is > 85%. If not, you can work on budget, bids, and/or quality score issues.

Search Top IS Metric: Who's on Top?

We all know that users tend to see and click on the ads shown at the top of a Google search. Google places up to four ads on the *top* of any search query, and then another three or four ads at the *bottom*. Those ads on the bottom **suck**; "suck" is a technical term meaning a) few people (if any) see them, and b) much of the traffic from ads at the bottom is bots and fraudulent clicks. I have no real evidence of this, other than common sense. *I mean, Google, C'mon – who sees or clicks ads at the bottom of a search?* No one.

> *For these reasons, I strongly recommend that you measure whether your ads are generally showing in the top four positions.*

The metric to do this is called "Search top IS" or "Search Top Impression Share." Like SIS, this metric measures how frequently you showed in a top position vs. the total available impressions. Shoot for 70% or more. To enable it, click into *Columns > Modify Columns* at the Campaign, Ad Group, or Keyword Level. Find *Competitive Metrics* and then click *Search Top IS*. Save this column set. I generally enable both SIS and Search Top IS and save the column set as "SIS." Here's a screenshot:

		Ad group	S	Impr.	Clicks	Search impr. share	Search top IS
☐	●	SEO Books	El	1,351	96	76.97%	71.27%
☐	●	Social Media - Amazon	El	1,668	144	60.94%	54.17%
☐	●	Social Media - Amazon - Dummies	El	1,009	63	77.68%	71.71%
☐	●	SEO for Dummies	E	457	30	47.73%	37.03%

Ad group status: All enabled

This tells me, for example, that my "SEO Books" Ad Group had 1,351 impressions, 96 clicks, and SIS of 76.97% and a Search Top IS of 71.27%. This means my ad showed about 75% of the time, and at the top about 70% of the time. I generally shoot for an SIS of > 85% and a Search Top IS of > 70% by raising (or lowering) my bids and spot-checking the ads each week. You can learn more about SIS and Search Top IS at **http://jmlinks.com/52t**.

While in the example above, conversion tracking is not enabled (because the ads go directly to Amazon), in a perfect world, I'd also measure my raw conversions, my CPA (Cost Per Action, or Conversion), and the revenue or profit generated by those conversions.

Your Goals

Ideally, you want an SIS score of > 85%, and a Search Top IS of > 70% as that is the "best value" position in my experience on Google Ads. You should increase your bid (or work on your Quality Score) to get these two metrics in optimum range. However, often you may need to increase your bid to get your SIS > 85% which will also propel your Search Top IS too high (> 90%), which means you are overpaying. Or, you bid too low, and then your SIS goes < 85%, meaning your ad isn't showing.

> The **art** of Google Ads is to optimize for an SIS > 85% and a Search Top IS of > 70%, which is not easy.

If you can't get a good top score, I would prefer an SIS > 85% as you need your ad to show to get results. In summary, using these metrics in combination with conversion tracking will tell you a) your ads are generally showing, b) your ads are generally showing at the top of the page, c) your ads are getting clicks as measured by a good click-thru rate (CTR), and d) your ads are getting conversions at a reasonable cost as measured by conversion tracking.

» CHECK YOUR SPENDING METRICS

It goes without saying that you should pay attention to your CPC (Cost Per Click), as you want to minimize your CPC. Check the columns:

Clicks = how many clicks your Campaign / Ad Group / Keyword / Ad received.

Impressions = how many impressions (how much it was seen) vs. SIS. If your SIS is > 85%, then essentially you are showing "all the time." If your SIS is < 85%, then there is more ad inventory, and you can show your ad more.

CTR = click-thru rate. Higher is better. Shoot for at least 1%, but I like to see 3, 4, or even 7% or higher CTRs for tightly focused *Keywords > Ad Groups > Ads*.

Cost = how much you've spent, total, for the time period you've selected in the Top Right.

Cost / conversions / cost per conversion. We'll discuss this in a moment, but this is your conversion data (meaning e-Commerce sales or completed feedback forms).

As you spot check your ads, you're seeking to REDUCE your bid per click YET get your ad to show (SIS > 85%) and maintain Search Top IS > 70%, and maintain a decent CTR. It's a see-saw and takes weekly or monthly maintenance at first. Once you have a good setup (Campaign > Keyword Focus > Ad Group > Keywords > Ads), then LET YOUR WINNERS RUN but KILL YOUR DOGS. Meaning, once you get an SIS > 85%, a Search Top IS > 70%, and a CTR of > 1% or more, LEAVE IT ALONE, whether this is a Campaign, an Ad Group, a Keyword, or an Ad.

If something is a dog, you either *fix it* (re-write the ads, reconfigure the Ad Group / bid / landing page) or you *kill it*. You don't just let it run and run, losing you money.

In summary, you're using these metrics to verify:

- Your ads are running vis-à-vis your target keywords by spot-checking with the preview tool.
- Your SIS is > 85% meaning your ads are running most of the time.
- Your Search Top IS > 70%, meaning you're in the #1, #2, #3, or #4 positions, at the top of the Google page.
- Your CTR is > 1% or better.

AND

- Your CPC is as low as possible by reducing your bid yet retaining the metrics above.

The Bid Simulator: A Useless and Misleading Tool

Note: at the Ad Group level in the Default Max CPC column (indicating your bid), you can click on the little zig-zag arrow to enable Google's **Bid Simulator**. Here's a screenshot:

The tool attempts to tell you if you increased your bid, what will happen to your clicks, cost, impressions, and conversions. Generally, the tool implies that the more you spend, the more clicks you'll get.

This might be the case, but I have had many instances that are just the opposite. I have found that often if you *reduce* your bid, your clicks stay the same or even increase as Google seems to "work harder" to spend "all your money" at the lower click bid (despite what bid simulator will tell you). <u>I find more success systematically lowering my bids over time yet paying attention to my SIS score and spot-checking my ads until I find the hidden "minimum bid" that Google wants to keep my ad running full blast.</u>

Don't believe everything Google tells you. Sometimes lower bids yield more clicks.

Remember as well that you care about *conversions*, not *clicks*, and even the tool shows that a substantial increase in CPC from $2.50 a click to $5.46 a click results in a huge increase in cost ($407-$188=$219), but just two more conversions, meaning a cost per conversion of $219/2 or $109.

Spending more isn't necessarily more efficient.

Another useless and much-hyped tool is Google's **Performance Planner**, available via the Tools menu. In my experience, Performance Planner will generally advise you to increase your bids / spend, add in useless keywords or otherwise expand your reach, etc. Unless you are running a very high volume, e-commerce campaign with robust conversion-tracking, Google's AI-based tools simply do not have enough data to be useful. Add in Google's nefarious motive to increase your spend, and I am deeply skeptical of Google's AI-based tools. But, hey, check them out and if they work for you, use them. If not, ignore them. You can learn more about Performance Planner at **http://jmlinks.com/52u**.

Bid Tuning Your Ads to Hit the Trifecta

Instead, I recommend you use the **manual bid strategy** and engage in what I call "bid tuning," which is ratcheting down your bids slowly until your SIS drops below 85%. In this way you find the true "minimum bid" you need to bid in order to get your ad to show at minimum cost.

Once you are running, *lower* the bids in any given Ad Group until your SIS falls below 85%, and then *raise* them back up until the SIS recovers. Pay attention to your ad position as well, as measured by Search Top IS.

You want to tweak your bids down, paying attention to your SIS, and you may find that by lowering your bids you actually get more impressions and more clicks – the *complete reverse* of what the official Google help files tell you!

On a weekly or monthly basis, you should:

1. Log in to Google Ads, and drill into your Ad Groups.
2. If an Ad Group has a good CTR (> 1 or 2%) and a good SIS (> 85%), then lower your bid just a tad (perhaps by fifty cents or so – it depends).

If an Ad Group has a poor CTR, then you need to re-write or improve the ads. If an Ad Group has a good CTR but a poor SIS, then you need to increase your bids. What you are doing is "tuning" your bids and ads to try to hit the *trifecta* of a good CTR, a good position, and a good SIS score at the lowest bid possible (plus a good conversion rate). Despite Google propaganda about "Smart Campaigns" and "Automated Bidding," I find better results with manual "bid tuning," but experiment yourself and do what works best for you. I also find that sometimes *lower* bids can generate *more* impressions, clicks, and conversions, which is really mind-blowing if you think about it vs. Google's propaganda.

Quality Score: Another Misleading Metric

Similarly, while there is a **Quality Score** metric available in Google Ads, it is also not reliable. To find it, you have to go to *Ad Groups > Keywords*, next click on *Columns > Modify Columns*. Find and enable Quality Score under *Quality Score*. Here's a screenshot:

That will enable it, so you can see it in your Google Ads Reporting. Once you're enable it, you'll see a column called *Qual. Score*. Generally speaking, you want a Quality Score of 4 or higher, except remember that Google gets paid "by the click" and you make money "by the conversion," so you can have a high Quality Score for a keyword that is a dog (*doesn't convert and/or doesn't make you money*). Conversely, you can have a low Quality Score for a star (*converts well, makes you a lot of money*) for a high-value keyword, and/or a keyword for which you have written a strong attract / repel ad.

You may even get a (misleading) message from Google that says "Rarely shown to low quality score" but your ad will actually still be running per SIS and/or spot-checking!

Take Quality Score with a huge grain of salt! I am more interested in a) is my ad running (SIS), b) is it in a good position (top of the page), and c) is it converting on my website?

Who cares about Quality Score if a, b, and c are all working?

» MONITOR THE DISPLAY NETWORK AND/OR YOUTUBE

If you're running on the Display Network or YouTube, many of the above-mentioned metrics don't apply. SIS (Search Impression Share), for example, isn't really available (though there is a fishy metric called "Display impression share"), and there's no easy way to spot-check to verify your ads are actually running. You have to rely on impressions and click data as reported by Google Ads directly. Position is also a bit misleading as on many sites in the GDN there is only one position, or perhaps two, and they don't easily line up as they do on Google. Most importantly on the GDN, you want to check (at least monthly if not more often), your **placements**.

Spot Check Your Placements

To do so, click into a *Display Network Campaign > Ad Group*, because placements "live" at the Ad Group level. Then click on *Placements* on the left. Then *See Where Your Ads Appeared* at the top. Sort by cost, and look for Placements that have lots of clicks, high costs, and/or few conversions. You're looking for "winners" or "dogs," meaning either placements that are performing well (high ROI as measured by a low CPC, high CTR, and good conversion rate) or performing poorly. If a placement is a "dog," then you probably want to block that placement by adding it to a negative placement list. I often look for outliers – placements that have a high spend and/or a high CPC, and few conversions.

Your very important **To-do** on the Display Network is to look for "dog" or "nefarious" placements and block them immediately.

You can use the Filter tab to create a filter to check for "stars" and "dogs." For example, here's a screenshot for a Display Network filter called "Conversion Stars" meaning high ROI:

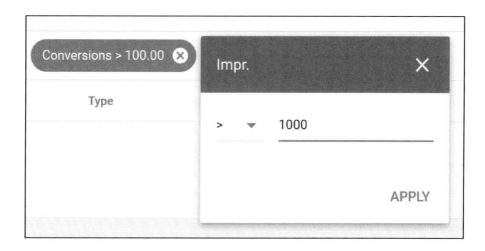

You can also create a filter for high impressions or cost, and low conversions to identify your "dogs." In this way, you can identify "winners" and "dogs," and continually improve your Google Display Network performance via placements.

YouTube

Remember that YouTube, parallel to the Google Search and Google Display Networks, has both a *Search* and a *Browse* functionality. Accordingly, if you are running YouTube ads using keyword targeting, click into an Ad Group, and then click *Keywords* on the left to view the keyword search queries on YouTube that generated impressions and views of your video. Here's a screenshot:

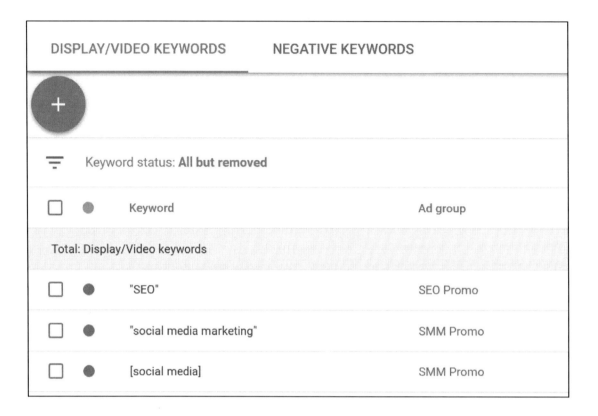

YouTube will also report clicks from the video to your call-to-action overlay, if enabled. If you're running on YouTube for browse (meaning "In-stream ads" or "Bumper ads"), you can click to the Placements tab and then see where your ads were run, either on YouTube or on the broader Google Display Network. To get even more detail, log in to your YouTube account and drill down to videos in Video Manager. To learn more about YouTube analytics, visit **http://jmlinks.com/51b**.

Using a Segment in Google Analytics for YouTube

Finally, inside of Google Analytics, you can set up a **Segment** to see, in more detail, how traffic from video ads on YouTube ended up on your website and whether it converted, as that data isn't easily available in Google Ads or in YouTube itself. To set up this Segment, log in to Google Analytics, click on the Grayed Out +*Add Segment* tab, then the red *+New Segment* button, then *Traffic Sources* and enter *youtube.com*. Here's a screenshot:

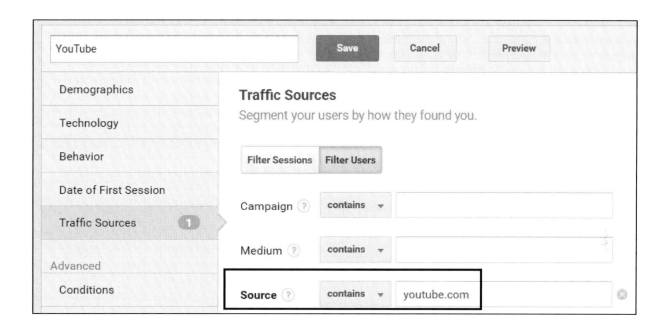

For the Google help file on how to create a Segment in Google Analytics, visit **http://jmlinks.com/25s**.

In summary, on both YouTube and the Google Display Network, you're looking to minimize your Cost Per Click (Cost Per View on YouTube), place your ads on the most relevant placements, secure the highest conversion rates and minimize total costs over time. I also strongly recommend that you continually monitor both the GDN and YouTube for "bad" or "nefarious" placements that just suck money out of your account.

» SET UP GOALS IN GOOGLE ANALYTICS

The Holy Grail for an advertiser on Google Ads is a conversion. When you first conceptualize your Google Ads strategy, you should identify what will constitute a conversion for you, such as:

These are "hard" goals –

A purchase on your e-Commerce store.

A completed inquiry form such as a sales inquiry.

These are "intermediate" goals –

A completed signup form such as an eLetter sign-up, free ebook or software download, etc.

A social media action such as "liking" your company's Facebook or LinkedIn page.

And these are soft goals –

Pageviews or time on site.

A video view

In most cases, the goal in Google Analytics can be measured as the *Thank You* page that the user hits AFTER they have completed the desired action. For example, after they fill out your inquiry form and hit send, they get to a *Thank You* page. Or, after they've made a purchase on your e-commerce store, they get a *Thank You* for your order page.

Once you've defined these goals, I highly recommend that you log into Google Analytics, and define them as a "goal" in Google Analytics. To do this, go to the view page for your Website in Google Analytics, and find the ADMIN tab on the far-left column. Click here, and then on the far right under "View," you should see Goals. Here's a screenshot:

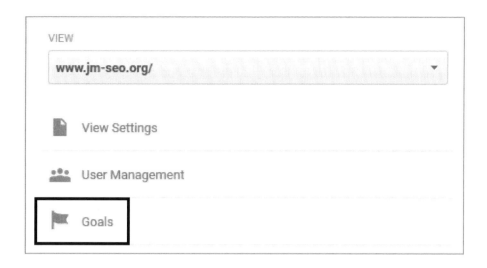

VIDEO. Watch a video on how to set up goals in Google Analytics at http://jmlinks.com/17z.

Once a goal is set up, you can go back to the main page in Google Analytics, and use **Segments** to slice and dice your data and thereby see what traffic is converting (i.e., completing your goal) vs. what is not. (For help with goals, visit the official explanation at **http://jmlinks.com/19a**).

» SET UP CONVERSION TRACKING IN GOOGLE ADS OR GOOGLE ANALYTICS

Google Ads provides two ways to track conversions. Remember that a "conversion" is simply the successful completion of your "goal" such as a completed purchase on your e-Commerce store or a completed feedback form on your website. Once you've defined these as goals on your website, you have two methods to track them.

Method #1: Google Ads Conversion Tracking

In Google Ads, click on *Tools* > *Measurement* > *Conversions*. Then click the blue circle. Next, select the conversion type. Here's a screenshot:

For most of us, it will be "Website." Fill out the elements as indicated:

Name. Give it a name such as "Contact Form"

Category. Assign it a category as indicated.

Value. Estimate its monetary value to your business.

Count. Count every conversion.

Conversion Window. Set it at the default of thirty days.

The default settings are generally fine. If you want to learn more, click on the "pencil icon" and then the "Learn more" link in blue. After you complete this, Google will give you some code to place on your website's *Thank You* page. Either copy/paste this yourself onto the "Thank You" page or have your developer install it. You can also use Google Tag Manager (**http://jmlinks.com/25u**) to manage this Google Ads tag. You can verify your installation is correct using Google Tag Assistant (**http://jmlinks.com/25v**).

VIDEO. Watch two good videos from Google on how to set up conversion tracking in Google Ads at **http://jmlinks.com/41p** and **http://jmlinks.com/41q**.

Once you've successfully installed the Google Ads Conversion tracking code, you should start to see conversions populating in your Google Ads reports.

Method #2: Google Analytics

The second method is to use Google Analytics. I'll assume you've signed up for a Google Analytics account, and implemented the tracking code across your website. I'll also assume that you've set up goals in Google Analytics as indicated above. In general, it's better to use Google Analytics for your tracking system rather than just the Google Ads code as it is more robust. You can get a lot more data in Google Analytics than in Google Ads!

Next, you'll need to link your Google Analytics to your Google Ads account.

Add Your Google Ads Login Email

If you use the same login for both accounts, this is pretty easy. I'd recommend, at a minimum, that you make sure that the Google Ads login you use is also listed as an Admin on Google Analytics. To do this (necessary only if your Google Ads login is not the same as your Google Analytics login email):

1. Log in to Google Analytics.
2. Click on the Admin tab / far lower left column.
3. Click on "User Management" at either the account, property, and/or view level.
4. Add your Google Ads login email to the list of users, and make sure it's added as a "Manage users, Edit, Collaborate, Read & Analyze" level account.

Here's a screenshot:

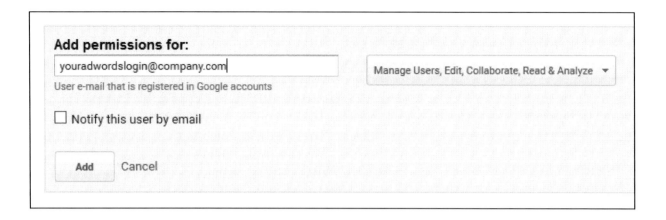

Link Google Ads to Google Analytics .

Next, you'll need to link your Google Ads account to your Google Analytics account. Login to Google Ads, and then click the Gear icon on the top right of the page. Then click *Setup > Linked Accounts* and then click Google Analytics on the left column. You should see your Google Analytics account and then click the "Set up link" icon.

This can be a little tricky, so don't hesitate to call Google Ads technical support by clicking on the Gear icon, and then finding the phone number. It's 866-246-6453 in the United States. The Google Ads tech support team can walk you through how to link your Google Ads to your Google Analytics account.

> **VIDEO.** Watch a video from Google on how to link Google Analytics to your Google Ads account at **http://jmlinks.com/26s**.

Finally, once you've linked the two accounts, you should start to see conversions populating into your Google Ads report. You should also **verify** that your account is linked by looking inside Google Analytics as follows:

1. Log in to Google Analytics.
2. Click on *Acquisition* on the left column.
3. Click on *Google Ads*.

4. Click on *Campaigns*. You should see your Google Ads Campaigns here.

5. Click on *Keywords* and *Search Queries*, and you should see those here.

6. **Important**: you should see Sessions data and Pages / Session data. This means that you can track behavior after the first page to see where people go on your website.

Finally, it's a good idea to create a Segment that is for just your Google Ads traffic. To do this, click on the grayed out +*Add Segment* link at the top of the page in Google Analytics. (It's a little hard to see, so you may have to hunt for it). Here's a screenshot:

Next, click on *System* in the left column, and then find the Segment called *Paid Tra*ffic (if you are only advertising on Google Ads). If you are advertising on other venues like Bing, Yahoo, or Facebook, click the red +*New Segment* button, give it a name like Google Ads, then click *Traffic Sources* on the left, then *Medium* contains **CPC**, and *Source* contains **google.** Here's a screenshot:

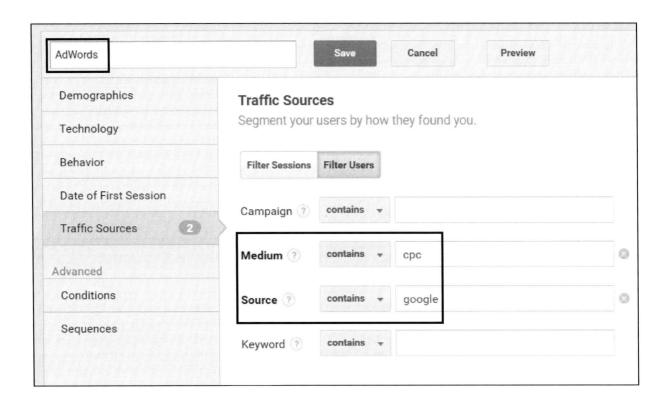

At this point, you've set up goals in Google Analytics, correctly linked Google Analytics to Google Ads, and set up a segment that allows you to examine the behavior of your Google Ads-originating traffic exclusively. Be proud!

» REVIEW YOUR CONVERSION DATA IN GOOGLE ADS

Now, let's return to Google Ads and view the data inside of Google Ads. Once you've activated goals and conversions in Google Ads and/or Google Analytics, you should start to see conversions show up in your Google Ads Reporting. If you remember that Google Ads is a hierarchy, you'll be able to keep oriented as you view the following:

Conversions vs. Campaigns. *Which Campaigns are performing the best?*

Conversions vs. Ad Groups. *Which Ad Groups are performing the best?*

Conversions vs. Keywords. *Which Keywords are your best performers?*

Conversions vs. Ads. *Which ads are your top performers?*

You may not see Conversions showing up in the Google Ads columns, so I recommend that at each level, you enable conversion data. At the Campaign level, for example, click on the *Columns icon*, then *Modify Columns*, and then click into *Conversions*. I recommend you enable:

Conversions. This will tell you the quantity of conversions. *More is better.*

Cost / conv. This will tell you how much you are paying to get a conversion. *Lower is better.*

Conv. rate. This will tell you the number of conversions / clicks. So, if you have 10 conversions out of 100 clicks, you have a $10/100 = 10\%$ conversion rate. *Higher is better.*

If you've assigned a value to a conversion, or enabled e-Commerce tracking in Google Analytics, you can also enable value metrics in Google Ads. These tell you not only the raw quantity of conversions but the value to you of a conversion as well. You can browse this data at the Campaign, Ad Group, Keyword, and Ad levels. You can also use the *Filter* tab to create a filter. For example, you can create a Filter to find Keywords for which you've spent more than $50 and the Cost per Conversion is > $10.

In this way, at any level (Campaign, Ad Group, Keyword, Ad) you can use a Filter in combination with Conversion data to identify "dogs" or "winners" and act accordingly.

If you've enabled the value metrics, you can use your conversion data to find out:

Quantity. Which Campaigns / Ad Groups / Keywords / Ads are generating the highest volume of conversions?

ROAS / ROI / Quality. Which Campaigns / Ad Groups / Keywords / Ads are generating the best *return on ad spend*, namely –

- o **Highest gross value.** Greatest dollar value as measured in sales volume.
- o **Most attractive performance.** Highest conversion rate, and highest revenue per conversion.
- o **Highest ROI.** Highest revenue per click as measured by highest value per conversion vs. click.

Time Horizons for Conversions

A Conversion in Google Ads / Google Analytics defaults to a thirty-day window, so remember that if you are looking at very fresh data (e.g., *yesterday*, *last week*), you will tend to underestimate your conversions and overestimate your cost per conversion. In addition, the tracking isn't perfect, so Google Ads / Google Analytics may significantly undercount conversions, not to mention fail to take into account lifetime customer value (LCV).

Use your gut instinct in combination with conversion data to verify that your Google Ads advertising is working.

Conversions in Google Analytics

Google Analytics will give you even more robust data on conversions than Google Ads. If you're using e-Commerce, for example, and you've linked your e-Commerce account to Google Analytics, Analytics will automatically populate e-Commerce sales as conversions and track the sales value. And, if Google Analytics is correctly linked to Google Ads, then this **conversion value** will be populated in Google Ads as well, automatically.

In this way, you can see the revenue per conversion data in Google Analytics as well as the raw conversion numbers.

You can also drill down into a Campaign, Ad Group, and/or Keyword to see which ones are generating the most clicks into your website and if the user fails to convert, you can follow the path from landing to bounce or exit. In this way, you can attempt to "debug" problems, wherein you are getting clicks from Google Ads but not conversions. You can even use Analytics' Funnel Visualization tool to graphically represent the path from landing to conversion (or bounce / exit). Inside of Google Analytics, therefore, you have an even more detailed window into not only who clicks on your ads on Google Ads, but what happens after the click, including those who convert easily at a high value and those who fail to convert or convert only at a low value.

» IDENTIFY PROBLEMS AND OPPORTUNITIES

I recommend that, at first, you check your Google Ads performance at least once a week. When you first start a new Campaign, I would even check it daily to make sure that it's actually running and that your spend and results are commensurate with your goals. Once you're up and running, then I find that – for most small business advertisers – checking twice a month is sufficient. (Obviously, if you are a large company or spending a significant amount, you'll want to check it more frequently).

Here's a list of things to check and opportunities to build out from; for each, at the *Campaign > Ad Group > Keywords > Ad level*. For our hypothetical Jason's Cat Emporium business, for example, we'd have at least two Campaigns (one selling cat accessories and one selling cat boarding & grooming). We'd then check each Campaign, as well as the Ad Groups inside them (both on the Search and on the Display Networks), especially with an eye towards keywords and conversions.

A Twice Monthly Checklist

At least once a week (at the beginning) and then twice-monthly, here are things to check at every level (Campaign / Ad Group / Keyword / Ad):

1. **Are your ads running?** Do a spot check using the Google Ads *Ad Preview and Diagnosis* tool (on the Tools tab) to verify that your ads are actually running vis-à-vis your target keywords. If you're geotargeting, be sure to spot-check various target cities. Check your recent performance to make sure you see impressions and clicks and check your **SIS score**.

2. **Double-check your Keywords**. What keywords are you running on as indicated by the "Search Terms" on the Keyword tab? Look for strong, valuable keywords vs. bad matches or low-converting keywords. If keywords are erroneous or poor performers, consider blocking them as "negative keywords."

3. **What are your Impressions, Clicks, Average CPC, CTR, and Costs?** Do they look to be in the ballpark of what you want?

4. **What's Your Budget / Spend Month-to-date?** Check your budget at the Account, Campaign, Ad Group, and Keyword level to make sure it's within your budget. If it's too high, pause or bid lower on less lucrative keywords. If it's still too high, consider re-optimizing. It's better to run "full blast" on your high ROI keywords and not at all on low performers than to spread yourself too thin.

5. Do you see any **messages from Google** such as "Limited by Budget," "Below first page bid," or "Rarely shown due to low quality score?" If so, investigate and fix.

6. **Is your SIS > 85%?** How does that compare with your **Search Top IS** (> 70%)? And what about your **CTR** (ideally, > 1%)? Adjust bids and/or re-write ads to attempt to hit the "happy medium" of SIS > 85% and CTR > 1%.

7. **How are your conversions**? Which Campaigns and Ad Groups have decent conversion quantities, conversion rates, and conversion values? Which ones are high ROAS, and which ones are low?

    a. Look at the Keyword level at your conversions. Which keywords have decent or better conversions, and which are below average? Investigate and fix as needed.

8. As for the **Google Display Network**, be sure to check your placements (looking for nefarious or "dog" placements) as well as check your CTR's and conversion rates and values.

In addition to the above, be on the lookout for "dogs" and for "winners." As for "dogs" – Campaigns, Ad Groups, Keywords, and/or Ads that are low performers – try to fix them as needed, and if necessary "kill" them. There's no shame in giving up on either non-winnable keyword patterns at an affordable price, or in realizing that some keywords are just "dogs." I will say it again:

KILL YOUR DOGS & LET YOUR WINNERS RUN

Pull Winners Out into their Own Special "Single Keyword Ad Group" or SKAG

As for "winners" or "opportunities," identify your best-performing Campaigns, Ad Groups, Keywords, and/or Ads and let them run. In particular, if you find keywords at the keyword level that are strong-performers, think of breaking them out into a special ad group called a "SKAG" or "Single Keyword Ad Group."

Remember that Google rewards a tight linkage between your Ad Groups and Keywords, so if there's a high performing keyword, breaking it out into a specialized Ad Group will generally boost its SIS, position, click-thru rate and even conversion rate.

If for example, we learn that the phrase "luxury cat boarding" generated a high return on ad spend, then we'd break it out into a special SKAG with special, unique ads just for it as well as a uniquely optimized landing page. Learn more about "Single Keyword Ad Groups" at **http://jmlinks.com/51c**.

Situate Google Ads ROI within Other Online Opportunities

Finally, don't forget to compare your return on investment through Google Ads with your ROI from other Internet marketing methods, such as SEO and/or Social Media. In particular, use a tool like FatRank for Chrome (**http://jmlinks.com/25w**) and/or the Google Ads Preview tool by city to see if you're ranking for "free" on Google with organic results. If you are ranking in the top three positions organically, then consider either cutting back on your Google Ads spend for that keyword, redeploy those funds to other more needy keywords, or just be happy that you're crushing it with visibility via Google Ads *and* via Organic for high-value keyword patterns.

If you're running on the Display Network or YouTube, consider trying out **social media advertising** on Facebook, Twitter, Instagram, or LinkedIn, as often performance on those social media networks will outperform that of the Google

Display Network with its plethora of nefarious site partners. The ROI on **email marketing**, in particular, is one people often miss. Another emerging options is ads on Amazon.com (if you sell on Amazon). Don't overspend on Google Ads yet starve other profitable opportunities for promotion online.

»» DELIVERABLE: AN GOOGLE ADS METRIC WORKSHEET

The **DELIVERABLE** for this chapter is a completed worksheet on Google Ads Metrics.

> For the **worksheet**, go to **http://jmlinks.com/adw2020**, then re-enter the password, "adw2020," and click on the link to the "Google Ads Metric Worksheet."

9
TOOLS FOR GOOGLE ADS

Google Ads is easier with free tools! To that end, I publish a massive list of SEO, Social Media Marketing, and Google Ads tools called the *Marketing Almanac*. Register your copy of the *Google Ads Workbook*, and you'll get full access to a PDF of all my favorite Google Ads tools plus my handy "dashboard" with easy, clickable links. In addition, here are the *best of the best* – my favorite Google Ads tools, ranked with the best ones first.

ADWORDS ACADEMY OF ADS - https://landing.google.com/academyforads/

Google's official training site for AdWords. Yes, a bit salesy and take it all with a huge grain of Google salt, but very good information by Google for Google about Google. #BeSkeptical.

Rating: 5 | **Category**: resource

TWINWORD KEYWORD TOOL - https://www.twinword.com/ideas/

Billed as the first "LSI" (Latent Semantic Indexing) tool and the first semantic keyword research tool that can sort by relevance. Useful for keyword discovery and finding related words, especially when writing a blog post.

Rating: 5 | **Category**: tool

ADWORDS YOUTUBE CHANNEL - https://www.youtube.com/user/learnwithgoogle

Official Google AdWords channel. Learn from the horse's mouth how to advertise on AdWords, why advertise, etc. Of course, be a bit skeptical as it is by Google, about Google, and ultimately for Google!

Rating: 5 | Category: resource

GOOGLE ADWORDS HELP CENTER - https://support.google.com/google-ads/

Your gateway to easy-to-use lessons about the Google AdWords advertising program. Whether you're just getting started with AdWords, seeking to improve your ad performance, or studying for the Google Advertising Professionals exam, you'll find lessons designed to help you learn at your own pace. You can also read the complete version (with all available lessons).

Rating: 5 | Category: resource

YOUTUBE ADVERTISING RESOURCES - https://www.youtube.com/yt/advertise/

YouTube wants you to advertise! But, it also hides some good free SEO-oriented resources here for how to use YouTube effectively. Worth a look, and a bookmark.

Rating: 4 | Category: resource

MOAT AD SEARCH - https://moat.com/

Want to snoop on competitors? Steal their ad ideas? Enter Moat Ad Search. Enter a competitor name and Moat goes and finds all sorts of ads that they've posted across the Internet. Mainly the Display ads, but excellent to see how a company brainstormed its ad strategy.

Rating: 4 | Category: tool

GOOGLE ADWORDS COMMUNITY

- https://support.google.com/google-ads/community

This is the official Google AdWords community group, wherein users post questions and get answers from Googlers or other AdWords gurus on AdWords.

It's a bit of a free-for-all but useful if you have a burning question about AdWords! Just remember that these are Google forums, so things can be on the salesy side.

Rating: 4 | **Category**: resource

KEYWORDSPY - http://www.keywordspy.com/

KeywordSpy currently operates in USA, United Kingdom, Australia and Canada. Through this keyword tool and keyword software, you can perform advanced keyword research and keyword tracking to study what your competitors have been advertising in their AdWords campaigns and other PPC campaigns. You can get complete in-depth analysis, stats, budget, affiliates & ad copies of your competitors.

Rating: 4 | **Category**: tool

SEED KEYWORDS - http://www.seedkeywords.com/

This is a wonderful human / machine tool. Gather your team together (or they can be in diverse cities). Create a prompt, such as 'you're hungry and you love Italian food, what would you search for?' This then creates a 'workspace' and as people type in their ideas it consolidates them into a master list. Excellent and fun tool for keyword brainstorming!

Rating: 4 | **Category**: tool

GOOGLE PARTNERS HELP CENTER - https://www.google.com/partners/about/

Google partners is Google's platform for agencies and consultants, particularly for AdWords. However, you can 'join' as an individual and thereby get access to many wonderful FREE Google AdWords learning resources. If you are a serious learner with respect to AdWords, this is a great way to go behind the scenes and learn even more about AdWords.

Rating: 4 | **Category**: resource

TAG ASSISTANT FOR CHROME - http://tinyurl.com/tagasst

If you're using AdWords and Google Analytics to track conversions, you need to verify you have the right 'tags' running as Javascript on your website. Ask your developer to get the conversion tracking code from AdWords and install on ALL pages of your website. Then use this Chrome extension to double-check / verify it actually is there.

Rating: 4 | **Category**: tool

ADWORDS EDITOR - https://ads.google.com/home/tools/ads-editor/

AdWords Editor is a free, downloadable (Windows or Mac) application for managing large Google AdWords accounts efficiently. Download campaigns, make changes with powerful editing tools, then upload the changes to AdWords.

Rating: 4 | **Category**: tool

GOOGLE ADWORDS KEYWORD PLANNER - https://adwords.google.com/ko/KeywordPlanner/Standalone/Home

Who got the data? Google got the data. Use the Keyword Planner for keyword discovery for both SEO and AdWords, but be sure to know how to use it. Not the easiest user interface, and remember it ONLY gives data for EXACT match types. NOTE: you MUST have a paid account to use, and be LOGGED IN.

Rating: 4 | **Category**: tool

GOOGLE INSIDE ADWORDS BLOG - https://blog.google/products/ads/

The official blog for Google AdWords. It's more for sophisticated users than for newbies, but - that said - you should pay attention to it if you are spending money with Google.

Rating: 4 | **Category**: blog

ADWORDS WRAPPER - http://www.adwordswrapper.com/

Use this tool to take your basic keyword list, and then wrap them with various characters to create each of seven target keyword match types in AdWords (such as quotes for phrase match, and brackets for exact match).

Rating: 3 | **Category**: tool

MICROSOFT BING ADVERTISING CENTER - https://about.ads.microsoft.com/en-us

Yes, Virginia, there is another search engine besides Google. It's called Bing, and it runs both Bing and Yahoo. And yes, Virginia, you can advertise on Bing, too. It's about 10% of the traffic on Google, on average, though public claims are more like 35%. Try it and see. Often the CPC is lower than on Google, so why not?

Rating: 3 | **Category**: resource

DELETE DUPLICATES KEYWORD TOOL

- http://angular.marketing/free-tools/delete-duplicates

If you are building a long list for rank-checking, or for AdWords input, you often will unknowingly generate duplicates. Then when you pull your reports, they will often not correspond to your original, because rank checker and other tools auto-delete duplicates. Use this tool to prevent this from happening in the first place.

Rating: 3 | **Category**: tool

MERGE WORDS - http://mergewords.com/

When you build your keywords list, especially for AdWords, you often want to take keywords and combine them into phrases. This is especially true for local search keyword phrases. This tool allows you to enter keywords and generate keyword lists.

Rating: 3 | **Category**: tool

LOCAL KEYWORD LIST GENERATOR - http://5minutesite.com/local_keywords.php

Don't know your local geography? What about all those pesky zip codes and small suburban towns? Enter a zipcode or city into this tool, and it generates a nifty list of possible nearby locales and zips for your SEO efforts. A time saver if local search is important to your SEO or AdWords.

Rating: 3 | **Category**: tool

USA ZIP CODE MAP (INTERACTIVE) - http://maps.huge.info/zip.htm

Free tool for browsing the USA by zip code. Enter a zip code and find nearby zip codes. Great to then pop into a local SEO tool and see if you show in a particular zip code for a "short tail" search like "divorce lawyer" or "plumber"

Rating: 3 | **Category**: tool

KEYWORD EVERYWHERE CHROME EXTENSION - https://chrome.google.com/webstore/detail/keywords-everywhere-keywo/hbapdpeemoojbophdfndmlgdhppljgmp?hl=en

Keywords via a nifty Chrome extension.

Rating: 3 | **Category**: tool

HERO CONFERENCE - http://www.heroconf.com/austin/

The event for quality, all-inclusive PPC education, Hero Conf brings you: Content for every level of PPC marketer – thoroughly vetted with a focus on innovation and relevance; Expert speakers who've done the work – engaging content from experts who do what you do daily; Actionable ideas & real-life examples – case studies with tips and tricks to immediately apply;

Rating: 3 | **Category**: conference

GOOGLE ADWORDS ON FACEBOOK - https://www.facebook.com/ENGoogleAds/

Google's official AdWords page on Facebook. If you are into AdWords, then you should 'like' the Google's AdWords page on Facebook to receive information as Google makes it available here.

Rating: 3 | **Category**: resource

LEAD PAGES - https://www.leadpages.net/

Another non-free app, LeadPages allows you to quickly and easily create landing pages (not just for AdWords but for Social Media Campaigns). Then you can split test which ones perform better.

Rating: 3 | **Category**: vendor

SPLIT TESTER BY PERRY MARSHALL - https://www.perrymarshall.com/splittester/

Is ad one better, or ad two better? AdWords allows you to set up experiments to 'split test' or 'A/B test.' But sometimes it's just as easy to run two ads and plug in the numbers. This tool will then 'do the math.'

Rating: 3 | **Category**: tool

ADWORD & SEO KEYWORD PERMUTATION GENERATOR -
http://seo.danzambonini.com/

Enter your keywords into this tool and it will cross-match them to generate a list. This is useful especially for AdWords when you want to create exact, phrase, or modified broad match keywords.

Rating: 3 | **Category**: tool

YOUTUBE AD PARTNERS - https://jm-seo.net/ytadpartners

Whether you have your own video or need to create one from scratch, these services can help bring your business to life on YouTube. Partners with YouTube who make ad creation easier if not easy.

Rating: 3 | **Category**: resource

DYNAMIC KEYWORD GENERATOR TOOL

- http://rustybrick.com/keyword-phrase-tool.php

This tool enables you to enter your primary, secondary and even tertiary keyword phrases separated by comma (,) into the appropriate fields and click Generate Keywords to receive a robust list of keywords to copy and paste into your program of choice. For rank-checking, it makes it easy to generate a longer keyword list.

Rating: 3 | **Category**: tool

SURVEY OFFER

CLAIM YOUR $5 SURVEY REBATE! HERE'S HOW –

- Visit **http://jmlinks.com/survey**.
- Take a short, simple survey about the book.
- Claim your rebate.

WE WILL THEN –

- Rebate you the $5 via Amazon eGift.

~ $5 REBATE OFFER ~

~ LIMITED TO ONE PER CUSTOMER ~

SUBJECT TO CHANGE WITHOUT NOTICE

RESTRICTIONS APPLY

GOT QUESTIONS? CALL 800-298-4065

Printed in Great Britain
by Amazon